sculpture

A Designer's Approach™

sculpture
A Designer's Approach®

© 2009 Pivot Point International, Inc.

ISBN 978-1-934636-06-0

1st Edition
7th Printing, January 2013
Printed in Hong Kong

Pivot Point International, Inc.
World Headquarters
1560 Sherman Avenue, Suite 700
Evanston, IL 60201 USA

847-866-0500 (Outside U.S.)
800-886-4247
pivot-point.com

Cover Design
Creative Director - Jennifer Eckstein
Graphic Designer - Dovile Riebschlager, Joanna Jakubowicz
Photographer - David Placek
Hair Designer - Vic Piccolotto
Makeup Artist - Amy Howard
Fashion Stylist - Beckett McMahan
Model - Kelly Kohnen

SEEING AND THINKING AS A DESIGNER

CREATING AS A DESIGNER

SEEING AND THINKING AS A DESIGNER

CREATING AS A DESIGNER

PREFACE: CHANGING A HAIR SCULPTURE

Throughout your career you will have many different opportunities to change and enhance many of your clients' hair sculptures. Whether going from long to short or from all one length to layers around the face, hair sculpture transformations enable your clients to wear hair designs that can be more flattering, more fashion-forward or more practical. A new hair sculpture may simply be more in synch with the image they want to project than their current hair sculpture.

This program has been specially developed to help you build your skill, proficiency and confidence in hair sculpture and prepare you for success in the salon. The foundation provided by the Pivot Point educational library you are using is built upon the individual designer's approach to learning new material and performing new skills. Understanding this approach will put you at the top tier of entry-level professionals when you complete your cosmetology training.

A Designer's Approach™ focuses on visualizing and creating hair designs that are as unique as each individual client. It includes the theory that gives you the thought process you'll need to guide your design decisions; procedures and techniques that will help you produce predictable results; and a language that allows you to think and communicate clearly with your clients and other designers. The goal is to give you confidence that comes with knowing that the final look you produce will be functional, aesthetic and correspond with the design you had envisioned for your client. Being able to align your final results with your design vision is the true benefit of using *A Designer's Approach*.

SEEING as a designer means that you have the ability to observe sculptures all around you—in fashion, nature and art as well as in hair—then connect these different expressions of sculpted form to one another and to the design elements and principles. Observing sculptures and making connections will give you the inspiration to see the range of possibilities that exist for transforming your clients' hair.

"IMAGINATION GIVES YOU THE PICTURE. VISION GIVES YOU THE IMPULSE TO MAKE THE PICTURE YOUR OWN."
— ROBERT COLLIER, AUTHOR

THINKING as a designer means that you know how to ***analyze*** your client's hair, features and lifestyle, ***visualize*** a final design, and ***organize*** a plan for achieving that design.

Sculpture transformation is all about changing the shape, the position of weight and the surface texture of your client's hair. As you visualize the form, you'll be determining which of the client's features you want to emphasize or balance, the lines you'll use, where you'll place volume and which sculpting techniques you will use to achieve your desired results.

CREATING as a designer means dedicating yourself to ***practice*** all aspects of hair design to build your expertise and to ***perform*** them with focus and precision. In hair sculpting, creating as a designer means that you are able to sculpt the four basic forms as well as combine them to give clients a professional salon result.

ADAPTING is the highest level of design proficiency. Adapting as a designer means that you are able to ***compose*** innovative and artistic hair designs by drawing upon your knowledge, skill and vision. Then you can ***personalize*** an overall design that complements your client's individual characteristics and needs.

With *A Designer's Approach* as your guiding principle, you have a framework for success that will last your entire career. You will see this guiding principle revealed throughout this sculpture design program, which begins by presenting you with the possibilities of sculpture and then teaching you the techniques and procedures for basic, advanced and men's hair sculpture.

LEARNING STRATEGIES WITHIN *SCULPTURE, A DESIGNER'S APPROACH*

The *Sculpture, A Designer's Approach Coursebook* has been specifically designed using state-of-the-art educational methods to make your learning process engaging as well as systematic and effective. To help you make the most of your time with *Sculpture, A Designer's Approach*, a brief description of these learning strategies is provided here so you can become familiar with them before diving into the chapters. You will begin to rely on them as learner-friendly threads that run throughout the *Coursebook*, giving you momentum and stability as you build your repertoire of professional skills.

" "WHAT WE HOPE TO DO WITH EASE, WE MUST LEARN TO FIRST DO WITH DILIGENCE"

— SAMUEL JOHNSON, POET "

The chapter overview is located on the first two opening pages of the chapter and provides a preview of the chapter in a concise, easy-to-read format. It contains seven elements that will orient you to the chapter so you are prepared and keyed-in to the important learning concepts.

1. **Chapter Title**—This is the overriding theme of the chapter.

2. **Advance Organizer**—A "mini-outline" of the chapter headings and subheadings that identifies the main content points and provides an overall view of the chapter in its entirety.

3. **Central Message**—A statement that highlights the critical value of the chapter.

4. **Learning Goals**—Learning targets that pinpoint exactly what you will learn as a result of working with the material in the chapter and preview how you will be evaluated.

5. **Essential Questions**—Thought-provoking questions that enhance and enliven the core chapter content by inviting you to expand your thinking, look at things from different perspectives, and challenge your assumptions. Essential Questions also help you to develop healthy skepticism and widen and deepen your understanding. Essential Questions are repeated within the chapter to tie them into the relevant content as it is presented.

6. **Key Terms**—Words and expressions that are most relevant to the chapter content. Key Terms are defined in the glossary at the end of the *Coursebook*.

7. **Color Bar**—A bar at the top of each right-hand page is color-coded for easy reference, following Pivot Point's color-coding system: Solid Form - Blue; Graduated Form - Yellow; Increase-Layered Form - Red; Uniformly Layered Form - Green; Combination Forms - Purple.

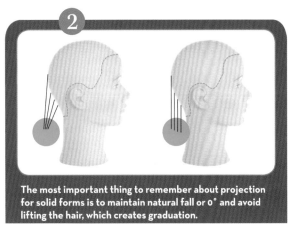

The most important thing to remember about projection for solid forms is to maintain natural fall or 0° and avoid lifting the hair, which creates graduation.

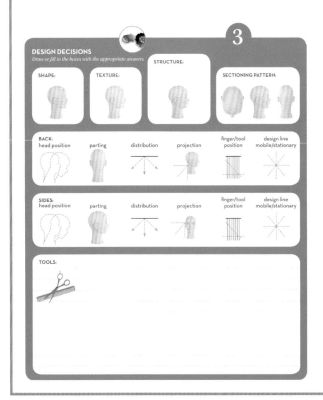

Immediately following the chapter overview is an **Introview (1)**, which is an introduction to the chapter that not only previews the content, but also relates the content to you in a personal way. The introview answers questions such as, "Why is this important to me?" "Why should I care about this?" and "How will I be better off in the future as a result of understanding this subject?"

Material contained in **Sidebars (2)** provides examples and additional information that make the content clearer and/or more relevant to real-life salon settings.

Following each full exercise is a **Design Decisions chart (3)** to guide you in planning the finished design before it is executed. By filling in each of the blank sections of the chart, you will be better able to visualize the finished design composition before you even begin.

At the very end of each full exercise, **Rubrics (4)** appear. Rubrics are self-assessment tools that help gauge your level of performance. These are designed to compare your skill and technique to industry standards.

Voices of Success (5) speak to you from four different and important points of view: the salon owner, the educator, the designer and the client. By capturing these industry voices, you have the advantage of discovering what is important to those people in a position to have a huge influence in your career. This creates a credible and personal bridge between your training and your career.

The primary assessment tool in each chapter is called the **Learning Challenge (6)**. This challenge allows you to test your recall and understanding of the most important material in the chapter.

Lessons Learned (7) provides a list of statements that recaps the chapter's critical messages and learning objectives. These are "words of wisdom" that you can take with you throughout your career.

In Other Words (8) summarizes the content with a brief statement at the end of every chapter.

Brainworks (9) are exercises that follow major learning topics and are designed to reinforce and build meaning. By working with exercises that reflect interesting or real-world situations, Brainworks allow you to relate personally to the topic and construct new meanings to affirm your understanding of the material. These exercises give you opportunities to engage in thinking about the ideas presented in the book and explore your ideas with other students.

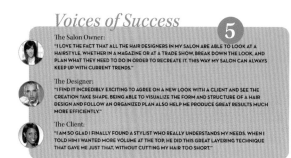

Voices of Success

The Salon Owner:
"I LOVE THE FACT THAT ALL THE HAIR DESIGNERS IN MY SALON ARE ABLE TO LOOK AT A HAIRSTYLE, WHETHER IN A MAGAZINE OR AT A TRADE SHOW, BREAK DOWN THE LOOK, AND PLAN WHAT THEY NEED TO DO IN ORDER TO RECREATE IT. THIS WAY MY SALON CAN ALWAYS KEEP UP WITH CURRENT TRENDS."

The Designer:
"I FIND IT INCREDIBLY EXCITING TO AGREE ON A NEW LOOK WITH A CLIENT AND SEE THE CREATION TAKE SHAPE. BEING ABLE TO VISUALIZE THE FORM AND STRUCTURE OF A HAIR DESIGN AND FOLLOW AN ORGANIZED PLAN ALSO HELP ME PRODUCE GREAT RESULTS MUCH MORE EFFICIENTLY."

The Client:
"I AM SO GLAD I FINALLY FOUND A STYLIST WHO REALLY UNDERSTANDS MY NEEDS. WHEN I TOLD HIM I WANTED MORE VOLUME AT THE TOP, HE DID THIS GREAT LAYERING TECHNIQUE THAT GAVE ME JUST THAT, WITHOUT CUTTING MY HAIR TOO SHORT."

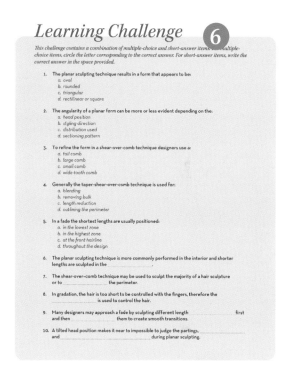

Learning Challenge

This challenge contains a combination of multiple-choice and short-answer items. For multiple-choice items, circle the letter corresponding to the correct answer. For short-answer items, write the correct answer in the space provided.

1. The planar sculpting technique results in a form that appears to be:
   a. oval
   b. rounded
   c. triangular
   d. rectilinear or square

2. The angularity of a planar form can be more or less evident depending on the:
   a. head position
   b. styling direction
   c. distribution used
   d. sectioning pattern

3. To refine the form in a shear-over-comb technique designers use a:
   a. tail comb
   b. large comb
   c. small comb
   d. wide-tooth comb

4. Generally the taper-shear-over-comb technique is used for:
   a. blending
   b. removing bulk
   c. length reduction
   d. outlining the perimeter

5. In a fade the shortest lengths are usually positioned:
   a. in the lowest zone
   b. in the highest zone
   c. at the front hairline
   d. throughout the design

6. The planar sculpting technique is more commonly performed in the interior and shorter lengths are sculpted in the _____.

7. The shear-over-comb technique may be used to sculpt the majority of a hair sculpture or to _____ the perimeter.

8. In gradation, the hair is too short to be controlled with the fingers, therefore the _____ is used to control the hair.

9. Many designers may approach a fade by sculpting different length _____ first and then _____ them to create smooth transitions.

10. A tilted head position makes it near to impossible to judge the partings, and _____ during planar sculpting.

Lessons Learned

Each form's specific qualities are more or less evident in a combination form.

Various criteria, such as the placement of the weight area in relation to the client's head shape and facial features as well as the proportion of the textures, must be considered when combining forms.

Specialized sculpting techniques can be performed with a variety of tools, such as shears, a razor, texturizing shears (also known as tapering or thinning shears) or clippers, and can be performed at the base, the midstrand, along the ends of the strand or a combination of the three depending on the desired effect.

IN OTHER WORDS:

Understanding sculpture transformations and making design decisions about hair sculpture will give you the ability to create the desired effects for your clients and expand your horizons, allowing you to see all the possibilities of hair sculpture.

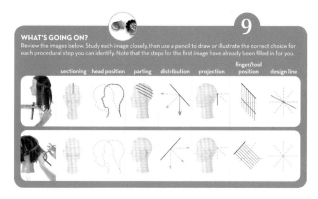

WHAT'S GOING ON?
Review the images below. Study each image closely, then use a pencil to draw or illustrate the correct choice for each procedural step you can identify. Note that the steps for the first image have already been filled in for you.

sectioning   head position   parting   distribution   projection   finger/tool position   design line

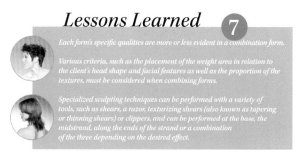

DIVING INTO *SCULPTURE, A DESIGNER'S APPROACH*

Sculpture, A Designer's Approach consists of two main areas of study: Seeing and Thinking as a Designer and Creating as a Designer. Each chapter within these two areas presents a discussion of key concepts, new insights on familiar topics, and practical examples. These themes build on one another from chapter to chapter. Immerse yourself in each chapter, take your time with the material, and enjoy the learning process.

Dex Images/Getty Images

SEEING AND THINKING AS A DESIGNER

In the first chapter, you will learn about many different aspects of sculpture—line, shape, weight, surface texture and structure—that occur in nature, fashion and art. These aspects can offer inspiration when it comes to sculpting hair. Whether short, medium or long, you will encounter clients who wish to change their styles through a new hair sculpture. Your professional knowledge and personal connection with your clients will assist you in making design decisions that will allow you to create the result you envision.

CREATING AS A DESIGNER

The second chapter of *Sculpture, A Designer's Approach* deals with essential skills for creating successful hair sculptures using the four basic forms. It is the four basic forms— solid, graduated, increase-layered and uniformly layered—that act as the foundation on which you will create successful hair sculptures with predictable results.

The third chapter applies these basic forms in a new way. It is in this chapter that you will learn to combine these basic forms within a hair sculpture to create more inspired and personalized designs that will earn your clients' loyalty.

In the fourth chapter, the concepts of combination forms introduced in Chapter 3 are used to create hair sculptures that are designed for the male client. The focus of this chapter is using new and different techniques to achieve variations on the combination forms as they relate to sculpting men's hair. You will apply these techniques to create longer, mid-length and short forms for men.

"ONE STEP—CHOOSING A GOAL AND STICKING TO IT— CHANGES EVERYTHING"

— SCOTT REED, AUTHOR

ADAPTING AS A DESIGNER

Pages 325-326 of this *Coursebook* give a brief preview of what it means to adapt a sculpture design. As skills improve, designers move beyond producing results to composing and personalizing new sculpture designs.

Now you are ready to learn about changing the hair's form and length through sculpting. Dive into Sculpture, A Designer's Approach *with enthusiasm and confidence in yourself and your teachers to prepare for a successful career. Your teachers understand the transition from student to professional. You can expect them to make sure you are ready for the challenges of creating all types of hair sculptures. Enjoy the journey.*

Executive Management Team

Leo Passage
Founder and
Chairman Emeritus

Karen Wilkin-Donachie
Chief Executive Officer

Corrine Passage
Senior Vice President, Production
and Systems Development

Robert Sieh
Senior Vice President,
Finance and Operations

Judy Rambert
Vice President,
Education and Research

Sarah Pirok
Vice President,
Franchise Development
and International Academies

Ken Angermeier
Vice President,
Global Marketing
and Customer Service

Susan Kier
Senior Director,
Sales and Education

Casey Swartz
Human Resources

Production Team

Sabine Held-Perez
Senior Director,
Program Development

Tina Rayyan
Production Director

Chris Cote
Creative Manager

Maureen Spurr
Editorial Manager

Brian Fallon
Educational Content Supervisor

Eileen Dubelbeis
Program Development Associate

Melissa Holmes
Program Development Associate

Vic Piccolotto
Program Development Associate

Csaba Zongor
Graphic Design Associate

David Placek
Photographer/Videographer

Janet Fisher
Senior Director,
Education and Research

Jen Eckstein
Creative Services Senior Manager

Marilyn Geary
Developmental Editor

Amy Howard
Program Development Associate

Joanna Jakubowicz
Graphic Design Associate

Deidre Glover
Editorial Associate

Charles Kushner
Production Associate

Anna Fehr
Educational Technology Manager

FrameOne Communications
DVD Production

Robert Richards
Fashion Illustrations

Markel Richards
Program Development Associate

Rick Russell
Graphic Design Associate

Benjamin Polk
Editorial Associate

Vasiliki A. Stavrakis
Art and Design Research Director

Mia Kim
Education and
Research Associate

Denise Podlin
New Products Manager

Dex Images/Getty Images

the POSSIBILITIES *of* SCULPTURE

- Shape
- Structure
- Weight
- Solid form
- Graduated form
- Increase-layered form
- Uniformly layered form
- Direction
- Line

Understanding the effects of transforming a hair sculpture leads to more creative possibilities for hair designers and clients.

Following this lesson on *The Possibilities of Sculpture*, you will be able to:

☐ List the aspects of a hair design that are influenced by a hair sculpture transformation

☐ Identify the observable differences among the four basic forms

☐ Describe the surface texture of the four basic forms

☐ Summarize the common lines along which each of the four basic forms can unfold

☐ Use design principles to describe the length arrangement of the four basic forms

☐ Explain ways in which a new hair sculpture can impact a person's appearance

ESSENTIAL QUESTIONS FOR THIS CHAPTER:

What are the things I need to consider before I can transform a client's look through sculpture?

How can I ensure that the sculpture I create matches my vision?

How do I choose the right lines for the sculpture I want to create?

How can I recreate a sculpture based on an image a client might show me?

As a professional hair designer, you will from time to time encounter clients who are looking for a dramatic change in their image. In some cases a client with longer hair may bring a picture of a celebrity who just recently sported a short style. Now this client would like you to sculpt her hair short as well. For many makeover cases like this, the hair sculpture is the first step to a completely new look. As you will learn in this program, *Sculpture, A Designer's Approach,* hair sculpting lays the foundation for all hair design compositions, while color and texture add support and enhance the sculpture.

Chapter 1, The Possibilities of Sculpture, will open your eyes and mind, helping you to envision and create a plan for your sculpture designs before the first strands of hair ever fall.

SCULPTURE: UP CLOSE AND PERSONAL

Consumers are always interested in finding out about new hair designs and haircuts. Many magazines notice an increase in sales when their cover states that the issue includes the "50 best haircuts for the season." Salon clients often read about the latest trends, even techniques, which cause many of them to come to their appointments with very clear expectations of the haircuts they want.

Most of your clients will be able to recognize short, medium and long hair very easily and can even distinguish between hair that is layered or not. As a designer, however, your understanding of hair sculpting will go far beyond that of your clients. You will understand how various aspects of a hair design are transformed by the sculpture. You will also be able to recognize the four basic sculpted forms and how they can be combined in unlimited combinations to create an endless variety of sculptures, including current trends.

What are the things I need to consider before I can transform a client's look through sculpture?

SCULPTURE TRANSFORMATION

When considering a new haircut, the first question clients usually want answered is how much shorter the hair will be. Although it is a fact that hair sculptures result in at least some, if not all, of the hair being somewhat shorter than before, length reduction is only one of the aspects hair designers will take into consideration.

What sculpture transformation is really about is changing the shape (or silhouette), the surface texture and the structure of a hair design. When you understand the effects of this transformation, it becomes clear that all short hair is not the same; all medium-length hair is not the same; and all long hair is not the same.

Designers can identify the ways in which hair sculptures differ by analyzing the shape, position of weight or volume, texture and length arrangement.

SHORT

MEDIUM

LONG

BRINGING SCULPTURE INTO FOCUS

Of all the services that you offer as a designer, hair sculpting is probably the one that has the greatest impact on the shape, or silhouette, of a hair design. You already know that the way the hair is sculpted immediately affects the shape and surface texture of a hair design.

One of the things to particularly notice is how each of the four basic sculpted forms results in a specific surface texture. Solid forms produce the most unactivated, or smoothest, surface texture. Uniformly layered forms, on the other hand, produce the most activated surface texture. Graduated and increase-layered forms produce sculptures that are partially activated and partially unactivated.

How can I ensure that the sculpture I create matches my vision?

Although the surface texture of a hair design can best be seen in natural fall, when visualizing the structure of a sculpture, the hair is imagined at a 90° projection (also known as normal projection) from the curve of the head. It is in this abstract view that the blueprint of the hair sculpture can be envisioned.

SOLID FORM

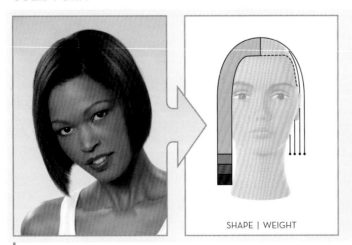

SHAPE | WEIGHT

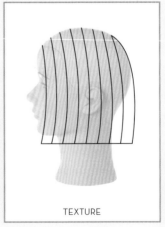

TEXTURE

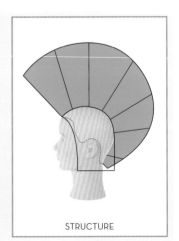

STRUCTURE

GRADUATED FORM

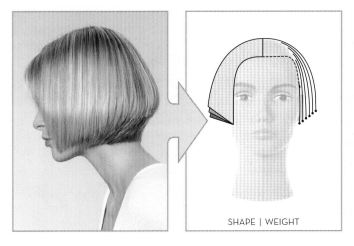

SHAPE	WEIGHT	TEXTURE	STRUCTURE

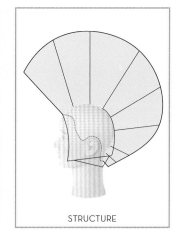

INCREASE-LAYERED FORM

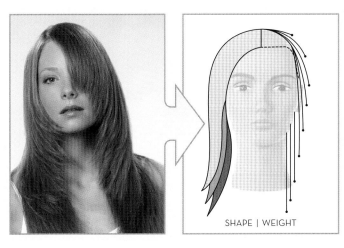

SHAPE	WEIGHT	TEXTURE	STRUCTURE

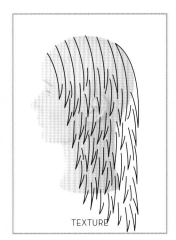

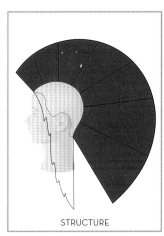

UNIFORMLY LAYERED FORM

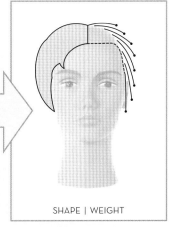

SHAPE	WEIGHT	TEXTURE	STRUCTURE

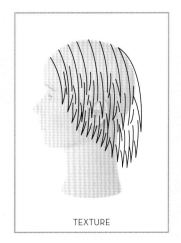

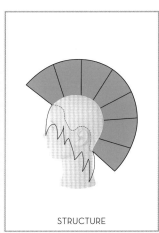

KEEP IN MIND THAT HAIR WITH CURLY TEXTURE APPEARS TO BE SHORTER. THIS CURL ACTIVATION ALSO INFLUENCES THE WAY THE SURFACE TEXTURE OF A SCULPTURE IS PERCEIVED.

In a solid form, all lengths reach the same level and although curly, the lines are still unbroken.

In an increase-layered form, hair ends disperse over the surface of the hair design featuring broken lines.

TELL IT LIKE IT IS!

Review the images to the right, then use a marker or pen and trace along the shapes of the designs. Then trace along the lines in the surface texture and circle the area of the designs where you notice a build-up of weight. Finally, use the space provided below each image to take note of the shape, texture and position of weight you have identified in each hair design.

Courtesy of DF 275.

1.2

How do I choose the right lines for the sculpture I want to create?

SCULPTURE: THE BIGGER PICTURE

Now that you have had an up-close look at hair sculpting, you are ready to take the next step—thinking about how to transform actual clients' hair designs by sculpting their hair.

To ensure that the new hair sculpture meets the physical and emotional needs of your client, you'll need to consider facial shape, body structure and hair qualities along with lifestyle and personal likes and dislikes.

To make sure that the hair sculpture matches the vision you and your client agreed upon, you will need to make several design decisions. Each of those decisions will greatly impact the resulting hair sculpture.

SCULPTURE DESIGN DECISIONS

Once you and your client have mutually agreed upon the overall hair sculpture, the decision-making process has just begun, especially for you as a designer. Before you can pick up your tools and sculpt the first strand of hair, you need to visualize the form and the structure of the final design. You'll also need to decide which lines you want to use throughout the design, which of the client's features you wish to highlight and which you'll try to balance. These considerations will lead you to decide which

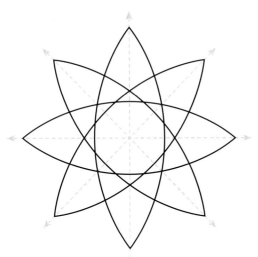

partings and design lines to use, i.e., horizontal, diagonal or vertical. Determining the placement of volume within the hair design will help you decide how to distribute and project the hair.

All these and more are hair sculpture design decisions. Understanding the nature of these decisions is what makes the difference between a stylist who cuts hair and a designer who sculpts hair.

VISUALIZING FORM

When visualizing the form of a hair design, it is helpful to use geometric shapes, such as the square, triangle, oval and circle, as references. Once you have identified the shape, take a look at the direction along which the form unfolds. Direction is especially important because it leads the eye through a design composition. It automatically draws attention to certain areas of the design and, in many cases, it determines where in a sculpture the surface of the hair displays unactivated (unbroken) lines or activated (broken) lines. Common lines used in sculpting are horizontal, vertical and diagonal.

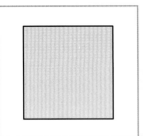

HORIZONTAL
SOLID FORM

DIAGONAL-FORWARD
SOLID FORM

DIAGONAL-BACK
SOLID FORM

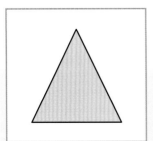

HORIZONTAL
GRADUATED FORM

DIAGONAL-FORWARD
GRADUATED FORM

DIAGONAL-BACK
GRADUATED FORM

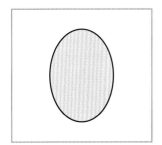

VERTICAL INCREASE-
LAYERED FORM

HORIZONTAL INCREASE-
LAYERED FORM

DIAGONAL-FORWARD
INCREASE-LAYERED FORM

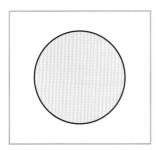

HORIZONTAL UNIFORMLY
LAYERED FORM

VERTICAL UNIFORMLY
LAYERED FORM

DESIGN PRINCIPLES

Design Principles are the patterns in which hair designers arrange length, texture and color within a design. Understanding these principles allows you to analyze a composition in order to recreate it or adapt it to suit your client.

Here are some examples of design principles that are used in sculpture:

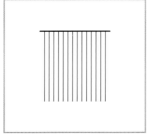

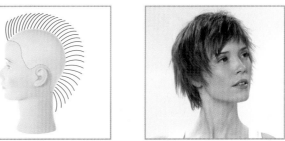

REPETITION
All lengths are equal throughout or within a given area.

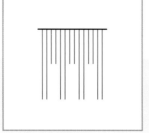  

ALTERNATION
Lengths alternate between short and long.

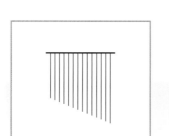 

PROGRESSION
Lengths progress from long to short or short to long.

CONTRAST
Lengths may be short in one area, and longer in another.

How can I recreate a sculpture based on an image a client might show me?

COMBINING FORMS AND STRUCTURES

In many cases you and your client will look at hair design images and will select a specific design. Then it is up to you to see as a designer—to analyze the shape and the position of weight, or volume, as well as surface texture. From there you will continue to think as a designer, envisioning the structure of a design, whether it consists of one pure form or, more commonly, a combination of forms.

Most often you will be combining forms to create the looks that your client desires. This means that you will sculpt one form in one area and another form elsewhere in the design. To combine forms successfully requires a great awareness of what each form will add to the overall design.

The images below help you to visualize how a pure version of any form (shown in the four corner images) can be combined into a combination form.

CHANGE THE SCULPTURE, CHANGE THE EFFECT

With your training as a hair designer you will have the power to transform your clients' appearance. A change in sculpture can impact the way people see themselves and are seen by others. Most sculpture clients will ask for a hair design of a certain length, or for layers to gain movement and texture. Or they may ask to make it easier for them to achieve volume in certain areas of the design. Some may even ask you to give them a completely new look.

A change in hair sculpture, as the foundation of an overall hair design, can transform a client's look in any number of ways—becoming more sporty, more sophisticated, more professional or more cutting edge, just to name a few.

Notice the changes created by sculpting the hair into different shapes and surface textures in the examples shown here, and the effects these changes in sculpture have on each client.

Hair designers are able to look at any person and have ideas on how to improve the way he or she looks. They can also look at an image in a hair magazine, maybe one of the latest trends, and apply the basic, detail and abstract levels of observation to identify the forms sculpted to create the style. Still thinking as designers, they create a plan that lets them reproduce what they see. When you take advantage of all the possibilities sculpture has to offer, you will increase your clientele and grow as a professional.

WHAT YOU KNOW NOW

In the spaces below, write as many characteristics about each one of the four basic forms as you can remember. Once completed, compare your notes with your classmates' and fill in any additional information that you may not have included.

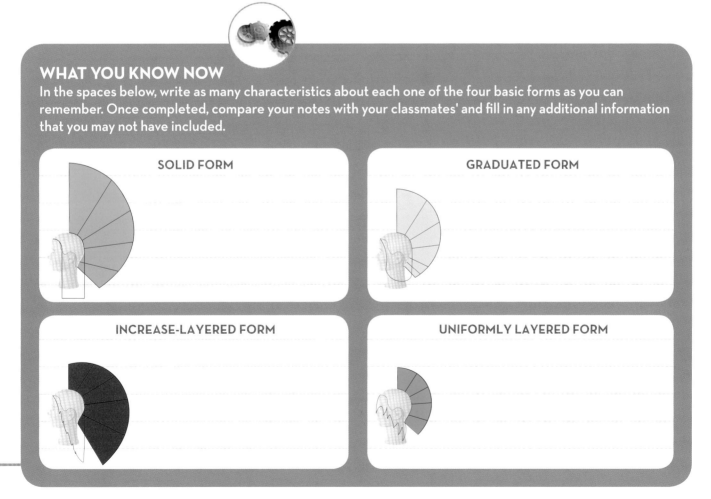

SOLID FORM

GRADUATED FORM

INCREASE-LAYERED FORM

UNIFORMLY LAYERED FORM

Voices of Success

The Salon Owner:

"I LOVE THE FACT THAT ALL THE HAIR DESIGNERS IN MY SALON ARE ABLE TO LOOK AT A HAIRSTYLE, WHETHER IN A MAGAZINE OR AT A TRADE SHOW, BREAK DOWN THE LOOK, AND PLAN WHAT THEY NEED TO DO IN ORDER TO RECREATE IT. THIS WAY MY SALON CAN ALWAYS KEEP UP WITH CURRENT TRENDS."

The Designer:

"I FIND IT INCREDIBLY EXCITING TO AGREE ON A NEW LOOK WITH A CLIENT AND SEE THE CREATION TAKE SHAPE. BEING ABLE TO VISUALIZE THE FORM AND STRUCTURE OF A HAIR DESIGN AND FOLLOW AN ORGANIZED PLAN ALSO HELP ME PRODUCE GREAT RESULTS MUCH MORE EFFICIENTLY."

The Client:

"I AM SO GLAD I FINALLY FOUND A STYLIST WHO REALLY UNDERSTANDS MY NEEDS. WHEN I TOLD HIM I WANTED MORE VOLUME AT THE TOP, HE DID THIS GREAT LAYERING TECHNIQUE THAT GAVE ME JUST THAT, WITHOUT CUTTING MY HAIR TOO SHORT."

IN OTHER WORDS:

Understanding sculpture transformations and making design decisions about hair sculpture will give you the ability to create the desired effects for your clients and expand your horizons, allowing you to see all the possibilities of hair sculpture.

Learning Challenge

This challenge contains a combination of multiple-choice and short-answer items. For multiple-choice items, circle the letter corresponding to the correct answer. For short-answer items, write the correct answer in the space provided.

1. The shape of a hair design describes the:
   a. texture
   b. structure
   c. silhouette
   d. length arrangement

2. The structure of a hair design can best be seen:
   a. on wet hair
   b. on short hair
   c. in natural fall
   d. in normal projection

3. The placement of volume within a hair design is also known as:
   a. *weight*
   b. *direction*
   c. *activation*
   d. *surface texture*

4. Sculpture transformation is about changing the hair's:
   a. *length*
   b. *surface texture*
   c. *shape and structure*
   d. *shape, surface texture and structure*

5. The surface texture of a hair design can best be seen:
   a. *on long hair*
   b. *on curly hair*
   c. *in natural fall*
   d. *in normal projection*

6. Pivot Point's hair sculpture education is built upon four basic forms, which are the solid form, graduated form, _____ _____ form and _____ _____ form.

7. In solid forms the lengths progress from shorter at the _____ to longer in the _____.

8. In natural fall the ends of a graduated form stack up along an _____.

9. The structure of uniformly layered forms features a _____ of lengths.

10. Hair sculptures that combine more than one of the basic forms are known as _____ _____.

Lessons Learned

An unlimited number of hair sculptures can be created using the four basic forms by themselves or in combination with one another.

Sculpting the hair influences the shape, position of weight, surface texture and structure of a hair design.

A series of design decisions needs to be made before beginning a sculpture service.

Sculpting peoples' hair can change how they see themselves and are seen by others.

2. A DESIGNER'S APPROACH TO
SCULPTING THE FOUR BASIC FORMS

a designer's approach to

SCULPTING *the* FOUR BASIC FORMS

2.1   ESSENTIAL SCULPTING TECHNIQUES

PREDICTABLE SCULPTING RESULTS
GUIDELINES FOR CLIENT-CENTERED SCULPTING

2.2   SOLID FORM

SOLID FORM OVERVIEW
HORIZONTAL LINE
DIAGONAL-BACK/CONVEX LINE
DIAGONAL-FORWARD LINE
FRINGE VARIATIONS

2.3   GRADUATED FORM

GRADUATED FORM OVERVIEW
DIAGONAL-FORWARD LINE
DIAGONAL-BACK/CONVEX LINE
FRINGE VARIATIONS

2.4   INCREASE-LAYERED FORM

INCREASE-LAYERED FORM OVERVIEW
VERTICAL LINE
DIAGONAL-FORWARD LINE
HORIZONTAL LINE

2.5   UNIFORMLY LAYERED FORM

UNIFORMLY LAYERED FORM OVERVIEW
HORIZONTAL/VERTICAL LINE
PIVOTAL LINE

Creating hair sculptures that match a designer's creative vision requires a step-by-step process.

Following this lesson on A Designer's Approach to Sculpting the Four Basic Forms, you will be able to:

☐ Describe the seven procedural steps used to create predictable sculpting results for the four basic forms

☐ Explain the guidelines for ensuring client satisfaction before, during and after the sculpting service

☐ Demonstrate the knowledge and ability to sculpt solid forms along a variety of lines

☐ Explain various fringe designs that can be incorporated into solid form sculptures

☐ Demonstrate the knowledge and ability to sculpt graduated forms along a variety of lines

☐ Explain various fringe designs that can be incorporated into graduated form sculptures

☐ Demonstrate the knowledge and ability to sculpt increase-layered forms along a variety of lines

☐ Demonstrate the knowledge and ability to sculpt uniformly layered forms along a variety of lines

ESSENTIAL QUESTIONS FOR THIS CHAPTER:

How does a procedure help produce predictable sculpture results?

How will I know when to use each of the basic sculpted forms?

Is there a way that I can know how the sculpture will turn out?

How can I make sure I don't cut my client's hair too short?

During the 1960s hairdressing evolved in a way our industry has yet to experience again. Prior to this evolution, the efforts spent to create a hair design were focused on cutting the hair in preparation for the more important roller set and comb-out.

During this time, industry leaders such as Leo Passage and Vidal Sassoon reinvented hairdressing through precision haircutting. Precision cutting created stunning, never-before-seen hair designs that took much less time to style. Precision cutting made the actual haircut the main aspect of the final design. It was at that time that Pivot Point started referring to the act of cutting the hair as *hair sculpting.*

Chapter 2, A Designer's Approach to Sculpting the Four Basic Forms will give you the essential foundations for sculpting hair. Along with learning the techniques you will also learn timeless, classic designs and beautiful hair sculptures that must be included in every successful hair designer's repertoire.

When you master these sculpture designs, you will be well on your way to becoming a sought-after designer.

ESSENTIAL SCULPTING TECHNIQUES

How does a procedure help produce predictable sculpting results?

At some point in your life you have probably flipped through the pages of a hair magazine, whether it was simply out of curiosity or to find a new look for yourself. Even if you looked at 100 hair magazines, you would have only seen a small fragment of the unlimited number of styles clients can choose from today. Despite the unlimited number of options, every hair sculpture is comprised of one or more of the four basic forms that you are about to learn. Knowing how to identify and create the four basic forms makes it possible for you to create almost any sculpture imaginable. These basic forms look so different because of the steps chosen to create a specific and predictable result.

PREDICTABLE SCULPTING RESULTS

Did you know that one of the most common reasons why a client may not go back to the same designer is that his or her hair was cut too short? When you think about it, a perm that's too tight can be loosened; color that's too light can be darkened; an up-do the client doesn't like can be redone; but a sculpture that is too short needs time—sometimes a lot of time—to grow out. Following a specific sequence of procedural steps, Pivot Point's Seven Sculpting Procedures allow you to produce exactly the hair sculpture that you and your client agree upon.

Designers follow the Seven Sculpting Procedures to create predictable sculpting results:

1. SECTION
2. POSITION HEAD
3. PART
4. DISTRIBUTE
5. PROJECT
6. POSITION FINGERS/SHEARS
7. SCULPT DESIGN LINE

SECTION

To ensure the correct proportional relationships between different forms, designers section, or divide, the hair to determine how they will create the new sculpted form. The established sectioning pattern helps to remember where techniques or design lines need to change, pointing the designer in the right direction to achieve the desired result. Even if the sculpture features only one form throughout, sectioning helps the designer control the hair to stay organized and achieve more accurate results.

Sectioning is performed with the wide-tooth end of the sculpting comb, and individual sections are kept neat and secured with sectioning clips. Sometimes hair may be too short to section effectively. That's when designers envision zones within the sculpted form. The zones act as sections do, separating between different techniques and design lines.

While sectioning is related to the intended design, it may also be related to the shape and size of the individual client's head and natural growth patterns.

Here are some common sectioning patterns:

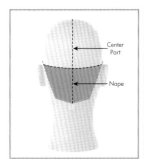

Center Part — Nape

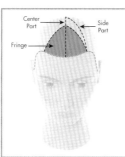

Center Part — Side Part — Fringe

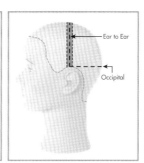

Ear to Ear — Occipital

Curved Section

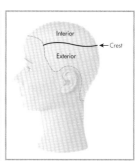

Interior — Crest — Exterior

How will I know when to use each of the basic sculpted forms?

POSITION HEAD

Many clients in the salon like to read a magazine during their service. This often results in a tilted head position. Hair designers pay attention to this and ensure that the head is in a correct position during the sculpture. Knowing how the head position influences the results of a sculpted form and communicating to the client why a certain head position is preferred helps clients cooperate with the designer. It often makes them appreciate their designer's skills even more and lets them feel they are taking part in the process.

The most common head positions are upright, forward and tilted to either side.

UPRIGHT

Since the upright head position allows the designer to best judge the angles of the design line, partings, projection and finger position chosen, it is the head position most frequently used, especially in solid and graduated form sculptures.

FORWARD

Tilting the client's head forward is often used when defining form lines or when sculpting the nape area very short. This position is also commonly used when sculpting increase-layered forms since it facilitates distributing and projecting the lengths upward.

TILTED TO EITHER SIDE

When sculpting short forms, designers may choose to tilt the client's head toward either side in order to refine the hairline at the ear and sideburn area or to refine the form line at the sides.

PART

To part the hair when sculpting means to subdivide the sections into separate individual partings for better distribution and control. These individual partings must be consistent and thin enough so that the design line that is followed while sculpting is still visible. Because the head is curved, it is essential for you to physically move around the head while parting, so that the angles and directions of the partings stay consistent, and so partings within a section remain parallel to one another. The direction of a parting is determined by the direction of the intended design line and the finished result.

The most common lines used to part the hair are:
horizontal, diagonal back, diagonal forward, vertical and pivotal.

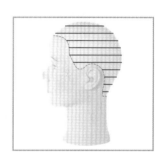

HORIZONTAL

DIAGONAL BACK

DIAGONAL FORWARD

VERTICAL

PIVOTAL

DISTRIBUTE

The direction in which the hair is distributed while sculpting makes a big impact on the final result and can't be overlooked. In general, use the fine teeth of the comb to distribute the hair. When the hair is curly or has a high density, the wide teeth of the comb can be used as well.

*The types of distribution identified by Pivot Point are:
natural, perpendicular, shifted and directional.*

NATURAL DISTRIBUTION

This distribution accommodates for growth patterns and is mainly used to sculpt solid forms. Designers may ask their clients to gently shake their head at certain times during the sculpture to see exactly how the hair falls naturally and retrace that direction with the sculpting comb. Natural distribution is often used to establish the perimeter of a sculpture, since it allows the designer to see where exactly the lengths will fall after sculpting.

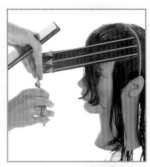

PERPENDICULAR DISTRIBUTION

Because this distribution can be measured and performed consistently, it is preferred for most graduated and increase-layered sculptures.

SHIFTED DISTRIBUTION

This distribution is used in many advanced sculptures to create exaggerated length increases. Many traditional sculptures can be personalized when shifted distribution is used.

DIRECTIONAL DISTRIBUTION

During planar sculpting directional distribution is used. Since the planar sculpting technique is popular for achieving angular forms for male clients, it is essential that hair designers develop a good eye and the skills needed to distribute directionally.

PROJECT

The way the hair is projected while sculpting is crucial to the final result. For example, when sculpting each parting with natural distribution and 0° projection, a solid form is achieved. When each parting is sculpted with natural distribution and 45° projection, a graduated form is achieved. When each parting is sculpted with 90° projection, a uniformly layered form is achieved.

When measuring projection, natural fall is used as a reference to sculpt solid and graduated forms, while the curve of the head is used as a reference to sculpt increase-layered and uniformly layered forms.

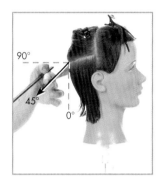

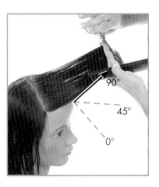
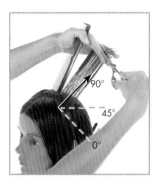

> **The higher the projection, the less weight build-up in the resulting form.**

POSITION FINGERS/SHEARS

When sculpting, the shears usually follow along the index and middle fingers of the opposite hand. In most cases, your fingers will be positioned parallel to the design line. This is especially important when the parting pattern and the design line are not parallel to one another, or for advanced sculpting techniques such as slide cutting.

SCULPT DESIGN LINE

At the beginning of each sculpture a parting pattern is chosen based on the intended or desired design line. In most cases, the design line will be sculpted parallel to the parting pattern. There are some instances, however, when the design line will be sculpted nonparallel to the parting pattern. One example would be when you want rapid length increases.

The type of design line you choose influences the amount of desired weight in the sculpted form. This design line is established and then used within the entire sculpture or within a component area.

In general, stationary design lines result in a faster length increase from one parting to the next. In turn, this creates more weight, especially in solid and graduated forms. Mobile design lines create a slower or no length increase from one parting to the next, such as when you are sculpting with a planar technique or when creating uniform layers.

STATIONARY DESIGN LINE

MOBILE DESIGN LINE

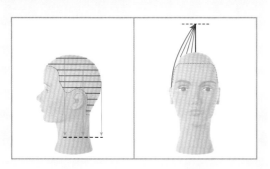

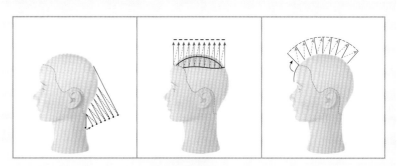

WHAT'S GOING ON?

Review the images below. Study each image closely, then use a pencil to draw or illustrate the correct choice for each procedural step you can identify. Note that the steps for the first image have already been filled in for you.

	sectioning	head position	parting	distribution	projection	finger/tool position	design line

Practice Makes Perfect

SOLID FORM

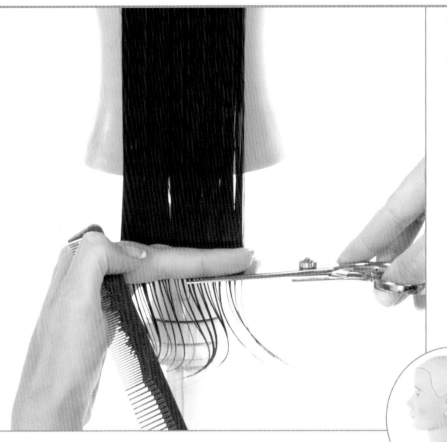

The focus of this exercise is to provide practice in sculpting a solid form along a horizontal line. The result will be smooth, unactivated texture in which the lengths fall to one level.

Practice this exercise to build skill and accuracy using an upright head position, horizontal partings, natural distribution, 0° projection, parallel finger/shear position and a stationary design line.

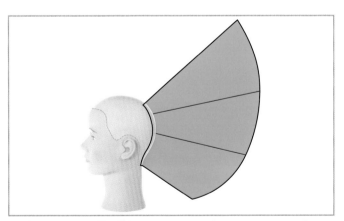

The structure graphic shows shorter lengths in the exterior, progressing to longer lengths in the interior.

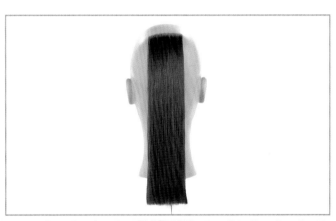

The smooth, unactivated texture is a result of the longest interior lengths falling to the same level as the shortest exterior length.

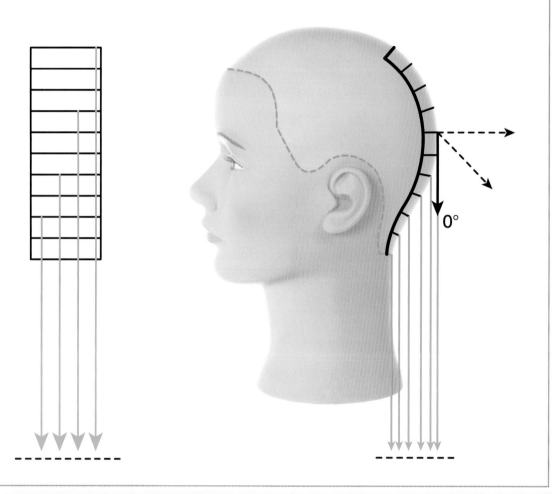

0°

Horizontal partings are used in this exercise. All lengths will be sculpted using a stationary design line.

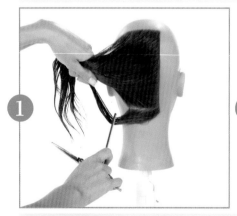

1 With the head in an upright position, release a horizontal parting using the wider teeth of the sculpting comb. Note that the hair is combed in the direction of the parting for ease.

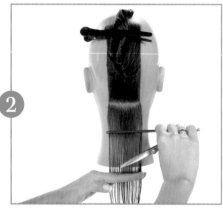

2 Distribute the hair using natural distribution with the fine teeth of the comb.

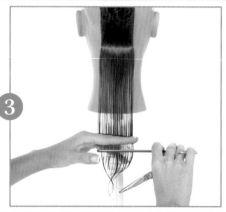

3 Control the lengths by following the comb with your fingers.

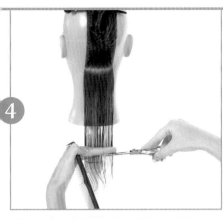

4 Position your fingers parallel to the parting. Sculpt parallel to your fingers to establish a stationary design line using minimal tension and no projection. Do not sculpt past your second knuckle.

5 Check the balance of the line before proceeding.

6 Release the next parting using the wide teeth of the comb. This parting needs to be thin enough to see the stationary design line through it.

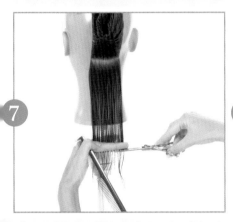

7 Continue to work upward as you sculpt parallel to the horizontal parting and the horizontal stationary design line.

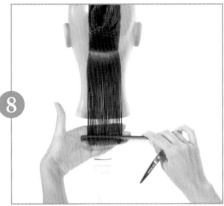

8 Note that there is a build-up of perimeter weight as you continue to sculpt.

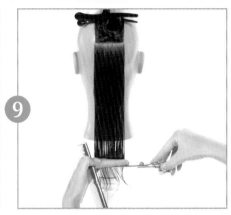

9 Avoid lifting or shifting the hair as you work toward the top, using the same sculpting technique.

10 For better control of the hair, distribute it using the wider teeth of the comb first, then use the finer teeth to refine the distribution.

11 Sculpt using minimal tension and no projection as you work over the curve of the head.

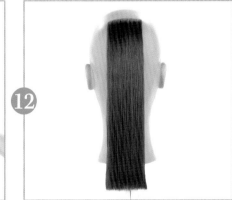

12 The solid form along a horizontal line features smooth, unactivated texture with a build-up of weight, while all the lengths fall to one level.

Practice Makes Perfect

GRADUATED FORM – PERPENDICULAR DISTRIBUTION

The focus of this exercise is to provide practice in using perpendicular distribution from diagonal-right partings to sculpt a graduated form. The result will be a combination of unactivated and activated textures along a diagonal-right line.

Practice this exercise to build skill and accuracy using an upright head position, diagonal-right partings, perpendicular distribution, parallel finger/shear position and a stationary design line.

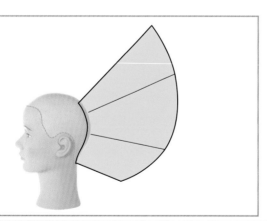

The structure graphic shows the length progression from the shorter exterior lengths to the longer interior lengths.

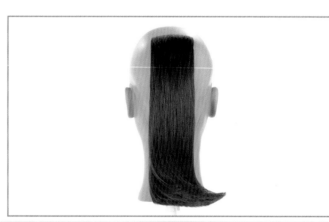

The combination of smooth, unactivated and activated textures is a result of using perpendicular distribution from a diagonal-right parting. A minimal amount of activation is achieved.

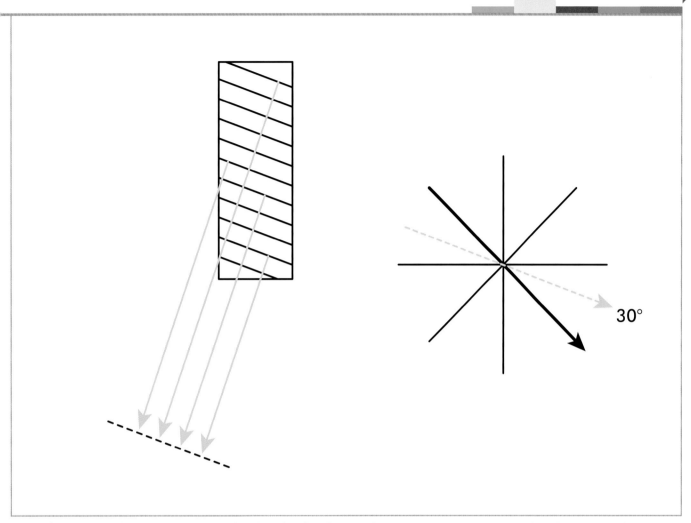

30° diagonal-right partings are used in this exercise. A stationary design line will be used throughout.

1 Release a diagonal-right parting using a 30° angle with the head in an upright position.

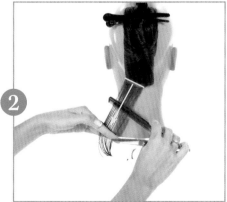

2 Distribute the hair using perpendicular distribution. No projection is used in this exercise.

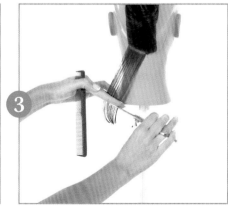

3 Position your fingers parallel to the diagonal-right parting. Sculpt parallel to your fingers to establish a stationary design line.

4

Continue to work upward as you sculpt parallel to the diagonal partings and the diagonal stationary design line.

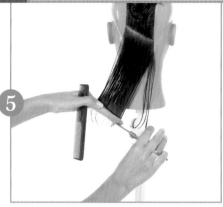

5

Continue to use the same techniques through the next partings. Note the palm-to-palm hand position.

6

Subdivide the partings for control as you work.

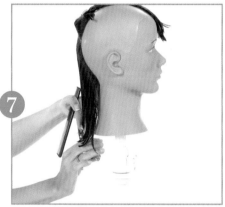

7

Continue to work upward using the same techniques. Avoid projecting the hair.

8

As you reach the top, distribute hair over the curve of the head and continue sculpting parallel to your fingers.

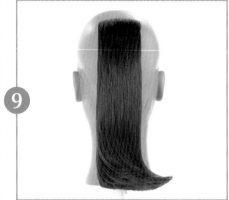

9

The finish shows the combination of unactivated over activated textures. A minimal amount of activation is achieved along a diagonal-right line.

Practice Makes Perfect

GRADUATED FORM – PROJECTION

The focus of this exercise is to provide practice in using projection in a graduated form. The result will be smooth, unactivated interior lengths over activated exterior lengths with a medium line of inclination.

Practice this exercise to build skill and accuracy using an upright head position, horizontal partings, 45° projection, parallel finger/shear position and a mobile design line in the exterior and a stationary design line in the interior.

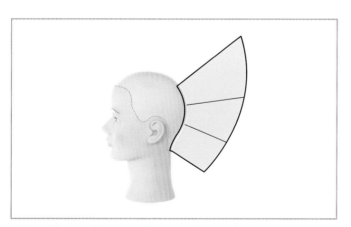

The structure graphic shows the length progression from the shorter exterior to the longer interior.

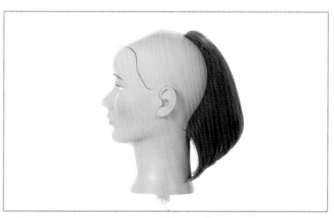

The combination of unactivated interior and activated exterior textures is a result of using a stationary design line to build weight and a mobile design line to create a more pronounced graduated texture.

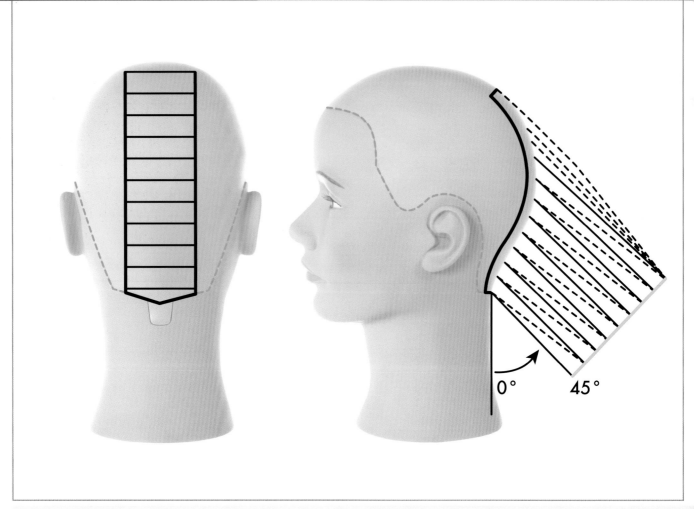

Horizontal partings are used in this exercise. A mobile design line will be used until the crest area is reached. A stationary design line is used for the remainder of the component.

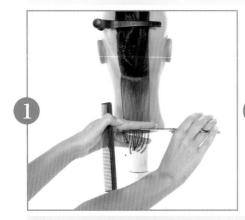

1 Release a horizontal parting and sculpt parallel to the part using perpendicular distribution and 1-finger projection. This will serve as a mobile design line.

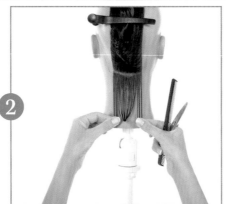

2 Check for symmetry before proceeding.

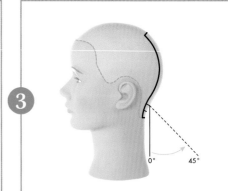

3 Project the next horizontal parting at approximately 45°.

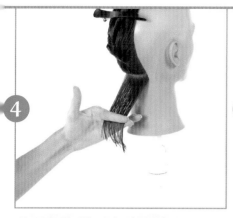

4 Note that by lifting the design line, you reduce the distance the remaining hair needs to travel, resulting in shorter lengths.

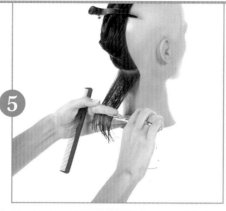

5 Sculpt parallel to the parting. The parting should be thin enough to see the mobile design line.

Many designers often turn their client's profile to the mirror to better assess projection while sculpting graduated lengths.

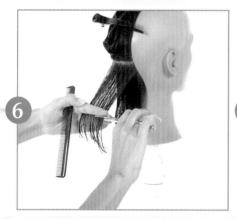

6 Release subsequent horizontal partings. Use each previously sculpted section as a mobile design line.

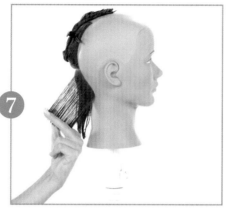

7 Note the resulting line of inclination created by using a mobile design line.

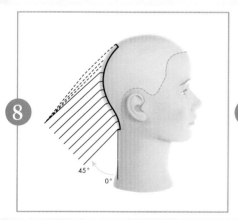

8 The art shows a stationary design line used to sculpt lengths above the crest.

9 Use the last projected section in the crest area as a stationary design line to build weight. All remaining sections will be brought down and sculpted at the stationary design line.

⑩ Work to the top using the same technique.

⑪ Distribute lengths over the curve of the head using perpendicular distribution. Sculpt parallel to your fingers at the stationary design line.

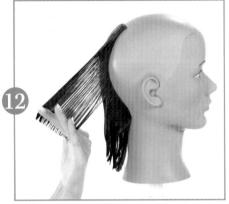

⑫ Cross-check for accuracy, taking vertical partings and angling your fingers along the line of inclination.

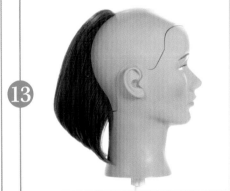

⑬ The finish shows a combination of unactivated texture in the interior and activated stacked lengths in the exterior.

Practice Makes Perfect

INCREASE-LAYERED FORM

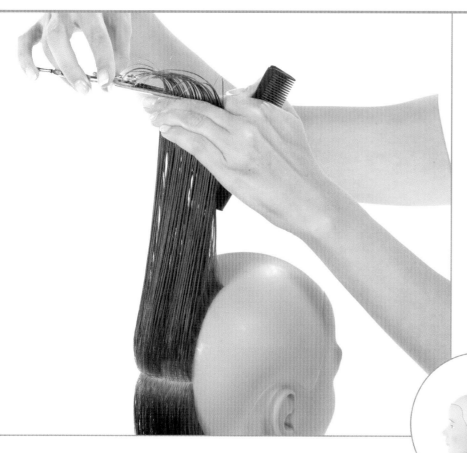

The focus of this exercise is to provide practice sculpting the increase-layered form, using the conversion layering technique with a stationary design line to create an increase in lengths from the interior to the exterior.

Practice this exercise to build skill and accuracy using an upright head position, horizontal partings, perpendicular distribution, 90° projection, parallel finger/shear position and a stationary design line that is positioned in the interior.

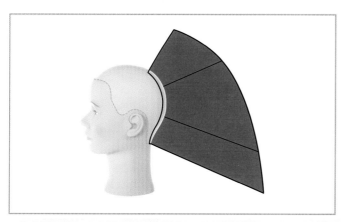

The structure graphic shows the length progression from shorter interior lengths to longer exterior lengths.

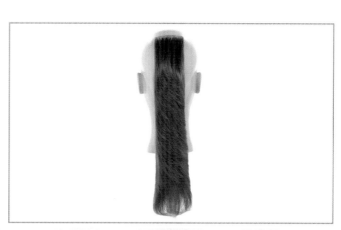

The totally activated texture is the result of the exterior lengths being converged to an interior stationary design line.

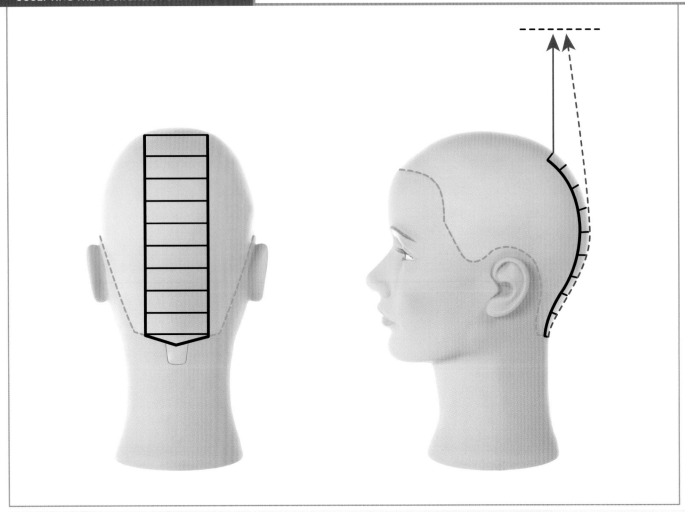

Horizontal partings are used in this exercise. All lengths are converged to an interior stationary design line. If there is a pre-existing length or if maximum length retention is desired, direct the perimeter length upward and measure the design line according to this length.

Release a horizontal parting at the top with the head in an upright position. Stand opposite of the intended length increase. Distribute the hair using perpendicular distribution and project the hair straight up. Sculpt parallel to the parting above your fingers. This will serve as a stationary design line.

Release the next horizontal parting.

3 Distribute the hair upward and converge lengths to the stationary design line. Sculpt parallel to the parting. This is the conversion layering technique.

4 Continue to converge subsequent partings to the stationary design line.

5 Subdivide partings for control while sculpting.

6 Continue to work toward the bottom, using the same techniques.

7 Maintain the projection of the stationary design line and perpendicular distribution throughout the exercise.

8 The activated texture of the increase layers from a horizontal line creates a diffused reflection of light on the surface.

Practice Makes Perfect

UNIFORMLY LAYERED FORM

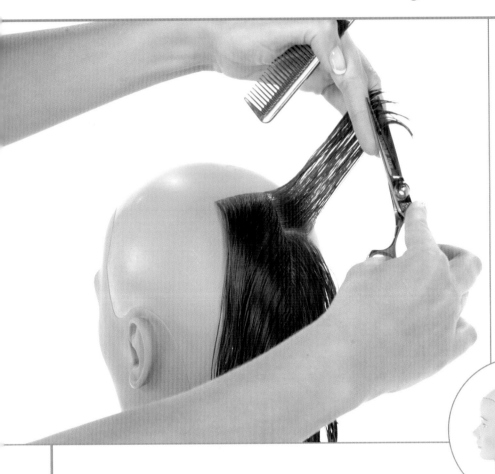

The focus of this exercise is to provide practice in using a mobile design line with vertical partings to create the rounded shape of the uniformly layered form. The result will be a totally activated texture with equal lengths throughout.

Practice this exercise to build skill and accuracy using an upright head position, vertical partings, perpendicular distribution, 90° projection, parallel finger/shear position and a mobile design line.

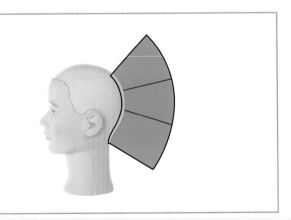

The structure graphic shows that equal lengths throughout create a rounded form that parallels the curve of the head.

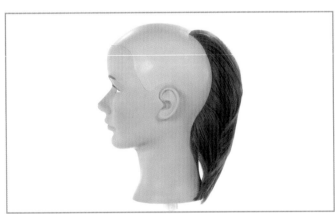

The activated texture of the uniformly layered form is the result of using a mobile design line throughout to create a rounded shape with no weight.

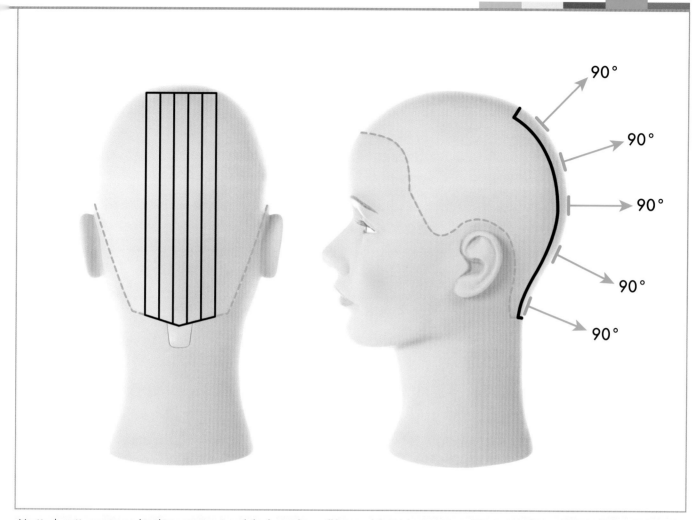

Vertical partings are used in this exercise. A mobile design line will be used throughout. A 90° projection angle is used to sculpt uniformly layered texture. Note the changes from one area to another.

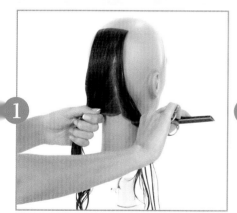

Release a vertical parting starting from the top with the head in an upright position.

Distribute using perpendicular distribution and a 90° projection angle. Sculpt parallel to the parting above your fingers. This will serve as the mobile design line.

Maintain the 90° projection angle as you continue to work toward the bottom.

4 Alter your hand position as you reach the bottom. Work with your palm away from the head. This position will help you to adapt and maintain the correct parallel finger position.

5 Release the next parting and use a portion of the previously sculpted parting as a mobile design line. Make sure your partings are thin enough to clearly see the mobile design line.

6 Follow the mobile design line while maintaining perpendicular distribution and 90° projection as you work toward the bottom.

7 Alter your hand position as you reach the bottom to maintain the correct finger position.

8 Continue to take thin, vertical partings as you work toward the other side.

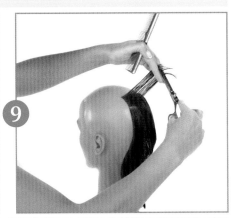

9 Any variance from the sculpting techniques will alter the equally rounded form.

10 Again, alter your hand position as you complete the last parting.

11 Cross-check for accuracy using horizontal partings, perpendicular distribution and a 90° projection angle.

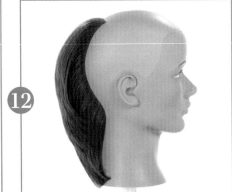

12 The finish shows activated texture of the uniformly layered form, which parallels the curve of the head.

GUIDELINES FOR CLIENT-CENTERED SCULPTING

Client-centered guidelines are designed to help you do everything possible to enhance your client's comfort during the service and satisfaction after the service.

Combining your experience with predictable sculpting results and client-centered guidelines will ensure your hair sculpting success as well as your client's appreciation of the final results.

PROCEDURAL GUIDELINES

The following chart will help you ensure your client's comfort and safety during the sculpting service.

SECTION
- Consider natural growth patterns and hair density
- Explain to client that you are using a sectioning pattern specific to achieving the desired result, e.g., taking growth patterns and hair density into consideration

POSITION HEAD
- Choose a head position that allows you to judge projection as well as angles of partings and finger position while sculpting
- Explain to clients why it is important that they maintain the same head position in order to achieve accurate results
- Move head slowly and gently when changing from one head position to another to ensure client safety and comfort

PART
- Avoid pulling hair by combing section into direction it will be parted prior to taking parting
- Gently draw the corner tooth of the wide-toothed side of sculpting comb across client's scalp to avoid discomfort

DISTRIBUTE
- In general, use fine teeth of comb to distribute a parting
- For thicker hair density or curly texture, wide teeth of comb may be used to distribute or to avoid pulling hair

PROJECT
- Ensure your client's head is in proper position when measuring or judging projection
- When sculpting solid or graduated lengths, measure projection from natural fall
- When layering, measure projection from curve of head

POSITION FINGERS/SHEARS
- Avoid applying excessive tension while holding hair with your fingers
- Avoid wearing rings that may get caught in client's hair
- Groom fingernails frequently to avoid scratching client or hair getting caught in broken or torn nails

SCULPT DESIGN LINE
- Whenever possible, establish length guide for your design line in natural fall first to ensure that lengths are not shorter than desired
- Take your time to establish design line, because it determines the length and directions of subsequent partings

2.2 SOLID FORM

The solid form sculpture has been and remains a popular style. Looking back at important figures in history with notable hair, Cleopatra comes to mind with a design that displayed all the characteristics of a pure solid form: maximum weight at the perimeter, unactivated texture with unbroken lines and all the lengths falling to the same level. Today many designers will agree that sculpting a solid form accurately is not an easy task and only skilled craftsmen are able to accomplish it.

On the pages that follow, you will learn the ins and outs of sculpting solid forms along horizontal, diagonal-back, convex and diagonal-forward lines. Keep in mind that solid form hair sculptures can be created along various lines and at many different lengths. Understanding and mastering the procedures needed to achieve solid lengths will be cornerstones in your repertoire as a hair designer.

SOLID FORM OVERVIEW

Also known as a blunt cut, one-length cut or bob, the solid form is in popular demand by many salon clients. It is now time to further explore the characteristics as well as the techniques used to create predictable solid form sculpture results.

Is there a way that I can know how the sculpture will turn out?

SHAPE

Analyzing the shape or silhouette of most solid forms will reveal similarities, which are most evident on straight hair. Near the top, the shape echoes the curves of the head. At the bottom of the shape, an angular form line is seen as a result of the weight build-up at the perimeter.

Permed or natural curl texture will expand the shape's dimension, particularly at the perimeter weight area.

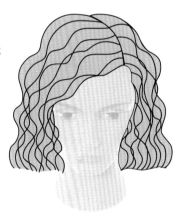

Solid forms can be sculpted at a variety of levels along horizontal, diagonal or curved lines.

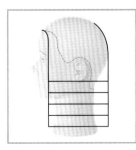 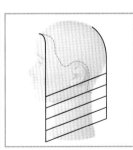  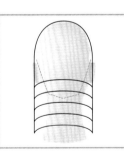 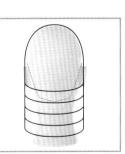

STRUCTURE

Solid form lengths progress from
shorter at the exterior to longer
in the interior. In natural fall, all
lengths fall to one level, creating
weight at the perimeter form line.

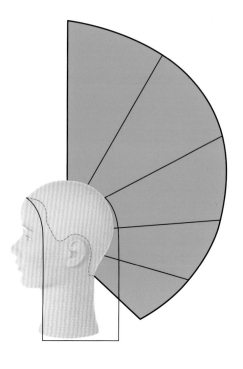

TEXTURE

The texture of the solid form is unactivated with smooth, unbroken lines on the
surface. This occurs because the longer lengths from the interior fall over the rest of
the hair and reach the perimeter of the design.

When sculpted on wavy or curly hair, the surface appears activated, even though the
lines are unbroken. The activation is a result of the curl pattern, not the sculpted form.

SOLID FORM SCULPTING PROCEDURES
SECTION
Sectioning is established for control and between design line changes.

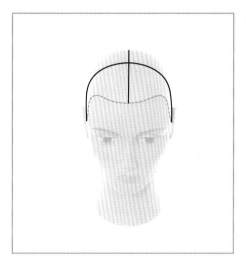

POSITION HEAD
When sculpting a pure solid form, the head is generally held in an upright position. When refining the nape hairline, the head may be tilted forward.

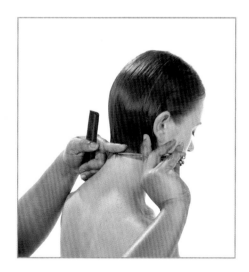

PART

Generally the parting pattern is parallel to the design line.

Common partings used to sculpt solid form designs are:

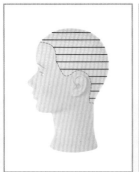

HORIZONTAL

DIAGONAL FORWARD

DIAGONAL BACK

CONCAVE

CONVEX

DISTRIBUTE

To sculpt solid forms, use natural distribution.

- Since natural distribution takes growth patterns into account, pay particular attention to the area above the crest. Place minimal tension on the hair and allow it to fall naturally over the curve of the head.

- Solid fringes require natural distribution around the front hairline to create a precise line. Often the freehand sculpting method is used to achieve a truly solid line in the fringe area.

- On solid sculptures without fringes, comb front lengths in the direction they will be worn before sculpting. This will ensure that the hair will fall to one level in the finished design.

PROJECT

The two projection angles used to sculpt solid forms are natural fall and zero degrees (0°).

NATURAL FALL

Remember when the hair is in natural fall, it is neither lifted away from the scalp nor moved toward it.

0° PROJECTION

This angle positions the hair flat against the surface of the head. In some areas of the head, natural fall and 0° may be the same.

To refine a solid form line, the hair can be sculpted on the skin at 0°.

To increase the underbeveled effect, the head can be tilted forward.

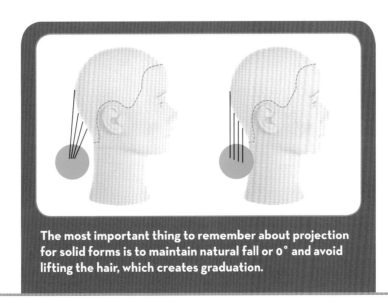

The most important thing to remember about projection for solid forms is to maintain natural fall or 0° and avoid lifting the hair, which creates graduation.

POSITION FINGERS/SHEARS

Most often fingers and shears are positioned parallel to the desired form line to sculpt the solid form. You may also choose to use the back of your hand or a comb to control the hair. The angle of the comb or hand establishes a guide to follow.

The sculpting hand may be turned with the palm up or the palm down. This will depend on the level of comfort relative to the length of the hair and the line being sculpted, as well as the area of the head in which you're sculpting.

DESIGN LINE

A stationary design line is used to sculpt solid forms. The direction of this design line is one of the foremost considerations in planning your design since it also establishes the perimeter form line. Once the stationary design line is established all subsequent partings travel to it.

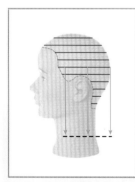    

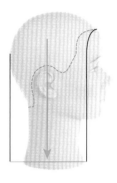

SOLID FORM GUIDELINES
TENSION

Whether sculpting on straight or curly hair, too much tension will result in a graduated appearance. This is especially true when sculpting over the ears. Variations in the hairline and the protrusion of the ears can cause uneven lengths if too much tension is applied.

One way to avoid tension around the ear is to use the back of the comb or your finger to compress the hair slightly toward the head, over the ear, before sculpting. The resulting slack will allow for the shape and protrusion of the ear.

How can I make sure I don't cut my client's hair too short?

COMB CONTROL

To sculpt a solid form with the least amount of tension on the hair, you may use the teeth of the comb to control the lengths while sculpting. The comb is placed parallel to the design line, and the shears are positioned parallel to the comb.

FREEHAND

Another way to avoid tension when sculpting solid forms is to use freehand sculpting techniques. Freehand sculpting allows you to sculpt the hair without holding or controlling the lengths with your fingers or any other tool.

CURLY HAIR

Note how much longer curly hair appears when tension is used. To maintain the shape of the solid form, you may use an overlapping technique. This is done by sculpting each section slightly longer as you work up the head form. The form line is then refined by sculpting with the tips of the shears if needed.

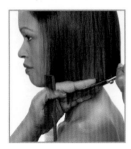

Remember that some hair textures require that the sculpting techniques be adapted. For instance, sometimes it is preferable to sculpt curly hair after it has been air formed straight.

LONGER LENGTHS

Often, the design decisions you make with your client will include lengths well below the shoulders. Since solid forms require sculpting a rather precise line, you may need to make slight adjustments in your technique.

Turning the client's head to one side and then to the other to sculpt the sides is helpful. You may then sculpt either in front or in back of the shoulders. When turning the head, keep the position of the chin consistent from one side to the other to maintain the line that you are sculpting.

To maintain a smooth horizontal line with a slight increase toward the sides, shift the hair toward the back. This allows you to sculpt on the flatter surface of the back.

SOLID FORM, HORIZONTAL LINE — WORKSHOP

The solid horizontal form is the most basic of all forms. It is essential to master before moving on to other forms. The solid horizontal form focuses on line and weight. As you learn to develop your eye for both of these, other forms will be easier to visually analyze.

The smooth, totally unactivated surface of the solid form helps to create a look of classic simplicity, which can be sculpted from a center or side part. Perimeter weight is accentuated by the horizontal form line.

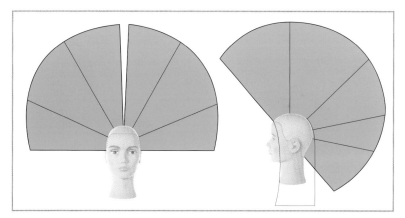

The structure graphics show the length arrangement, which is shorter in the exterior and gets progressively longer in the interior. This allows the hair to fall to one level.

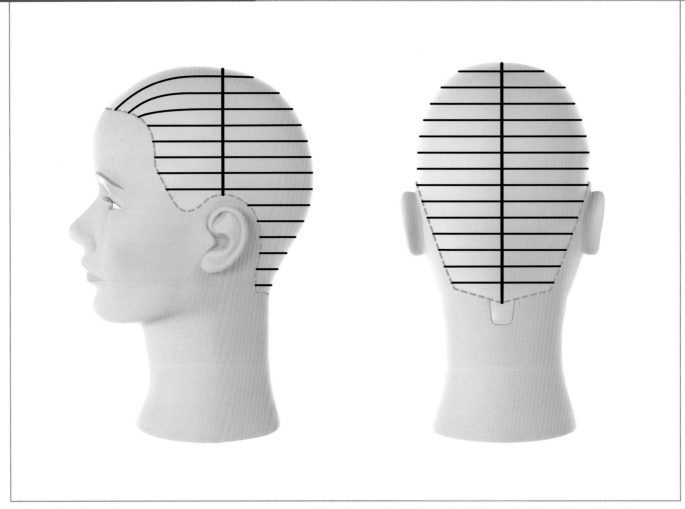

The art illustrates the horizontal parting pattern that will be used to sculpt this form. Note that the partings are consistent in width and parallel to each other.

1 Begin with the head in an upright position. Section the hair with a center part from the forehead to the nape.

2

3 Place the comb on the top of the head to determine the apex, or the highest point of the head.

4 Section from the apex down to the top of each ear.

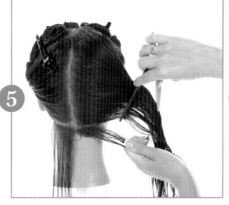

5 Use the wide teeth of the comb to take the first horizontal parting in the nape.

6 Then flip the comb and use the fine teeth to comb the hair in natural distribution.

NOTE: *Designers most commonly choose the palm-up or palm-down hand position based on comfort. The key is to avoid strain on the wrist of the sculpting hand.*

7 With the hair in natural fall, position your fingers parallel to the horizontal parting. Position the shears parallel to your fingers and begin sculpting in the center of the parting.

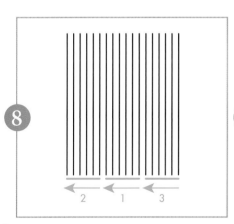

8 Sculpt from the center to the left side and then from the right side to the center.

9 Check the design line for accuracy before continuing.

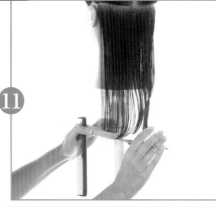

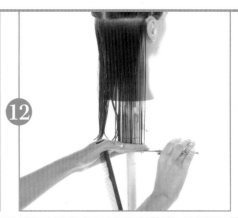

Continue working up the back of the head, using consistent horizontal partings, natural distribution and no projection. Sculpt parallel to the partings, sculpting the center and then either side. Avoid excessive tension and projection, which will cause activation.

When you begin to sculpt above the ears, distribute the hair, then use the back of the comb to push the hair toward the head. The resulting slack helps to compensate for the protrusion of the ear and ensures an accurate horizontal line in the final sculpture.

Sculpt parallel to the horizontal design line.

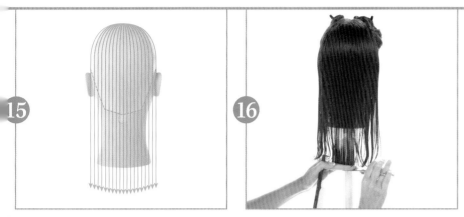

In the crown area, maintain natural distribution. Sculpt horizontally with no projection and no tension.

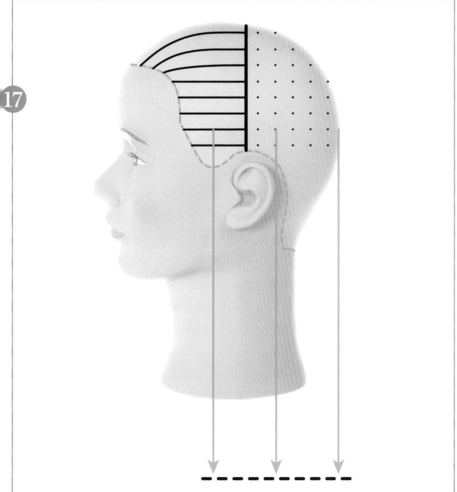

The art shows that the horizontal side partings will be extended into the previously sculpted back sections. This will maintain the continuity of the line from the back to the front.

Use natural distribution and no projection while releasing tension above the ear. Notice that the closed shears may also be used.

Sculpt parallel to the horizontal partings.

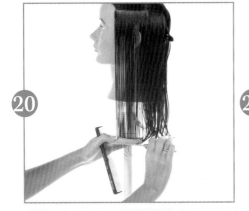

Work toward the top of the section using the same technique.

When you reach the recession area, begin to distribute the hair as it will be worn, before you begin sculpting. In some cases this will be in a slight curve around the hairline. This maintains length toward the face, avoiding any activation in the finished design. Sculpt with very little tension as you work to the top of the head.

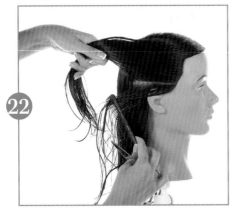

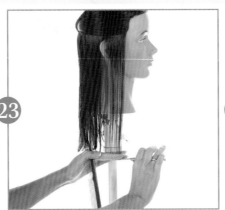

Move to the opposite side and take the first horizontal parting, extending it to the back section. Use the same steps as on the first side, being especially careful to avoid tension over the ear.

Check the symmetry of both sides before continuing.

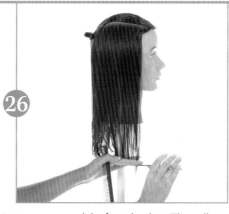

Work to the center part, distributing the hair in a curve around the front hairline. This will maintain the solid form when the hair is worn slightly off the face.

Use very little tension as you sculpt this last section following the horizontal lines of the previous partings.

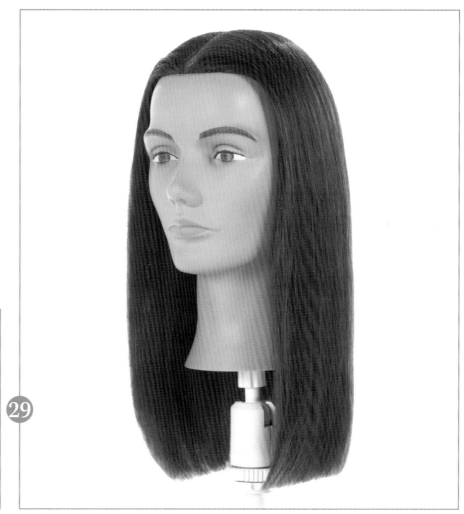

This sculpture may also be styled using a side part.

After air forming, the solid form displays a totally unactivated surface with maximum perimeter weight.

DESIGN DECISIONS

Draw or fill in the boxes with the appropriate answers.

STRUCTURE: solid

SHAPE: Square

TEXTURE: unactivated

SECTIONING PATTERN:

BACK: head position	parting	distribution	projection	finger/tool position	design line mobile/stationary

SIDES: head position	parting	distribution	projection	finger/tool position	design line mobile/stationary

TOOLS:

Shears , Clips , all purpose comb

variation
SOLID FORM, HORIZONTAL LINE

As an option, you may choose to establish the entire perimeter design line before proceeding to sculpt individual horizontal partings. This technique is especially effective in helping to establish symmetry in the design from the very beginning of the sculpting process. Many designers use this method to begin sculpting mid-length and longer sculptures that feature a distinct perimeter form line.

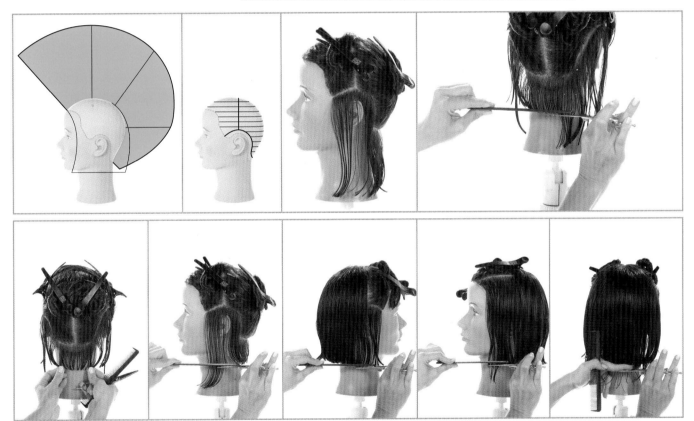

As the hair is sectioned, a perimeter hairline parting is released. The thickness of this parting, which does not include the front hairline, is often adapted to work with density and hairline growth patterns. The design line is sculpted from the center back using natural distribution, no projection and a horizontal comb position. Sculpt with comb control. It is essential to check symmetry as the design line is sculpted from the center to one side and then the other. Then, sculpt both sides using natural distribution, no projection and a horizontal comb position. Some designers choose to sculpt from the center back to the front hairline on either side.

NOTE: *Fingers could also be used to control the hair.*

SCULPTURE DESIGN RUBRIC

Chapter 2: Solid Form, Horizontal Line

This Rubric is a performance assessment tool designed to measure your ability to **create** Pivot Point sculpture designs.

Name _____ ID Number _____ Date _____

	In Progress Level 1	Getting Better Level 2	Entry-Level Proficiency Level 3
PREPARATION			
• Assemble sculpting essentials	☐	☐	☐
CREATE			
• Section hair with center part from hairline to nape and from apex to each ear	☐	☐	☐
• Position head upright	☐	☐	☐
• Part horizontally in nape from center to each side using wide teeth of comb	☐	☐	☐
• Distribute hair in natural fall with fine teeth of comb	☐	☐	☐
• Position fingers and shears parallel to the parting	☐	☐	☐
• Sculpt horizontal stationary design line using palm-up hand position and no projection	☐	☐	☐
• Check design line for accuracy before proceeding	☐	☐	☐
• Sculpt subsequent partings parallel to first using natural distribution with minimal tension above ear	☐	☐	☐
• Sculpt crown area using natural distribution	☐	☐	☐
• Check design line for accuracy before proceeding	☐	☐	☐
• Part hair horizontally on one side, extending to back, using wide teeth of comb	☐	☐	☐
• Sculpt horizontal stationary design line using natural distribution and no projection	☐	☐	☐
• Sculpt with minimal tension over ear	☐	☐	☐
• Distribute hair at top as it will be worn before sculpting	☐	☐	☐
• Sculpt up to center part using same procedures	☐	☐	☐
• Sculpt first parting on opposite side using horizontal partings, natural distribution and no projection; check symmetry with first side	☐	☐	☐
• Work toward center part using equal horizontal partings, natural distribution and no projection	☐	☐	☐
• Sculpt remainder of side using same procedures	☐	☐	☐
• Check for balanced horizontal line with no activation at perimeter form line	☐	☐	☐
• Finish sculpture design	☐	☐	☐

TOTAL POINTS = ☐ + ☐ + ☐

TOTAL POINTS _____ ÷ HIGHEST POSSIBLE SCORE 63 = _____ %

Record your time in comparison with the suggested salon speed. _____

To improve my performance on this procedure, I need to: _____
_____

SOLID FORM, DIAGONAL-BACK/CONVEX LINE – WORKSHOP

Salon professionals strive to help clients achieve the looks they want. As a designer, you can offer this diagonal-back/convex sculpture to clients with longer lengths who want a classic look that showcases shiny, healthy hair. The diagonal-back perimeter allows clients to maintain the sleekness of "one length" hair while the shorter lengths around the face create interest.

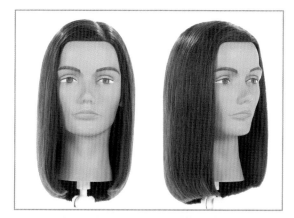

Artistic elements are composed in this solid form design to combine diagonal-back and convex lines. Note that the design is sculpted from a side part.

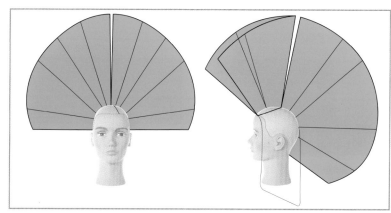

The structure graphics show that the lengths are shorter in the exterior and longer in the interior. Diagonal-back lines at the sides create a length increase toward the back.

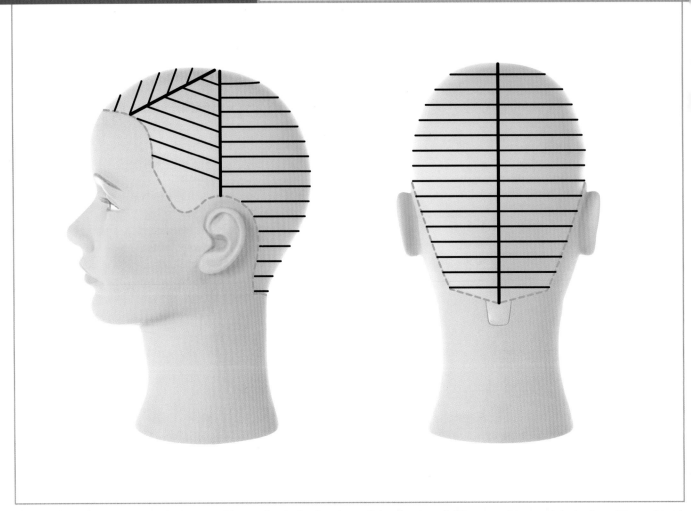

The art indicates that horizontal partings will be used in the back with parallel and nonparallel finger positions and design lines. Diagonal-back partings are used on the sides with parallel finger positions and design lines.

1 **2** Section with a side part from the center of the left eye to the center of the crown and down the center back. Use the center of the ear as a guide to section the front from the back on either side.

3 Position the head upright and take a horizontal parting in the nape.

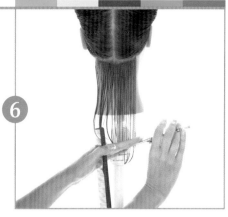

Using natural fall, begin sculpting the center horizontally, parallel to the parting. Move to one side and sculpt diagonally with a nonparallel finger position. Then move to the other side and repeat the same technique, sculpting along the opposite diagonal line.

Note that the convex line consists of a horizontal line at the center, combined with diagonal lines at the sides. This line now serves as the stationary design line for the back section of this sculpture.

Take subsequent horizontal partings as you work upward.

For consistency in sculpting, always sculpt the center of the convex line before moving to the sides.

Continue working up the back of the head using horizontal partings with natural fall. Position your fingers parallel to the parting to sculpt the horizontal center of the convex line and nonparallel to sculpt the diagonal lines at the sides.

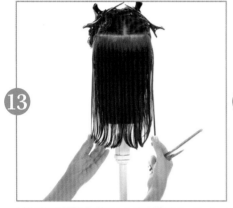

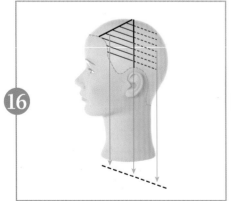

Check for symmetry before you proceed.   Maintain natural distribution as the back section is completed.

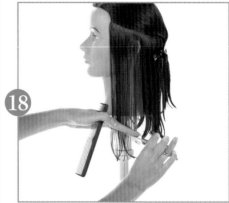

Next, move to the lighter side of the sculpture. Take diagonal-back partings that are compatible with the convex line in the back. Extend these partings to the back to ensure blending. Use natural fall and sculpt parallel to the diagonal-back parting.

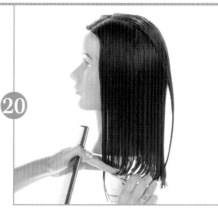

Work up to the side part avoiding excessive tension, especially over the ear. Distribute the hair as it will be worn, especially in the recession area, prior to sculpting. Continue to sculpt along the diagonal-back line with no projection.

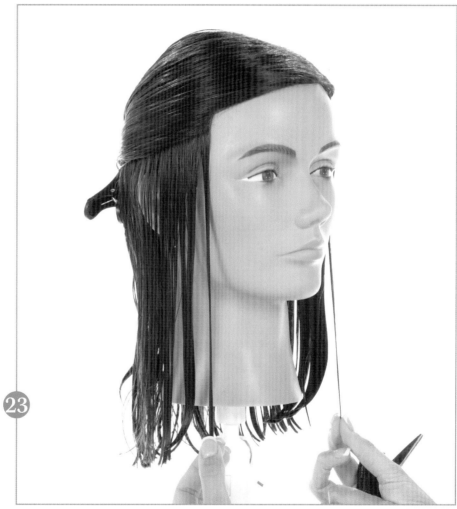

Move to the heavier side of the design. Use the same technique to sculpt the design line.

Check for symmetry before continuing on this side.

24

Continue using natural distribution and no projection. Maintain accuracy when distributing around the hairline.

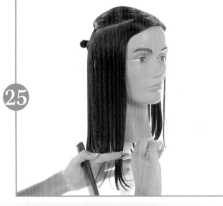

25

At the top of the head, distribute the hair in a slight curve around the hairline. Sculpt parallel to the diagonal-back partings.

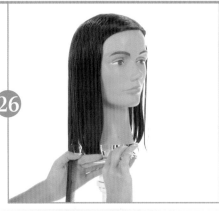

26

Maintain this distribution while sculpting with as little tension as possible.

27

After air forming, distribute the lengths in natural fall. Use the shears to refine the perimeter and remove any unwanted hair that may remain due to natural growth patterns.

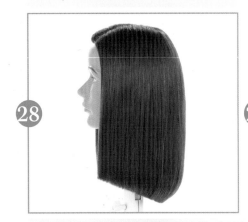

28

29

The surface appearance of the solid form enhances the convex line in the back of this design. The diagonal lines at the sides are flattering for many clients.

DESIGN DECISIONS
Draw or fill in the boxes with the appropriate answers.

STRUCTURE: Solid

SHAPE: Rectangle

TEXTURE: unactive.

SECTIONING PATTERN:

BACK:

head position	parting	distribution	projection	finger/tool position	design line mobile/stationary

design line mobile/(stationary)

SIDES:

head position	parting	distribution	projection	finger/tool position	design line mobile/stationary

TOOLS:

SCULPTURE DESIGN RUBRIC

Chapter 2: Solid Form, Diagonal-Back/Convex Line

This Rubric is a performance assessment tool designed to measure your ability to **create** Pivot Point sculpture designs.

Name _____ ID Number _____ Date _____

	In Progress Level 1	Getting Better Level 2	Entry-Level Proficiency Level 3
PREPARATION			
• Assemble sculpting essentials	☐	☐	☐
CREATE			
• Section hair with side part that extends through center crown to nape and from ear to ear	☐	☐	☐
• Position head upright	☐	☐	☐
• Part horizontally in nape from center to each side using wide teeth of comb	☐	☐	☐
• Distribute hair in natural fall	☐	☐	☐
• Position fingers and shears parallel to parting	☐	☐	☐
• Sculpt a convex stationary design line using no projection and a parallel finger position at center that adjusts to a nonparallel finger position at sides	☐	☐	☐
• Sculpt upward to crown using consistent horizontal partings and natural distribution	☐	☐	☐
• Check design line for symmetry before proceeding	☐	☐	☐
• Part hair on lighter side using diagonal-back partings that extend to back	☐	☐	☐
• Sculpt a stationary design line using natural distribution, no projection and a parallel finger position with minimal tension over ear	☐	☐	☐
• Distribute hair as it will be worn before sculpting, beginning in recession area	☐	☐	☐
• Sculpt up to side part	☐	☐	☐
• Sculpt first parting on heavier side using a diagonal-back parting, natural distribution and a parallel finger position; check symmetry with lighter side	☐	☐	☐
• Sculpt remainder of side using same procedures	☐	☐	☐
• Check for an equally balanced diagonal-back line with no activation at perimeter form line	☐	☐	☐
• Finish sculpture design	☐	☐	☐
• Sculpt to refine perimeter	☐	☐	☐

TOTAL POINTS = ☐ + ☐ + ☐

TOTAL POINTS _____ ÷ HIGHEST POSSIBLE SCORE 54 = _____ %

Record your time in comparison with the suggested salon speed. _____

To improve my performance on this procedure, I need to: _____

_____

SOLID FORM, DIAGONAL-FORWARD LINE — WORKSHOP

The diagonal-forward solid form is a classic favorite among designers and clients. Many trends begin with this sculpture as the foundation; endless variations of the basic form can suit a wide variety of clients. The smooth surface and progression of lengths from the back to the front lead the eye toward the face, giving the classic a little fashion edge.

The elements in this diagonal-forward solid form create harmony and symmetrical balance. This design is most effective when sculpted above the shoulders.

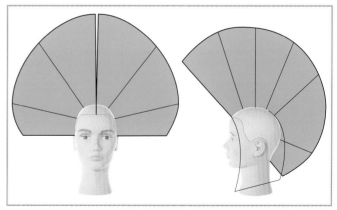

The structure graphics show shorter exterior lengths and longer interior lengths, falling to a single perimeter form line.

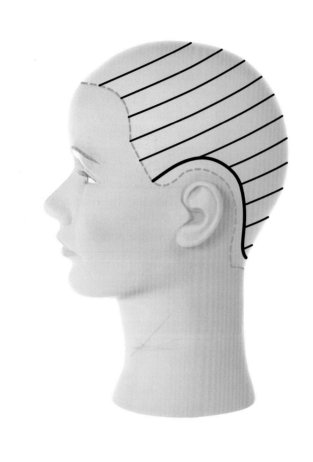
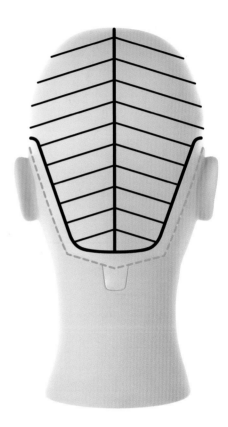

The art indicates that a center part, consistent diagonal-forward partings and a hairline parting are used. The hairline parting will be used to create the diagonal-forward design line and length guide. The diagonal-forward partings should be parallel to the intended design line and can vary from the standard 45° angle.

Begin with a center part that extends from the forehead to the center nape.

Release a ½" (1.25 cm) parting along the hairline. Take the parting from the center of the nape to the front hairline on either side.

Then use the comb to determine the lengths at the front and to envision the angle of the line you will sculpt.

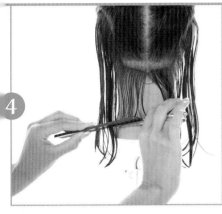

4 With the head upright, use natural distribution and comb control to sculpt the design line. Position the comb diagonally on one side, and sculpt parallel to the comb with no projection and no tension.

5 Use the same technique on the opposite side. Note that your comb and shears will be positioned along the opposite diagonal line to create a concave line. Check the angle of your comb and shears before sculpting.

6 Check balance and symmetry, observing the line in natural fall. Then gently pull down the strands on either side to check the lengths for symmetry.

7 Return to the left side and continue sculpting a diagonal-forward line, working toward the front hairline. Continue using natural distribution and comb control following the diagonal form line.

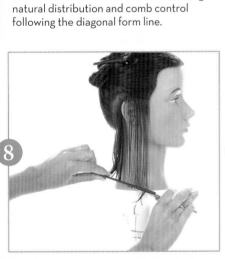

8 Move to the right side and complete the design line by sculpting from the back toward the front using the same technique.

9 Check the completed design line for symmetry before proceeding. If you are working in front of a mirror, check the line in the reflection as well. This method of checking will be very helpful to you when you are working on clients.

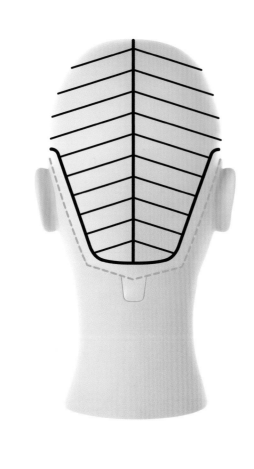

10 The art shows diagonal-forward lines connecting in the center. Note that you will alternate from one side of the head to the other throughout the exercise.

11 Release a parting parallel to the previously sculpted design line on both sides. Beginning on the left side, use natural distribution, minimal tension and no projection. Position fingers parallel to the design line and sculpt.

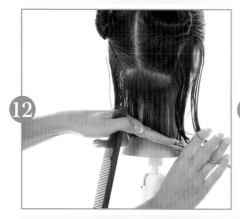

12 Repeat the same technique on the right side.

13/14 Take subsequent partings parallel to the initial diagonal-forward parting on each side. Work from the center nape outward continuing to use natural distribution, no projection and minimal tension. Sculpt parallel and continue to check for symmetry as you work.

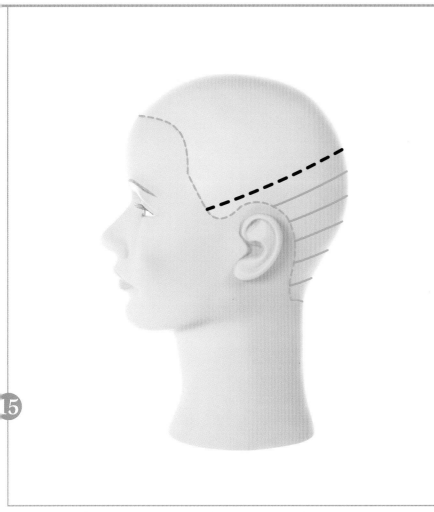

15 When you reach the first parting above the ear, extend partings to the front hairline on both sides.

16 Begin sculpting at the center back of the left side and work toward the front hairline.

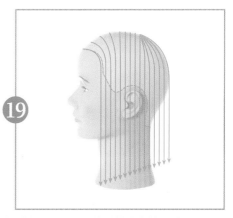

17 Continue using natural distribution and no projection. Avoid tension, especially when sculpting hair that is distributed over the ear. Repeat the same technique on the right side.

18 Continue to work toward the top of the head using the same technique. Alternate from one side to the other, sculpting each parting from the center back toward the front hairline.

19 The art shows that the hair is distributed in a slight curve around the hairline to avoid activation and create a pure diagonal-forward line when the hair is finished.

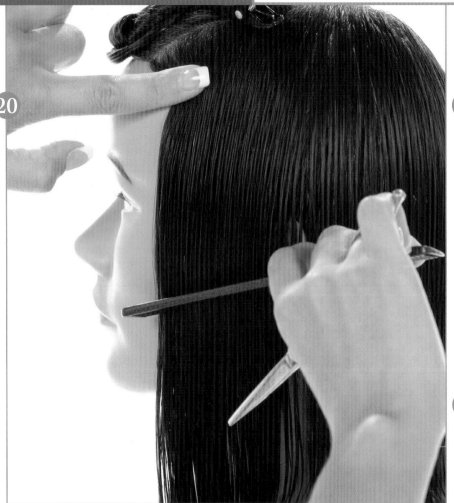

20

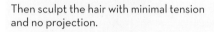

21

Then sculpt the hair with minimal tension and no projection.

22

Beginning at the recession area of the hairline, distribute the hair in a slight curve around the hairline to ensure that no activation occurs when the hair is worn slightly off the face.

Repeat the same technique on the right side.

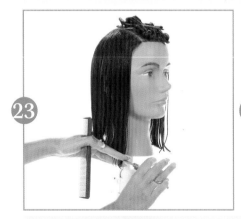

23

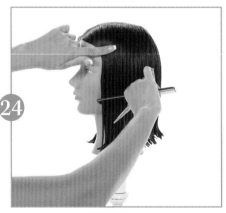

24

25

Distribute the hair around the hairline beginning at the top of the recession area. Use no projection and sculpt parallel to the design line.

Continue alternating sides, distributing the hair in a slight curve around the hairline. Work up to the center part on one side and sculpt with minimal tension.

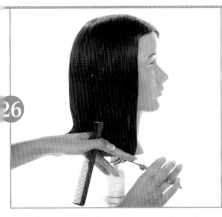

Use the same technique to complete the other side. Maintain minimum tension and no projection as you sculpt.

To soften the front corners, direct the front lengths forward and sculpt a slightly curved line. To avoid activation use as little projection as possible when sculpting this area.

Air form the sculpture, then check and refine the nape form line. Tilt the head forward and sculpt using comb control.

This sculpture can be styled with a center or a side part.

The completed design has a smooth surface with shorter lengths in the back and longer lengths near the face.

DESIGN DECISIONS

Draw or fill in the boxes with the appropriate answers.

STRUCTURE:

SHAPE:

TEXTURE:

SECTIONING PATTERN:

BACK: head position	parting	distribution	projection	finger/tool position	design line mobile/stationary

SIDES: head position	parting	distribution	projection	finger/tool position	design line mobile/stationary

TOOLS:

variation
SOLID FORM, DIAGONAL-FORWARD LINE

Clients with curly or tightly curled hair often prefer to wear their hair in straight styles. Dry-sculpting techniques are used to ensure accuracy and precision in the completed sculpture when it is worn straight. The same technique can be used to sculpt hair that has been chemically relaxed.

After shampooing and conditioning, the hair is air formed straight with minimal volume, as it will be worn. Generally, a 7- or 9-row brush is used. Some designers choose to use a flat iron to straighten the hair further before sculpting. The hair is sectioned appropriately and the perimeter hairline is isolated. Clients with curly or tightly curled hair may have less density at the hairline, so a wider hairline parting may be required. The comb is used to determine the angle of the diagonal-forward design line. With the head upright, the design line is sculpted using natural distribution with no projection, positioning the fingers along the diagonal-forward line. Diagonal-forward partings are then used to sculpt the remainder of the solid form.

SCULPTURE DESIGN RUBRIC

Chapter 2: Solid Form, Diagonal-Forward Line

This Rubric is a performance assessment tool designed to measure your ability to **create** Pivot Point sculpture designs.

Name _____ ID Number _____ Date _____

	In Progress Level 1	Getting Better Level 2	Entry-Level Proficiency Level 3
PREPARATION			
• Assemble sculpting essentials	☐	☐	☐
CREATE			
• Section hair with center part from forehead to nape	☐	☐	☐
• Position head upright	☐	☐	☐
• Part hair ½" (1.25 cm) wide parallel to hairline from nape to front hairline on each side	☐	☐	☐
• Distribute in natural fall	☐	☐	☐
• Use the comb to check angle of line with lengths at front to determine angle of design line	☐	☐	☐
• Sculpt a stationary diagonal-forward design line using natural distribution, no projection and comb control, working from center of nape to front on either side	☐	☐	☐
• Check design line for symmetry before proceeding	☐	☐	☐
• Part hair using a diagonal-forward line parallel to design line on each side of nape	☐	☐	☐
• Distribute hair in natural fall	☐	☐	☐
• Position fingers and shears parallel to parting	☐	☐	☐
• Sculpt using minimal tension and no projection; repeat on opposite side	☐	☐	☐
• Sculpt upward using consistent diagonal-forward partings and natural distribution, alternating between both sides	☐	☐	☐
• Extend diagonal-forward partings from back to front hairline above ears	☐	☐	☐
• Sculpt from center back toward hairline on both sides using minimal tension above ear	☐	☐	☐
• Check design for symmetry before proceeding	☐	☐	☐
• Sculpt toward top of head alternating from one side to the other using same procedure	☐	☐	☐
• Distribute hair in slight curve around hairline in recession area before sculpting	☐	☐	☐
• Sculpt up to center part using same procedures	☐	☐	☐
• Sculpt opposite side using the same procedures	☐	☐	☐
• Sculpt front corners by directing front lengths forward and sculpting slightly curved line	☐	☐	☐
• Check for symmetrical balance with shorter lengths at back and longer lengths near face	☐	☐	☐
• Finish sculpture design	☐	☐	☐
• Check and refine nape form line using comb control	☐	☐	☐

TOTAL POINTS = ☐ + ☐ + ☐

TOTAL POINTS _____ ÷ HIGHEST POSSIBLE SCORE 72 = _____ %

Record your time in comparison with the suggested salon speed. _____

To improve my performance on this procedure, I need to: _____

_____

SOLID FORM FRINGE VARIATIONS

Solid designs may be customized with the addition of a solid fringe or different types of fringes. There are many options available and here are a few examples. Remember that all fringe designs should be personalized to adapt to the features of your client's face as well as growth patterns and hair density in the fringe area.

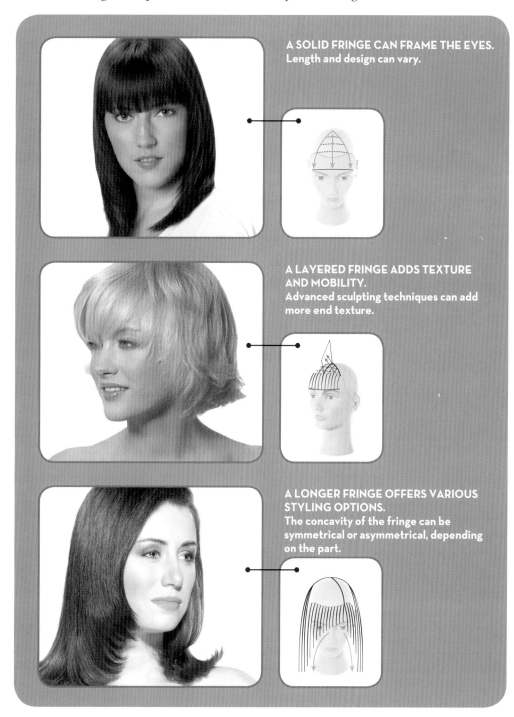

A SOLID FRINGE CAN FRAME THE EYES.
Length and design can vary.

A LAYERED FRINGE ADDS TEXTURE AND MOBILITY.
Advanced sculpting techniques can add more end texture.

A LONGER FRINGE OFFERS VARIOUS STYLING OPTIONS.
The concavity of the fringe can be symmetrical or asymmetrical, depending on the part.

2.3 GRADUATED FORM

Graduated sculptures have grown in popularity especially since the 1960s, and names have been given to these designs such as "wedge" or "firefly." Despite the many different technical approaches that can be used to create graduated sculptures, they all have a striking geometric character that features a triangular shape—the trademark of this form.

Now you will learn a variety of techniques used to create graduated sculptures. Understanding and developing proficiency in these procedures will continue to build your foundation as a hair designer.

GRADUATED FORM OVERVIEW

In the previous section of this chapter you learned all about the solid form and that the sculpting procedures for it are so specific that any deviation from them will result in something other than a solid form. What you are about to find out is that a lot of the things you *couldn't do* when sculpting a solid form are exactly what you *need to do* to achieve a graduated form.

On the following pages you will learn more about the characteristics of the graduated form as well as techniques used to create predictable, graduated sculpture results.

SHAPE

Graduated forms tend to be triangular in shape. The appearance of width is accentuated when the graduated form is sculpted on wavy or curly hair.

Note how the shape is influenced by the degree of graduation:

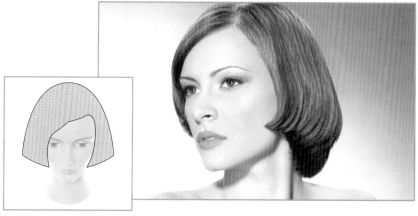

LOW GRADUATION

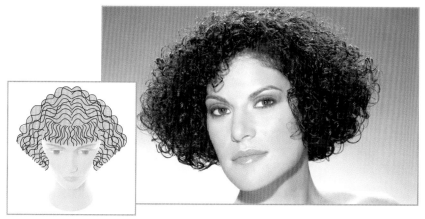

MEDIUM GRADUATION

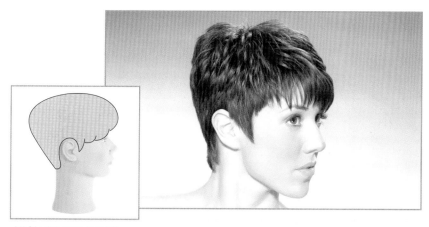

HIGH GRADUATION

WEIGHT

The weight within a graduated form occurs above the perimeter form line. A weight line develops at the location where the longest lengths fall to rest and is usually defined and easy to see.

 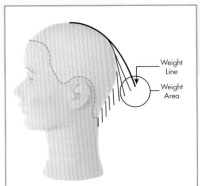

A weight area occurs at the widest angular corner of the shape. Sculpting on textured hair will expand the shape and the weight area.

STRUCTURE

In the graduated form, shorter exterior lengths progress toward longer interior lengths. In natural fall the ends of the hair fall close to one another and stack up along an angle. Note how this progression varies in low, medium and high graduated forms.

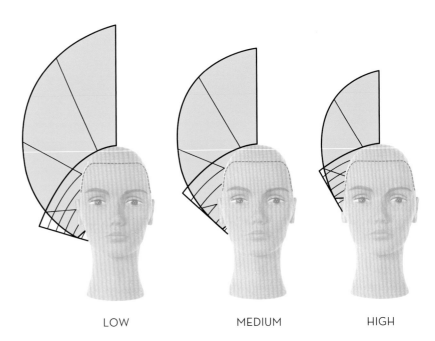

LOW   MEDIUM   HIGH

TEXTURE

The combination of unactivated texture at the interior and activated texture in the exterior of a graduated form is created by the visible stacking of the hair ends. The line that visually separates the two textures is called the ridge line. This visual texture contrast is reduced when sculpted on wavy or curly hair.

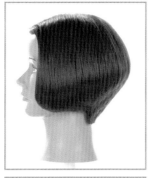

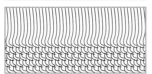
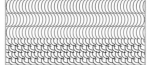

GRADUATED FORM SCULPTING PROCEDURES

SECTION

Graduated forms are usually sectioned between design line or projection changes. You may also section to subdivide large areas for control while sculpting.

POSITION HEAD

The head position used to sculpt graduated forms is generally upright. The position may vary when sculpting certain areas, such as the nape. If the head position is altered, be especially careful of the distribution and projection used.

UPRIGHT

TILTED FORWARD

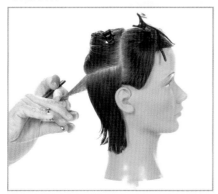

PART

Common partings used are horizontal, vertical, diagonal forward and diagonal back. Generally the partings will be parallel to the intended form line.

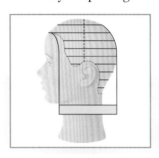 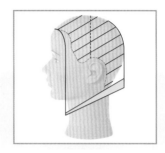 

The exception is sculpting from vertical partings, which can be used with any form line. In this case, the partings are not necessarily parallel to the form line; however, your finger position must remain diagonal.

DISTRIBUTE

Natural, perpendicular and shifted distribution can be used to create varying degrees of graduated texture.

Natural distribution from horizontal and diagonal partings must be combined with projection to create graduated texture.

Perpendicular distribution from diagonal partings will result in a small amount of graduation. The steeper the angle of the parting the greater the amount of graduation. Projection increases the amount of this graduation.

Shifted distribution is used in graduated forms to create length increases for blending or establishing the form.

PROJECT

Projection for graduated forms involves lifting the hair out of natural fall prior to sculpting. It is the most commonly used method to achieve graduation.

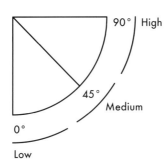

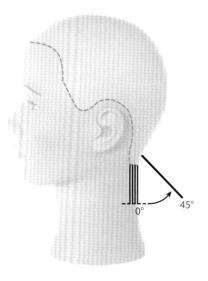

Lower projection angles create low graduation, and higher projection angles produce high graduation.

Often a medium (approximately 45°) angle is used as a standard.

LINE OF INCLINATION

Since graduation is sculpted from the perimeter upward, the first section that is projected will determine the progression of lengths. This establishes the line of inclination. This line describes the angular silhouette that the graduated form reveals as it is being sculpted. At the beginning of the sculpture, the line of inclination is an imaginary line that guides you in the development of the form. All subsequent sections travel to this line and exposed hair ends stack up along the angle of this line. The celestial axis can be used to maintain consistent projection when directing the hair to the desired line of inclination.

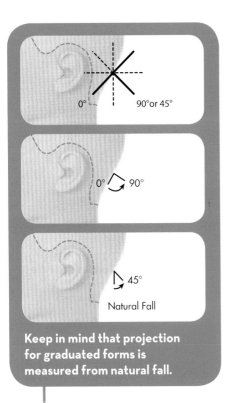

0°   90° or 45°

0°   90°

45°

Natural Fall

Keep in mind that projection for graduated forms is measured from natural fall.

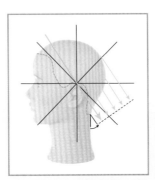

A low projection angle results in a low line of inclination. More weight is maintained in the form with a small amount of activation.

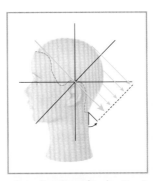

A medium line of inclination is created by sculpting with a medium projection angle. The amount of activation increases and expansion occurs with a defined weight area.

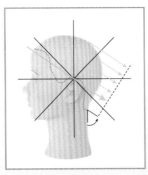

A high line of inclination is created with a high projection angle. The amount of activation and expansion is greater with the higher degree of projection.

PROJECTION COMBINATIONS

Low, medium and high projection angles can all be combined within a single hair sculpture if varying degrees of graduation are desired. As the projection angle is lowered, the line of inclination drops and the amount of weight increases. When the projection angle is raised, more activation and expansion in the interior of the form are created.

 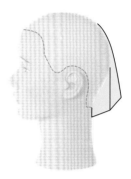

POSITION FINGERS/SHEARS

In most instances, your finger/shear position will be parallel to your partings while sculpting graduation. The sculpting position generally positions your hands "palm to palm."

 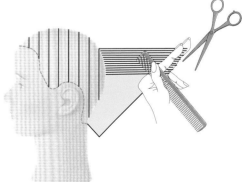

Graduation can also be created by using a vertical parting pattern and positioning your fingers along the intended line of inclination. Depending on the length of the hair and the area of the head, you may position your hand palm up or palm down.

DESIGN LINE

Generally, graduated forms are sculpted with a horizontal or diagonal design line. The design line may be stationary, mobile or a combination of the two, depending on the amount of weight desired in a given area.

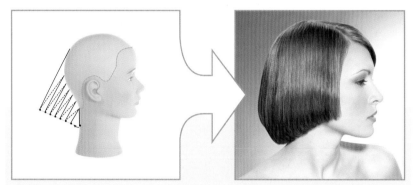

When projecting each section consistently along the line of inclination, a mobile design line is used. As you progress, pick up a small amount of the previously sculpted hair as a guide.

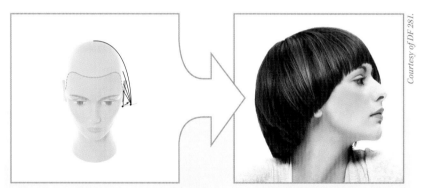

Courtesy of DF 281.

It is also possible to project all lengths to the first projected section when a weightier low graduation is desired. This involves the use of a stationary design line.

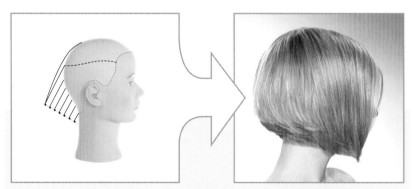

In many instances, a combination of mobile and stationary design lines may be used. The stationary design line may be used where additional weight is desired.

GRADUATED FORM GUIDELINES

CROSS-CHECKING

Vertical partings are often used to cross-check graduated forms. The hair is sectioned vertically and directed out from the head, while the fingers are aligned with the line of inclination. Pay special attention not to remove the weight corner while checking for irregularities along the sculpted line.

SOFTENING THE WEIGHT AREA

It is often desirable to soften the weight area of a graduated form. Generally, this is done by taking vertical partings and sculpting the weight corner to remove it or texturize within it. To remove the weight corner, the hair is projected out and sculpted vertically or notched. Taper shears or a razor may also be used to remove the desired amount of weight.

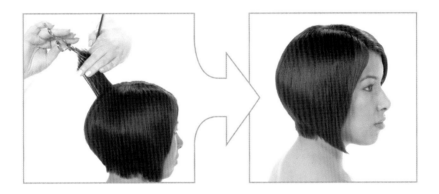

PRESSURE GRADUATION

Graduation can also be achieved by placing tension, or pressure, on wet hair. Pressure graduation is especially effective on wavy or curly textures. The amount of activation and expansion is greatly influenced by the degree of curl texture in the hair. The hair may be controlled between the fingers, or it may be held flat to the head with the back of the hand or the spine of the comb.

GRADUATED FORM, DIAGONAL-FORWARD LINE — WORKSHOP

In the salon you'll work with many clients who prefer the ease of shorter hairstyles but also like the feeling of some length. This graduated sculpture creates closeness in the nape while maintaining longer lengths toward the front.

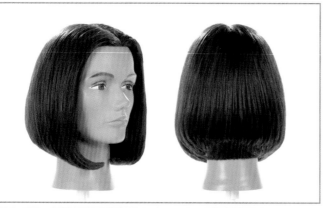

This classic sculpture features unactivated and activated textures and flows along a diagonal-forward line.

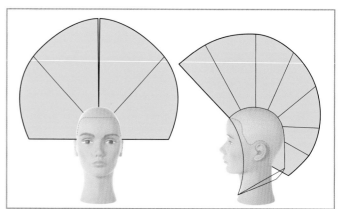

The structure graphics show the length progression from the shorter exterior to the longer interior. This allows lengths to stack upon one another to create the graduated texture.

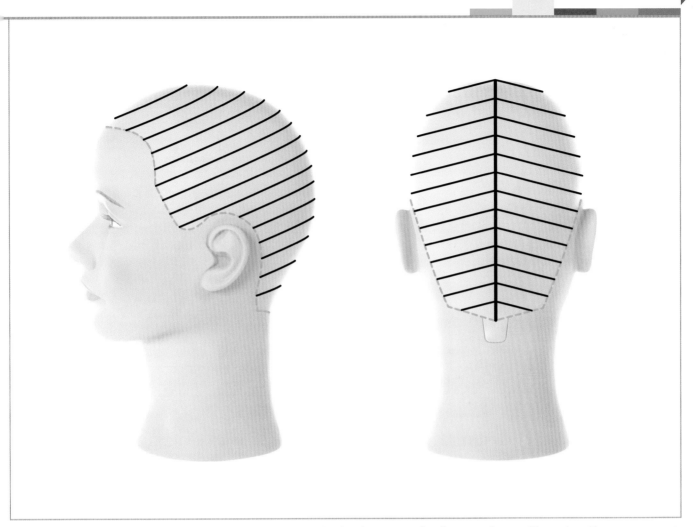

The art indicates that diagonal-forward partings will be used to sculpt this design. Note that this entire design will be sculpted from a center part.

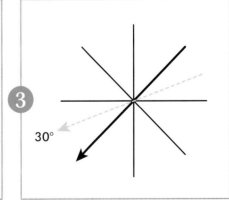

Section the head with a center part that extends from the forehead to the nape. Each section will be clipped out of the way while sculpting.

The art indicates the approximate angle at which diagonal-forward partings will be taken.

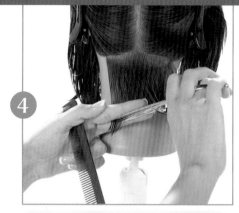

4

Release a diagonal-forward parting at either side of the nape and begin sculpting one side. Use perpendicular distribution and 0° projection. Position your fingers and sculpt parallel to the diagonal-forward parting.

5

Then sculpt the other side. This will now serve as a mobile design line until the crest area is reached.

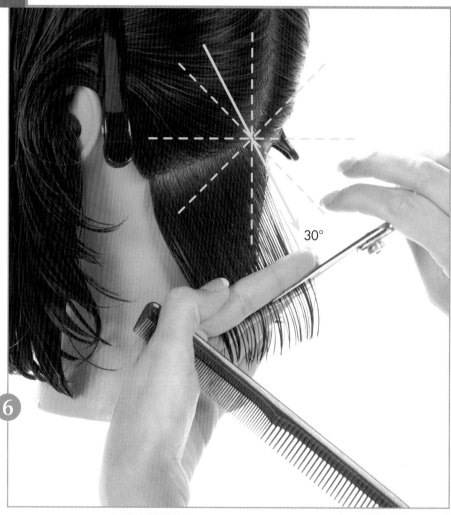

6

30°

Release the next diagonal-forward partings parallel to the first and begin sculpting one side. Project approximately 30° using perpendicular distribution. Position your fingers and sculpt parallel.

7

Use the same technique to sculpt the other side. Sculpt one side and then the other to maintain symmetry in the design.

8

Continue working upward, subdividing partings for control. Sculpt each parting from the center toward the hairline; maintain perpendicular distribution and 30° projection while sculpting.

9

Alternate sides to maintain balance. It is essential that distribution and projection are consistent throughout.

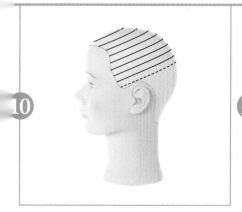

10

The art shows consistent diagonal-forward partings extended to the front hairline in the area above the ear.

11

When you reach the top of the ear, extend the diagonal-forward partings from the back through the front.

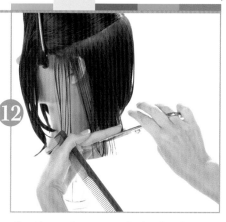

12

Continue using perpendicular distribution with 30° projection and a mobile design line. Subdivide the parting for control.

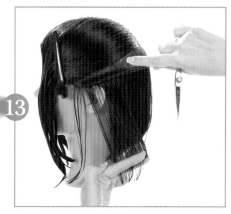

13

To avoid tension over the ear and maintain the sculpted line, you may use the back of the comb, your fingers or your shears to compress the hair toward the head.

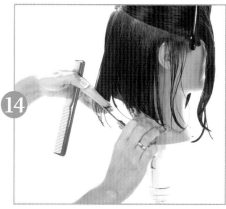

14

Continue to alternate sides using consistent distribution and projection.

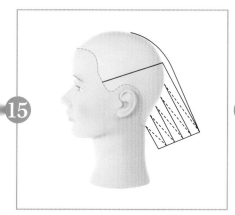

15

The art indicates that a stationary design line will be used once the crest area is reached. The design line is projected at the established 30° angle.

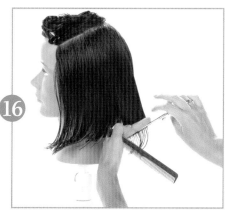

16

At the crest area, distribute and project partings to the stationary design line. Continue to use perpendicular distribution and sculpt along the diagonal-forward line.

17

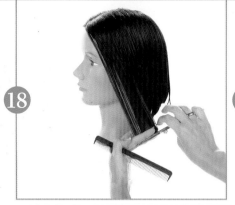

Since there are no diagonal-forward partings at the top, distribute the lengths following the perpendicular distribution used in the previously sculpted parting. This ensures consistency in the graduated form.

To soften the front corners, distribute the hair forward using minimal projection and sculpt horizontally to soften the point.

After air forming, distribute the nape lengths in natural fall. Use the tips of the shears to refine the perimeter and remove any unwanted hairs that may remain due to hairline irregularities or natural growth patterns.

The finished sculpture shows graduated texture along diagonal-forward lines.

DESIGN DECISIONS
Draw or fill in the boxes with the appropriate answers.

STRUCTURE:

SHAPE:

TEXTURE:

SECTIONING PATTERN:

BACK:
head position

parting

distribution

projection

finger/tool position

design line mobile/stationary

SIDES:
head position

parting

distribution

projection

finger/tool position

design line mobile/stationary

TOOLS:

variation

GRADUATED FORM, DIAGONAL-FORWARD LINE

In the salon you'll have clients who prefer maintenance-free designs. This graduated sculpture is the perfect option. The graduation in the nape will give the illusion of an elongated neck, flattering to many clients. The horizontal lines on the sides will allow the client to maintain length around the face and provide many styling options.

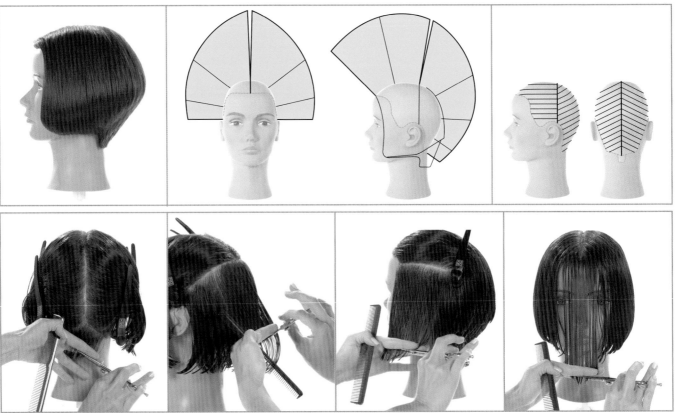

Diagonal-forward partings are used to sculpt the back and horizontal partings are used at the sides. Perpendicular distribution and medium projection are used to sculpt the back with a stationary design line at the crest area to build weight within the design. Horizontal partings with perpendicular distribution, low projection and a mobile design line are used to sculpt the sides. Medium and low projection angles result in a combination of graduated textures.

SCULPTURE DESIGN RUBRIC

Chapter 2: Graduated Form, Diagonal-Forward Line

This Rubric is a performance assessment tool designed to measure your ability to **create** Pivot Point sculpture designs.

Name _____ ID Number _____ Date _____

	In Progress Level 1	Getting Better Level 2	Entry-Level Proficiency Level 3
PREPARATION			
• Assemble sculpting essentials	☐	☐	☐
CREATE			
• Section hair with a center part that extends through center crown to nape	☐	☐	☐
• Position head upright	☐	☐	☐
• Part hair at nape along a diagonal-forward line on each side	☐	☐	☐
• Distribute perpendicular	☐	☐	☐
• Position fingers and shears parallel to parting	☐	☐	☐
• Sculpt a diagonal-forward mobile design line using no projection and palm-to-palm hand position	☐	☐	☐
• Check for balance before continuing	☐	☐	☐
• Sculpt subsequent partings using approximately 30° projection, perpendicular distribution and parallel finger position	☐	☐	☐
• Work up to crest area alternating from side to side, using mobile design line	☐	☐	☐
• Extend diagonal-forward partings from back to front hairline in area above ear	☐	☐	☐
• Sculpt using minimal tension over ear	☐	☐	☐
• Sculpt a stationary design line beginning in crest area using last projected section as length guide	☐	☐	☐
• Sculpt up to top using diagonal-forward partings, stationary design line and perpendicular distribution	☐	☐	☐
• Finish sculpture design	☐	☐	☐
• Check and refine nape perimeter	☐	☐	☐

TOTAL POINTS = ☐ + ☐ + ☐

TOTAL POINTS _____ ÷ HIGHEST POSSIBLE SCORE 48 = _____ %

Record your time in comparison with the suggested salon speed. _____

To improve my performance on this procedure, I need to: _____

_____

GRADUATED FORM, DIAGONAL-BACK/CONVEX LINE — WORKSHOP

The diagonal-back graduated form allows clients to enjoy a short hair sculpture while retaining interior lengths for styling versatility. This particular graduated form design has been a classic for decades and remains popular in salons today.

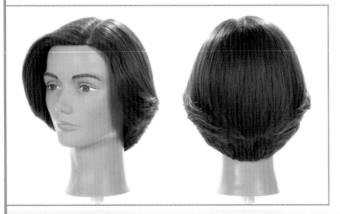

In this exercise, graduated texture is sculpted along a diagonal-back line.

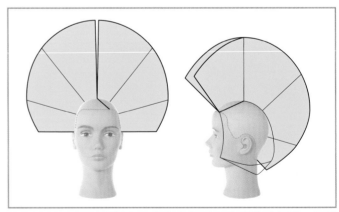

The structure graphics show the progression of shorter exterior lengths to longer interior lengths. This progression allows the lengths to stack upon one another and create graduated texture.

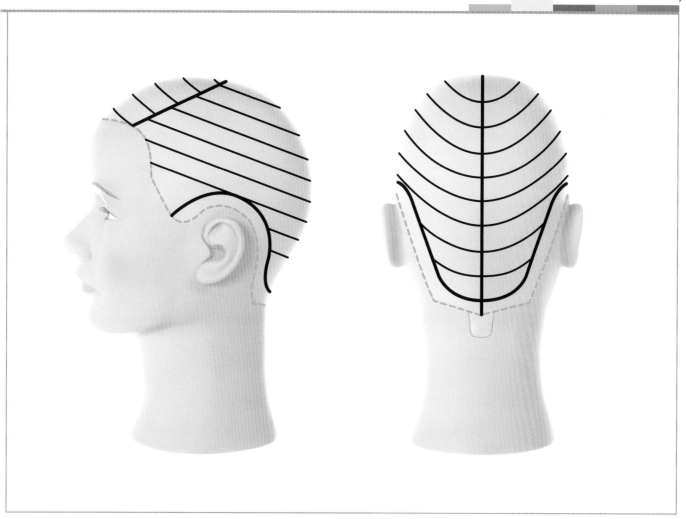

The art indicates that a side part and consistent diagonal-back partings are used. Partings are slightly rounded at the center back to avoid a point. A hairline parting is used to establish the diagonal-back design line. Partings should be parallel to the intended design line and may vary from the standard 45° angle.

1 Begin with a side part that extends from the center of the left eye at the hairline through the center of the crown, and down to the center nape.

2 Release a 1" (2.5 cm) parting along the hairline. Take the parting from the hairline to the center of the nape on both sides.

Sculpture · 101

4

Then use the comb to determine the angle and the length of the intended line.

5

6

With the head upright, begin sculpting at the front hairline on the right side. Use natural distribution and no projection. Position your fingers at a medium angle and sculpt parallel to your fingers toward the center back.

7

Move to the left side and use the same techniques to establish the diagonal-back design line.

8

Note that your fingers and the shears will be positioned on the opposite angle to create a convex line in the nape area.

9

Check the design for symmetry before you proceed. This design line will be used as the mobile design line in the rest of the exercise.

In the nape, release a parting parallel to the previously sculpted design line on both sides. Use perpendicular distribution and medium projection. Position your fingers and shears parallel to the parting and sculpt using the previously sculpted hairline parting as a guide. Sculpt alternating from side to side.

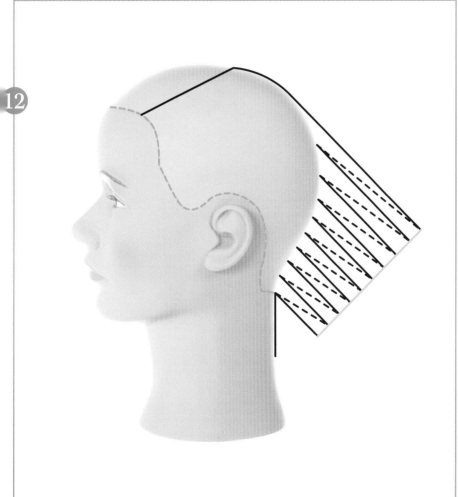

The art indicates that all subsequent partings will be sculpted using a medium projection angle and a mobile design line.

Continue working upward using the mobile design line, perpendicular distribution and medium projection. As you work up the head, note that the lower lengths will drop out.

Repeat the same technique on the other side using perpendicular distribution.

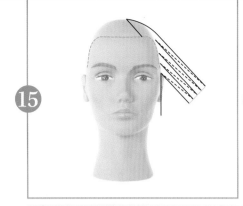

15

The art indicates that a consistent line of inclination is maintained throughout the exercise. As you work from the crest to the crown, envision your line of inclination to ensure accuracy.

16 17

When the diagonal-back partings extend to the front hairline, complete the lighter side before moving to the heavier side. Continue using perpendicular distribution and medium projection. Sculpt parallel from the front hairline to the center back.

18

Continue working up the left side using the same techniques.

19

As you reach the last parting, be careful to maintain the correct distribution and projection angle.

20

Move to the right side and sculpt from the front hairline to the back using perpendicular distribution, medium projection and a mobile design line.

21

To connect the two sides in the back, extend the partings into the previous side.

22

When you reach the parting that extends to the fringe area, begin sculpting over the ear using the mobile design line as a guide. Sculpt toward the front of the parting and then from the ear to the center back.

23

As you work to the front hairline, shift the hair back slightly to compensate for the hairline and to retain length.

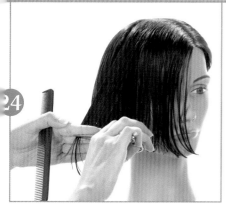

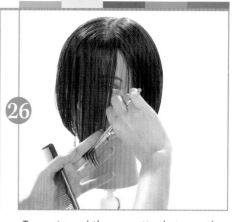

Continue working through the top using the same techniques.

To create a subtle connection between the two sides, direct the front lengths forward with minimal projection. Sculpt a steep diagonal line from the lighter side blending to the heavier side.

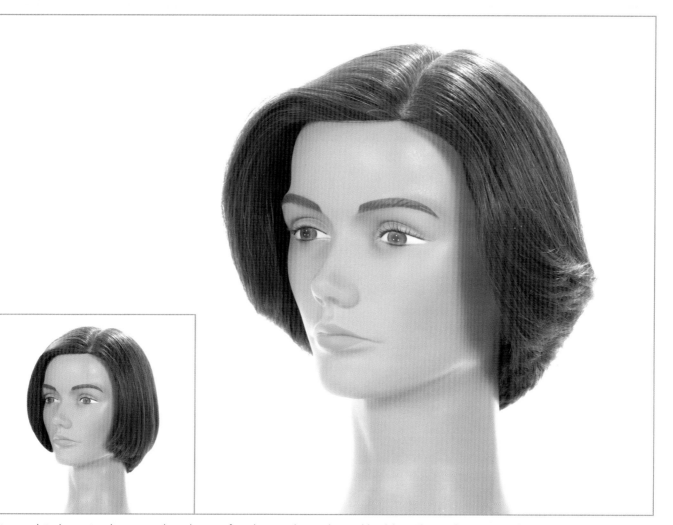

This completed exercise shows a medium degree of graduation along a diagonal-back line. The resulting activated texture can be more or less visible, depending upon the styling.

DESIGN DECISIONS

Draw or fill in the boxes with the appropriate answers.

STRUCTURE:

SHAPE:

TEXTURE:

SECTIONING PATTERN:

BACK: head position	parting	distribution	projection	finger/tool position	design line mobile/stationary

SIDES: head position	parting	distribution	projection	finger/tool position	design line mobile/stationary

TOOLS:

variation
GRADUATED FORM, DIAGONAL-BACK LINE

Many clients will appreciate the styling ease of this face-framing sculpture. As a designer, your expertise will be called upon to find the right focal points to accentuate your client's best features. The diagonal-back line is contrasted with diagonal-forward lines at the back of the design.

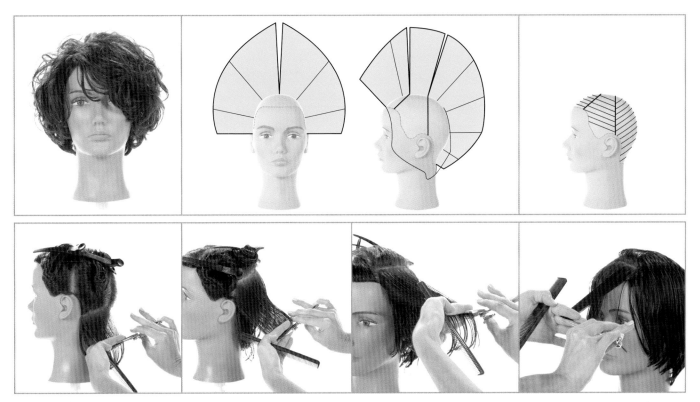

The back of this graduated variation is sculpted using diagonal-forward partings with perpendicular distribution. 30° projection is used in the exterior and 60° projection is used in the interior. On the sides, diagonal-back partings are used with the same distribution and projection combinations as in the back. The fringe, which is sectioned from in front of the apex to the outside corner of each eye, is sculpted with horizontal partings, perpendicular distribution and medium projection. A mobile design line and combinations of projection angles give this sculpture more movement and less weight.

SCULPTURE DESIGN RUBRIC

Chapter 2: Graduated Form, Diagonal-Back/Convex Line

This Rubric is a performance assessment tool designed to measure your ability to **create** Pivot Point sculpture designs.

Name _____ ID Number _____ Date _____

	In Progress Level 1	Getting Better Level 2	Entry-Level Proficiency Level 3
PREPARATION			
• Assemble sculpting essentials	☐	☐	☐
CREATE			
• Section hair with side part that extends through center crown to center nape	☐	☐	☐
• Position head upright	☐	☐	☐
• Part a 1" (2.5 cm) parting parallel to hairline from front to center nape on each side	☐	☐	☐
• Distribute in natural fall, use comb to determine angle and length of design line	☐	☐	☐
• Sculpt length guide in natural fall along a diagonal-back line in nape area	☐	☐	☐
• Check for balance then continue to finish length guide on one side then the other	☐	☐	☐
• Part diagonal-back parting parallel to design line in nape area on both sides	☐	☐	☐
• Sculpt hair using perpendicular distribution, medium projection and a parallel finger position	☐	☐	☐
• Work in nape area alternating sides using same technique	☐	☐	☐
• Part above ear area extending diagonal-back partings to front hairline	☐	☐	☐
• Sculpt lighter side from hairline to center back	☐	☐	☐
• Sculpt subsequent partings using same techniques up to side part	☐	☐	☐
• Part heavier side, extending diagonal-back partings into previously sculpted section to ensure blending	☐	☐	☐
• Sculpt from front to back using perpendicular distribution, medium projection and parallel finger position	☐	☐	☐
• Sculpt subsequent partings using same techniques	☐	☐	☐
• Sculpt over the ear when partings reach fringe area, working toward hairline	☐	☐	☐
• Distribute hair back slightly at front hairline to retain length; complete this side using same techniques	☐	☐	☐
• Distribute front lengths forward	☐	☐	☐
• Sculpt front corners from light to heavy side using minimal projection and steep diagonal line	☐	☐	☐
• Check for symmetrical balance	☐	☐	☐
• Finish sculpture design	☐	☐	☐

TOTAL POINTS = ☐ + ☐ + ☐

TOTAL POINTS _____ ÷ HIGHEST POSSIBLE SCORE 66 = _____ %

Record your time in comparison with the suggested salon speed. _____

To improve my performance on this procedure, I need to: _____

_____

GRADUATED FORM FRINGE VARIATIONS

A variety of fringes can alter the overall appearance of the graduated form.

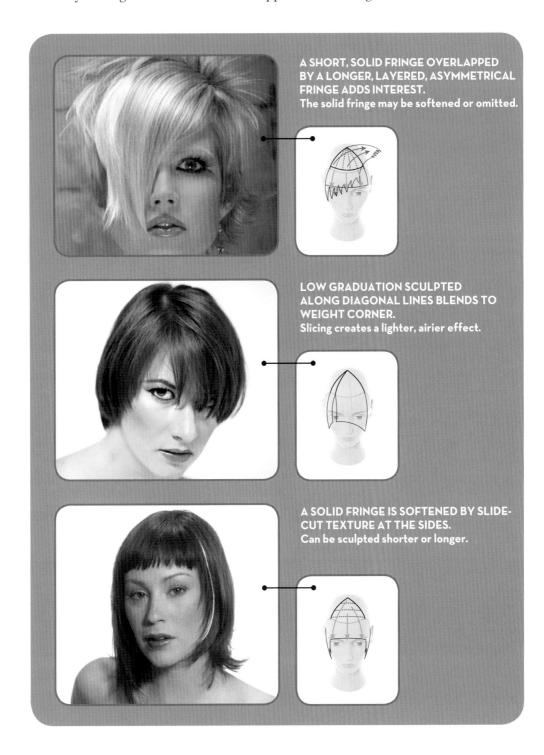

A SHORT, SOLID FRINGE OVERLAPPED BY A LONGER, LAYERED, ASYMMETRICAL FRINGE ADDS INTEREST.
The solid fringe may be softened or omitted.

LOW GRADUATION SCULPTED ALONG DIAGONAL LINES BLENDS TO WEIGHT CORNER.
Slicing creates a lighter, airier effect.

A SOLID FRINGE IS SOFTENED BY SLIDE-CUT TEXTURE AT THE SIDES.
Can be sculpted shorter or longer.

2.4

INCREASE-LAYERED FORM

The increase-layered form is a popular and versatile form that allows clients to keep length, yet still have layers that create volume, texture and directional movement. Since this sculpture is usually performed on longer lengths, a systematic approach is even more critical to achieving successful results.

INCREASE-LAYERED FORM OVERVIEW

Increase-layered texture may comprise the entire form or a component area of a design. Before creating these designs, you will learn to recognize the characteristics of this form and understand the techniques used to sculpt it.

SHAPE

The shape or silhouette of the increase-layered form has many variations, but overall it is elongated. If the form is not combined with another one, there will be no build-up of weight and no area of accentuated width.

STRUCTURE

Generally the length arrangement of an increase-layered form will progress from shorter interior lengths toward longer exterior lengths. The shorter lengths create the interior fullness, which is characteristic of the increase-layered form.

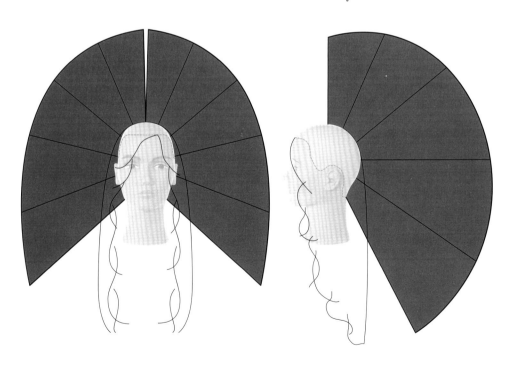

TEXTURE

The texture of the increase-layered form is activated with visible hair ends that do not stack upon each other. When sculpting most increase-layered forms, the curve of the head influences the dispersion of lengths. This creates a more spread-out, airier texture, as compared to the compact stacking effect seen in graduated forms.

If the interior is sculpted at a longer length, the result is longer layers. Proportionately, more of the strands will be visible, creating a combination of activated and unactivated textures.

Sculpting increase-layered forms on wavy or curly hair will tend to accentuate the activated appearance of the sculpture. Since we generally sculpt on damp to wet hair, be aware of the length reduction that will take place as curlier textures dry. This length reduction might be especially apparent on shorter interior lengths.

INCREASE-LAYERED FORM SCULPTING PROCEDURES
SECTION

Minimal sectioning is necessary to sculpt increase-layered forms. In many cases the hair will be sectioned along a side or center part, depending on how the client wears his or her hair.

POSITION HEAD

The head is generally positioned upright when sculpting the increase-layered form. The exception is when you are sculpting longer lengths. Then, a forward head position gives you more control. In either case, it is important to remain consistent once you establish your stationary design line.

PART/DISTRIBUTE

The parting pattern can be vertical, horizontal or diagonal. Often the parting pattern establishes the direction in which the hair is converged or distributed, since perpendicular distribution is generally used.

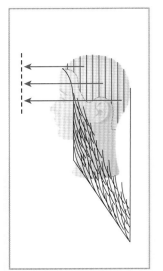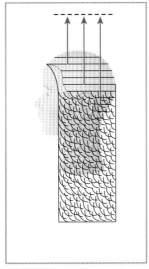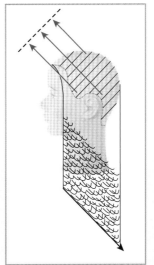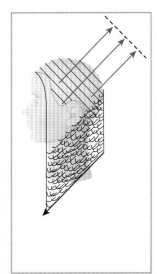

Distributing the hair forward from vertical partings positions shorter lengths around the face and decreasing layered texture toward the back.

Distributing the hair upward from horizontal partings will position layered texture equally around the head.

The hair is parted along the opposite diagonal line when increase-layered texture is designed to fall along a specific diagonal line.

PROJECT

In the increase-layered form the projection angle of the stationary design line is most important because it establishes the location to which all other lengths are converged. The farther hair travels to reach the design line, the longer the result.

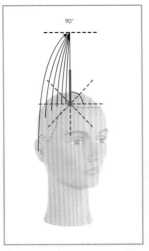
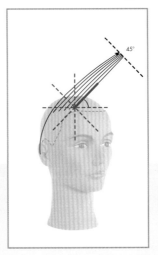

The projection angle of the stationary design line is usually 90°. You can, however, vary the projection angle to either increase or decrease the distance that lengths travel to reach it.

POSITION FINGERS/SHEARS

The finger and/or shear positions used to sculpt increase-layered forms may be parallel or nonparallel, depending on the design and the desired length increase.

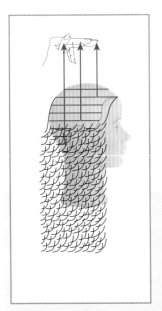
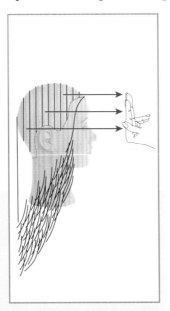
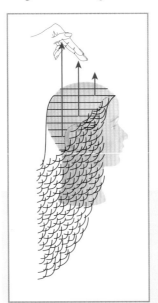
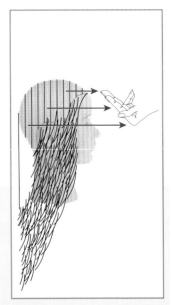

The finger position used is relative to the area of the head that is being sculpted.

A nonparallel finger position is used to sculpt these examples. The fingers are angled from the initial length guide (the shortest point of the sculpture) to the perimeter length.

Increase-layered texture may also be sculpted by slide cutting with the shears. The shortest length is established and the shears are closed as they glide through the hair toward the longest length. This is a more freeform cutting line, often curved in nature.

Standing opposite the length increase and directing hair toward the stationary design line will help maintain a consistent projection angle.

SCULPT DESIGN LINE

The most common increase-layering technique is conversion layering. This technique uses stationary design lines. Once the design line is sculpted, remaining lengths are converged to this line in order to create a length progression that increases in the opposite direction.

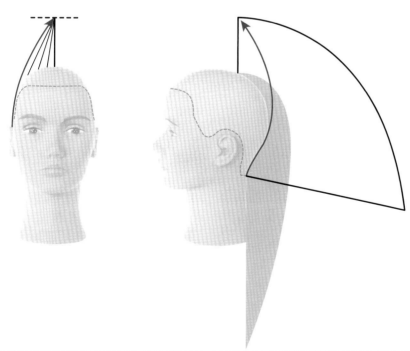

When lengths in the exterior are not long enough to reach a single stationary design line and full texture activation is desired, multiple design lines may be used. Since the rate of increase changes within the design, the form will tend to be less elongated.

TWO STATIONARY DESIGN LINES

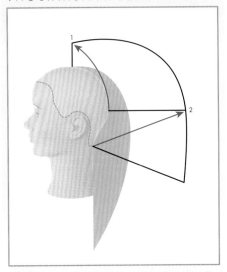

In this example, the hair on the lower half of the head travels a reduced distance to the second design line.

THREE STATIONARY DESIGN LINES

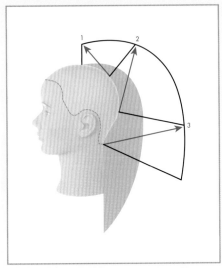

The progression of length changes according to the number of design lines used. Also, the perimeter length is affected by establishing additional design lines.

INCREASE-LAYERED FORM GUIDELINES
CUSTOMIZING THE PERIMETER DESIGN LINES

For many clients it is desirable to have some perimeter weight, which is often achieved by sculpting the perimeter design line in natural fall before or after the increase-layered texture is sculpted. This will produce a small amount of solid texture around the perimeter. If distinctly more weight is desired, proportionately more solid or graduated texture may be sculpted in the exterior.

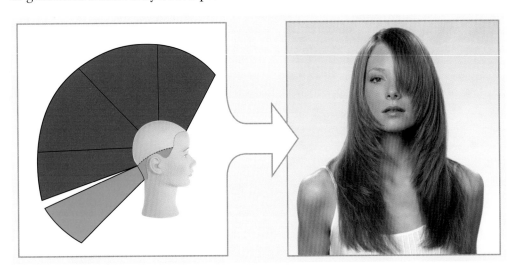

This example shows increased layers in the interior, sculpted over a graduated exterior.

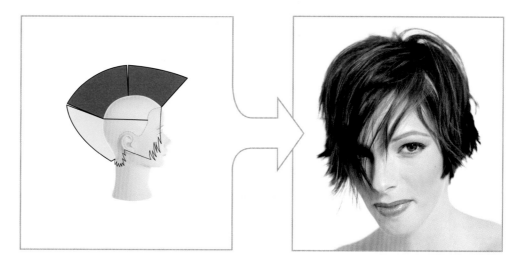

ESTABLISHING THE DESIGN LINE

When establishing the interior design line, a small strand of hair can be selected in the area where the shortest layers are desired. This strand is distributed naturally and sculpted while it falls freely without tension. The strand is then projected according to the desired length increase and serves as a length guide to sculpt the initial design line.

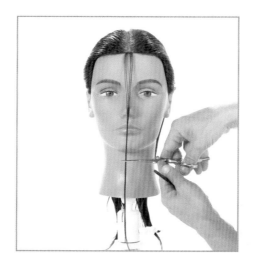
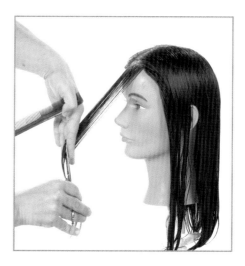

INCREASE-LAYERED FORM, VERTICAL LINE – WORKSHOP

As a designer, creating hair sculptures to meet your clients' needs is a must in any salon! This increase-layered sculpture produces a length increase toward the exterior maintaining the most length at the center back. Depending on the length of the initial sculpted design line and the direction in which the hair is styled, a combination of textures will be more or less apparent. This increase-layered form is ideal for clients who want layered texture along the front with more length in the back.

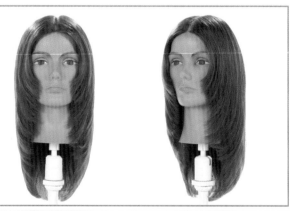

This increase-layered form is sculpted from vertical partings using a parallel finger position. Lengths are shortest around the face with extreme length increases toward the nape. Although this design was sculpted from a center part, it can be styled from a slight side part as well.

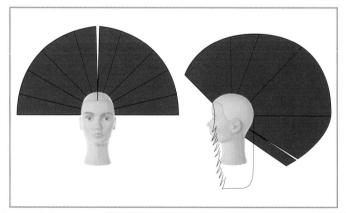

The structure graphics show shorter lengths in the interior progressing to longer lengths in the exterior.

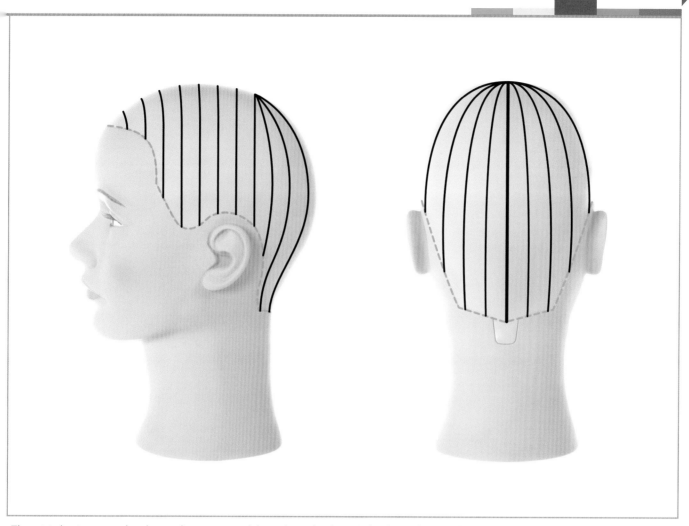

The art indicates vertical and pivotal partings used throughout the design. The design line and finger position are parallel to the partings.

1 Section with a center part that extends from the front hairline to the nape.

2 Release a small, thin section at the center front hairline. With the hair in natural fall, sculpt a length guide below the lip.

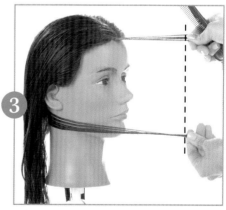

3 Use this length guide and compare to the nape length to determine the position of the intended vertical design line.

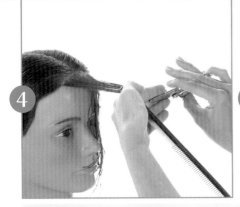

Release a vertical parting at the center front hairline that includes the previously sculpted length guide. Distribute the hair straight forward with perpendicular distribution. Position your fingers parallel to the parting and sculpt from the center to one side. Then sculpt from the other side to the center to establish the stationary design line.

Release the next parting on one side. Project the hair straight forward to the stationary design line. Sculpt parallel from the top of the parting to the bottom.

Continue using vertical partings as partings extend to the hairline. Continue sculpting from the top following the established stationary design line.

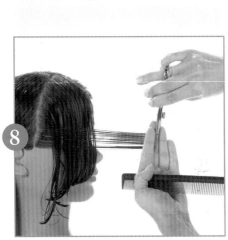

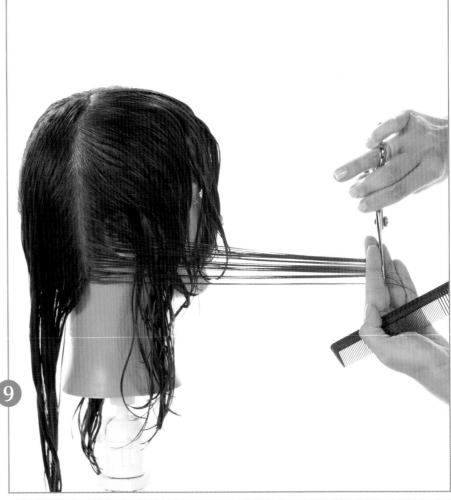

Maintain perpendicular distribution and the vertical finger position while working toward the bottom of each parting. Work toward the back of this side.

When you reach the crown area, begin to take pivotal partings. Continue directing the hair to the stationary design line using the conversion layering technique. Use 0° projection as you direct each parting around the curve of the head to the stationary design line.

Continue to use pivotal partings working to the center back. Partings may increase in size due to the thickness of the stationary design line. Work to the center back, using the same sculpting technique.

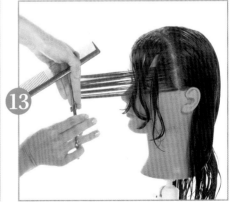

Move to the opposite side and release a vertical parting that includes the initially sculpted length guide. Distribute the hair straight forward and position your fingers vertically. Sculpt parallel following the stationary design line.

Subdivide partings for control and work from the top of the parting to the bottom. Note that the sculpting position has changed.

Continue working toward the back, using the conversion layering technique. Use perpendicular distribution and 0° projection as you direct each parting to the design line. Work to the center back.

Once the conversion layering is completed, distribute the hair in natural fall and refine the perimeter lengths.

The completed exercise shows the increase-layered form sculpted from vertical partings. This design can be styled straight or curly.

DESIGN DECISIONS
Draw or fill in the boxes with the appropriate answers.

SHAPE:

TEXTURE:

STRUCTURE:

SECTIONING PATTERN:

RIGHT SIDE:

head position	parting	distribution	projection	finger/tool position	design line mobile/stationary

---

LEFT SIDE:

head position	parting	distribution	projection	finger/tool position	design line mobile/stationary

---

TOOLS:

variation
INCREASE-LAYERED FORM, VERTICAL LINE

In this variation, the same vertical (and pivotal) parting pattern is used with perpendicular distribution as in the previous exercise. A nonparallel finger position is used to retain more perimeter lengths toward the back. This technique is highly desired by clients with extra-long hair.

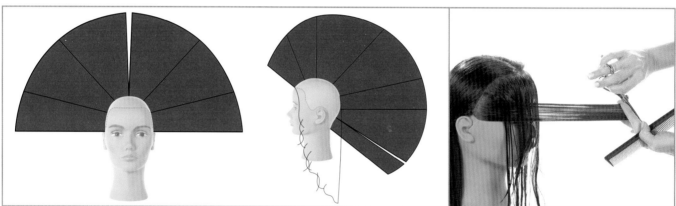

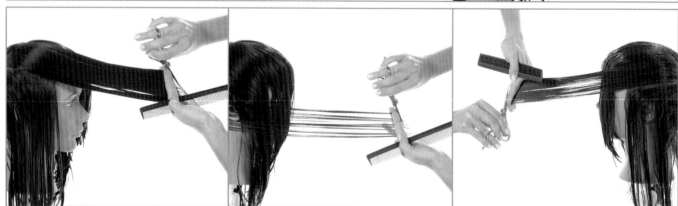

Vertical partings, perpendicular distribution and a nonparallel finger position are used to sculpt this increase-layered form. The nonparallel finger position allows for greater length retention in the exterior, which is important to many clients. A comparison between the shortest intended length at the forehead and the existing nape length will determine the nonparallel finger position to be used. This comparison will ensure that the longest lengths are retained. All lengths are distributed forward to the nonparallel stationary design line and sculpted.

SCULPTURE DESIGN RUBRIC

Chapter 2: Increase-Layered Form, Vertical Line

This Rubric is a performance assessment tool designed to measure your ability to **create** Pivot Point sculpture designs.

Name _____ ID Number _____ Date _____

	In Progress Level 1	Getting Better Level 2	Entry-Level Proficiency Level 3
PREPARATION			
• Assemble sculpting essentials	☐	☐	☐
CREATE			
• Section hair down center from forehead to nape	☐	☐	☐
• Part small section at center front hairline	☐	☐	☐
• Sculpt length guide using natural fall and no tension	☐	☐	☐
• Compare lengths at nape with length guide	☐	☐	☐
• Part vertically at center front hairline	☐	☐	☐
• Distribute hair straight forward including length guide	☐	☐	☐
• Sculpt stationary design line using perpendicular distribution and parallel finger position	☐	☐	☐
• Part vertically from center part	☐	☐	☐
• Distribute hair straight out using perpendicular distribution	☐	☐	☐
• Sculpt one side using conversion layering technique and parallel finger position	☐	☐	☐
• Sculpt working toward back using same techniques	☐	☐	☐
• Distribute hair around curve of head from pivotal partings at crown as work continues to center back	☐	☐	☐
• Repeat on opposite side	☐	☐	☐
• Refine back perimeter along a convex line in natural fall to blend to front	☐	☐	☐
• Check for layered texture around face that diminishes toward back	☐	☐	☐
• Finish sculpture design	☐	☐	☐

TOTAL POINTS = ☐ + ☐ + ☐

TOTAL POINTS _____ ÷ HIGHEST POSSIBLE SCORE 51 = _____ %

Record your time in comparison with the suggested salon speed. _____

To improve my performance on this procedure, I need to: _____

_____

INCREASE-LAYERED FORM, DIAGONAL-FORWARD LINE — WORKSHOP

Clients love the benefits of added volume while still being able to maintain maximum length. Increase layers sculpted from diagonal-forward partings create texture and movement around the face and can be sculpted in a variety of lengths.

This classic increase-layered form is sculpted using a diagonal-forward stationary interior design line. Lengths are shortest near the forehead and longest at the nape. This versatile sculpture can be air formed for a variety of finishes.

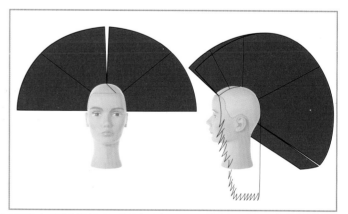

The structure graphics show the progression of lengths from the shortest lengths at the forehead to the longest lengths at the nape.

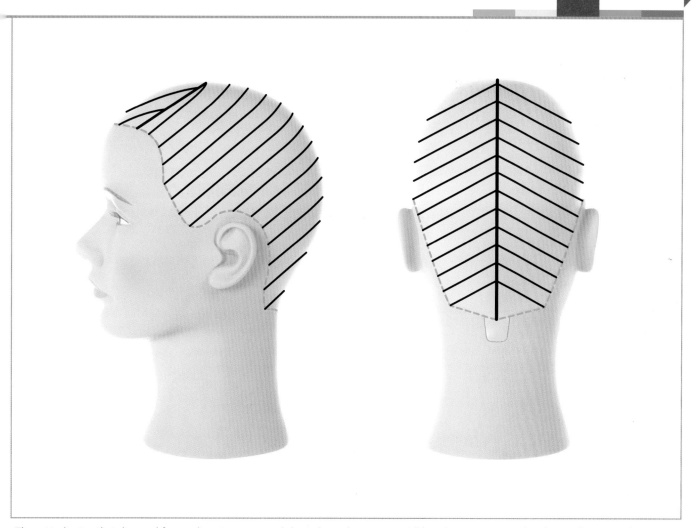

The art indicates that diagonal-forward partings are used throughout the exercise. All lengths are converged to the predetermined stationary design line to ensure that layering does not remove perimeter length, which will later be refined.

With the head in an upright position, create a side part to the center crown. Extend this parting from the center crown to the center nape.

Using the tip of the nose as a reference point, sculpt a length guide.

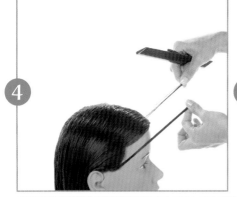

Now compare lengths at the sideburn and the crown with the length guide. If all lengths reach the guide, a pure increase-layered form can be achieved. If lengths from the perimeter do not meet the length guide, this ensures that the perimeter lengths will not be reduced.

Tilt the head slightly forward and begin sculpting on the heavier side. Take a diagonal-forward parting, distribute perpendicular and project 90° from the curve of the head. Sculpt parallel to establish the stationary design line.

Take subsequent partings parallel to the first. Use perpendicular distribution and direct the hair to the stationary design line, which is still projected at 90°. Subdivide partings for control and check that the stationary design line is visible before sculpting.

Sculpt from the top of each parting to the bottom.

Continue working through this side of the head. Maintain consistent diagonal-forward partings and perpendicular distribution as you work over the curves of the head.

10 Continue projecting the stationary design line at 90° from the curve of the head.

11 As you work toward the back of this side, note that lengths are directed around the curve of the head to the stationary design line.

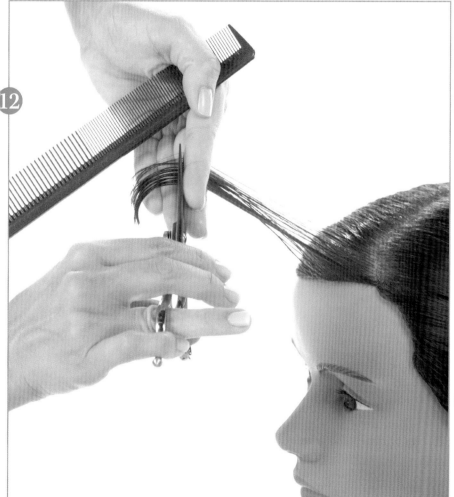

12 Now take a diagonal-forward parting on the opposite side of the head. Use perpendicular distribution and project 90° from the curve of the head. Use a small section of the previously sculpted side as a length guide and sculpt parallel to the parting.

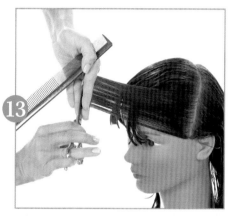

13 Take subsequent partings parallel to the first. Maintain perpendicular distribution as you project the lengths to the stationary design line.

14 Continue toward the center back to complete this side.

After air forming the hair to fall naturally, envision the angle and amount of length to be sculpted to refine the perimeter.

Sculpt a convex line that blends to the diagonal-back form line at the sides, refining to create more weight and definition.

This increase-layered form works well with both curly and straight hair textures.

DESIGN DECISIONS
Draw or fill in the boxes with the appropriate answers.

STRUCTURE:

SHAPE:

TEXTURE:

SECTIONING PATTERN:

RIGHT SIDE:
head position

parting

distribution

projection

finger/tool position

design line mobile/stationary

LEFT SIDE:
head position

parting

distribution

projection

finger/tool position

design line mobile/stationary

TOOLS:

variation
INCREASE-LAYERED FORM, DIAGONAL-FORWARD LINE

This increase-layered form has been adapted to suit clients with curly hair. The techniques used in the previous exercise are adapted to accommodate the visual length reduction that occurs with curly hair.

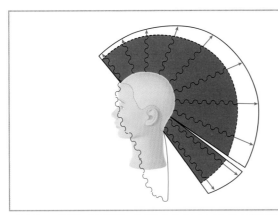

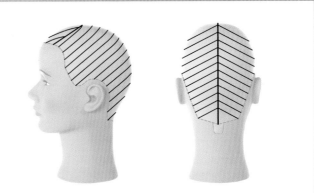

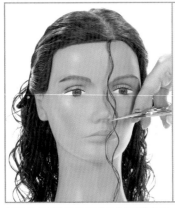

This increase-layered form is sculpted using diagonal-forward partings, perpendicular distribution, and a parallel finger position with the stationary design line projected at 90°. The length guide at the tip of the nose was sculpted freehand in natural fall with no tension. This allows the hair to assume its natural curl configuration and makes allowances for the visual length reduction that occurs as curly hair dries. While sculpting, the hair is distributed using the wide teeth of the comb to avoid tension and stretching.

SCULPTURE DESIGN RUBRIC

Chapter 2: Increase-Layered Form, Diagonal-Forward Line

This Rubric is a performance assessment tool designed to measure your ability to **create** Pivot Point sculpture designs.

Name _____ ID Number _____ Date _____

	In Progress Level 1	Getting Better Level 2	Entry-Level Proficiency Level 3
PREPARATION			
• Assemble sculpting essentials	☐	☐	☐
CREATE			
• Section hair with side part that extends through center crown to nape	☐	☐	☐
• Position head upright	☐	☐	☐
• Sculpt length guide using small portion of hair from heavy side of part	☐	☐	☐
• Compare lengths at sideburn and crown with length guide	☐	☐	☐
• Position head slightly forward	☐	☐	☐
• Part hair along a diagonal-forward line on heavier side	☐	☐	☐
• Distribute hair using perpendicular distribution and project hair at 90º from curve of head	☐	☐	☐
• Sculpt a diagonal-forward stationary design line using a parallel finger position	☐	☐	☐
• Sculpt remainder of heavier side using conversion layering technique; work toward center nape	☐	☐	☐
• Determine length guide for lighter side using a portion of previously sculpted side	☐	☐	☐
• Sculpt a diagonal-forward stationary design line on lighter side using perpendicular distribution, 90º projection, and a parallel finger position	☐	☐	☐
• Sculpt remainder of lighter side using same procedure as heavier side	☐	☐	☐
• Check for symmetrical balance	☐	☐	☐
• Finish sculpture design	☐	☐	☐
• Sculpt a convex line in nape area to refine perimeter line	☐	☐	☐
TOTAL POINTS =	☐ +	☐ +	☐

TOTAL POINTS _____ ÷ HIGHEST POSSIBLE SCORE 48 = _____ %

Record your time in comparison with the suggested salon speed. _____

To improve my performance on this procedure, I need to: _____

_____

INCREASE-LAYERED FORM, HORIZONTAL LINE — WORKSHOP

This planar/conversion-layered sculpture is ideal for clients who want more volume in the interior, while maintaining enough exterior length to elongate the form. Because the form isn't sculpted from a specific part, it allows for great styling options.

This classic increase-layered form incorporates planar sculpting in the interior and conversion layering in the exterior. The result is a slower rate of increase in the interior and a faster rate of increase in the exterior.

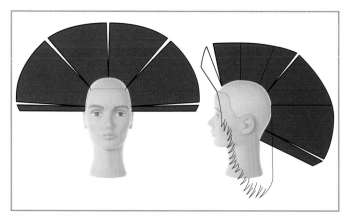

The structure graphics show the shortest lengths at the center top. The rate of increase changes according to the sectioning taken, with a faster rate of increase in the exterior portion of the sculpture.

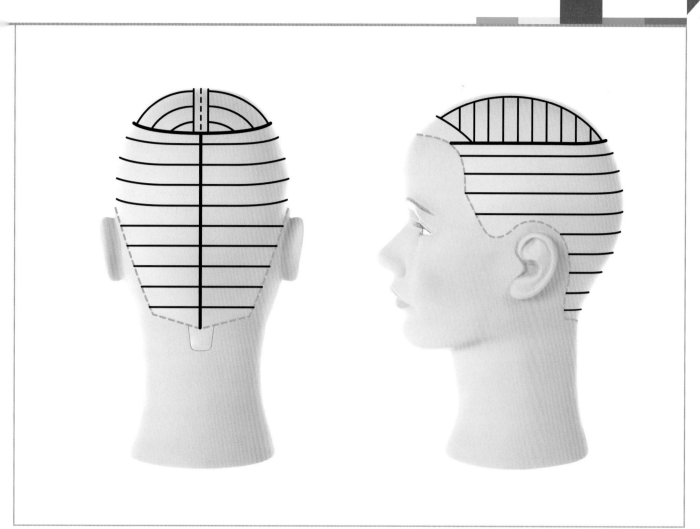

The art shows the interior sectioned above the crest. A center parting from the forehead to the crown will serve as a guide to sculpt the remainder of the interior, which will be sculpted from horizontal partings. The exterior is divided vertically at the center back and horizontal partings will be used to sculpt. The front hairline has been isolated to accommodate the shorter fringe.

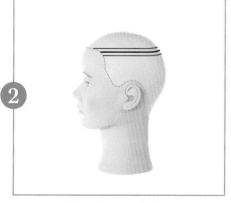

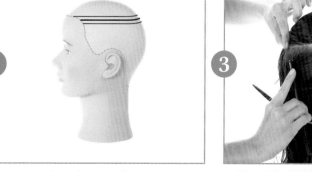

Begin by creating a defined back perimeter form line. Use natural distribution and sculpt a horizontal form line.

Next, section the interior from the exterior using a horseshoe-shaped parting. This sectioning may vary depending on the head shape and the desired proportional rates of increase.

Position the head upright and compare the lengths at the forehead and the back of the section. To accommodate the shorter fringe from the previous sculpture, isolate a 1" (2.5 cm) parting at the front hairline to allow for more length retention. Compare the lengths behind the hairline section and the back of the section to determine the finger position to be used.

Release a center parting from 1" (2.5 cm) behind the front hairline to the crown. Project the lengths straight up. Position your fingers horizontally and sculpt parallel to the fingers.

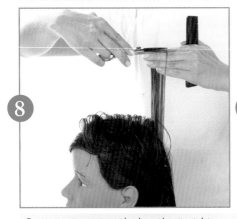

Continue to project the lengths straight up, with fingers positioned parallel to the floor, as the remainder of the length guide is sculpted.

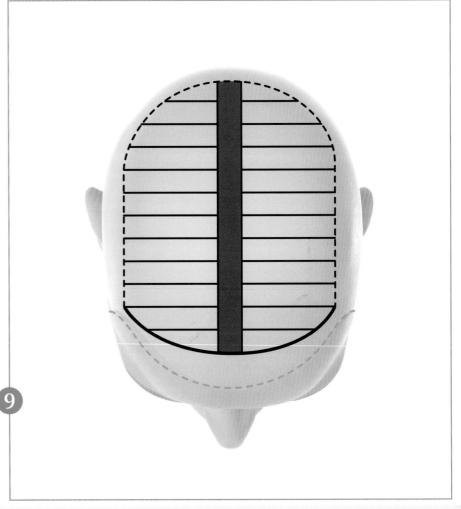

The art indicates that horizontal partings will be used to sculpt the remainder of the interior with the center parting as a guide. Each subsequent horizontal parting is projected straight up, with both the center parting and the previous horizontal parting serving as guides.

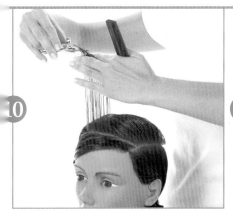

Take a horizontal parting behind the front hairline section. Project the hair straight up and position your fingers horizontally. Use the previously sculpted center parting as a guide and sculpt parallel to your fingers.

As you work with the planar sculpting technique, you may choose to complete one side of the interior section and then the other, or sculpt each horizontal parting straight across.

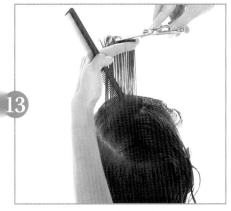

Continue using the same sculpting technique as you work toward the back of the interior section. It is important to maintain an upright head position and consistent projection while sculpting.

Work to the back of the section using the same technique. Note that the hair in each parting is projected vertically straight up, not at 90° from the curve of the head. This would result in a more rounded form.

When the interior is completed, direct the hairline that was originally isolated straight up. Position your fingers horizontally and sculpt any lengths that may extend beyond the horizontal plane.

Cross-check the interior section along the opposite line, still positioning your fingers parallel to the floor.

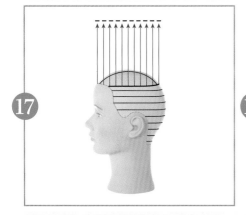

The art shows horizontal partings that extend from the front to the center back.

After releasing a length guide along the perimeter of the interior section, move to one side of the exterior and take a horizontal parting that extends from the front to the center back. One side of the exterior will be sculpted first and then the other.

NOTE: *Various techniques can be used in the exterior to alter the proportions of the finished design. For instance, slide cutting will maintain more exterior length than blunt sculpting.*

Using the perimeter of the interior section as a stationary design line, direct the hair straight up with perpendicular distribution and sculpt horizontally. Generally, you should stand opposite the intended length increase to clearly see the stationary design line. Use the conversion layering technique to sculpt the remainder of this side. As an alternative, you may also stand on the side of the head that you are sculpting.

22 Continue to use the same sculpting technique to complete this side.

23 Move to the other side of the exterior. Use a guide from the perimeter of the interior section and direct the hair straight up while sculpting.

24 Continue taking horizontal partings using perpendicular distribution and directing the hair to the stationary design line.

25 Work to the bottom of this section making sure both sides blend.

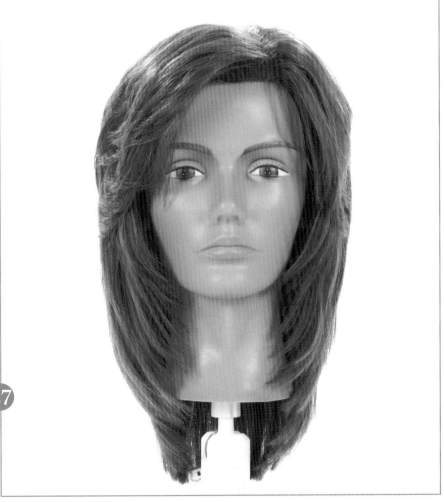

26 To refine the perimeter, first air form the hair. Then use low projection, position your fingers along a steep diagonal-back line and sculpt only the ends.

27 As in all increase-layered forms, lengths progress from short to long, but here we see two different rates of increase. A slower rate in the interior allows for shorter length and more volume. The faster rate of increase in the exterior creates elongation.

DESIGN DECISIONS

Draw or fill in the boxes with the appropriate answers.

SHAPE: oval

TEXTURE: acti vated

STRUCTURE: increased layered

SECTIONING PATTERN:

INTERIOR:

head position	parting	distribution	projection	finger/tool position	design line mobile/stationary

EXTERIOR:

head position	parting	distribution	projection	finger/tool position	design line mobile/stationary

TOOLS:

SCULPTURE DESIGN RUBRIC

Chapter 2: Increase-Layered Form, Horizontal Line

This Rubric is a performance assessment tool designed to measure your ability to **create** Pivot Point sculpture designs.

Name _____ ID Number _____ Date _____

	In Progress Level 1	Getting Better Level 2	Entry-Level Proficiency Level 3
PREPARATION			
• Assemble sculpting essentials	☐	☐	☐
CREATE			
• Sculpt horizontal-back perimeter form line using natural distribution	☐	☐	☐
• Section interior from exterior above crest using horseshoe-shaped parting	☐	☐	☐
• Compare lengths at forehead and back of section	☐	☐	☐
• Isolate a 1" (2.5 cm) parting at front hairline to retain more length	☐	☐	☐
• Part vertically behind front hairline to crown	☐	☐	☐
• Position head upright	☐	☐	☐
• Project center panel straight up and position fingers horizontally	☐	☐	☐
• Sculpt entire center panel parallel to fingers to establish length guide	☐	☐	☐
• Part hair horizontally at front across horseshoe-shaped section	☐	☐	☐
• Project hair straight up and position fingers horizontally	☐	☐	☐
• Sculpt parallel to fingers using planar sculpting technique and center panel as guide	☐	☐	☐
• Sculpt subsequent sections working toward back using previously sculpted parting and center panel as length guide	☐	☐	☐
• Cross-check interior section along opposite line	☐	☐	☐
• Release perimeter of interior section as a length guide for exterior	☐	☐	☐
• Extend a horizontal parting in exterior, just below interior, from front hairline to center back	☐	☐	☐
• Project hair straight up from exterior horizontal parting using perpendicular distribution	☐	☐	☐
• Sculpt horizontally, parallel to floor, using perimeter of interior section as a stationary design line	☐	☐	☐
• Sculpt subsequent horizontal partings using the conversion layering technique; work toward perimeter	☐	☐	☐
• Sculpt opposite side using same technique, extending partings in back to ensure blending	☐	☐	☐
• Check for two different rates of increase: slower in interior, faster in exterior	☐	☐	☐
• Finish sculpture design	☐	☐	☐
• Refine perimeter using steep diagonal-back lines on each side sculpting ends only	☐	☐	☐

TOTAL POINTS = ☐ + ☐ + ☐

TOTAL POINTS _____ ÷ HIGHEST POSSIBLE SCORE 69 = _____ %

Record your time in comparison with the suggested salon speed. _____

To improve my performance on this procedure, I need to: _____

_____

2.5

UNIFORMLY LAYERED FORM

The fourth of the four basic forms, the uniformly layered form, is the true "one-length-cut." In other words, all the lengths are uniform. Despite how simple this sculpture may appear, sculpting this form accurately takes a lot of skill and precision. The results are consistent layers and a rounded silhouette throughout the sculpted area, which is flattering and easy to style for female and male clients alike.

UNIFORMLY LAYERED FORM OVERVIEW

After you learn the characteristics that define the uniformly layered form, you will also learn to understand the techniques used to create predictable, uniformly layered sculpture results.

Uniformly layered forms are curvilinear and have an activated surface texture. Personalizing the perimeter lengths allows you to customize the form.

SHAPE

Uniformly layered forms are characterized by a rounded shape that parallels the curve of the head and features no discernible weight within the form.

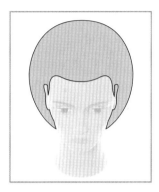

STRUCTURE

All lengths in a uniformly layered form are equal. Uniformly layered forms may be sculpted at a variety of lengths; however, they usually fall into the short- to mid-length category.

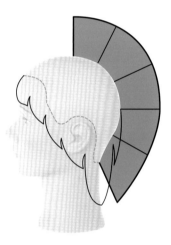

TEXTURE

Generally the sculpted texture of a uniformly layered form is totally activated. Curl texture, whether natural or permed, will accentuate the textural effect while enhancing volume and dimension.

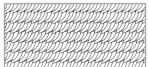

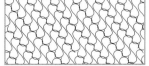

UNIFORMLY LAYERED FORM SCULPTING PROCEDURES

POSITION HEAD

The head is most often positioned upright while sculpting uniformly layered texture. However, it can be positioned forward when layering in the nape.

SECTION/PART

In uniform layers the hair is mainly sectioned for control. Common sectioning lines are center part, parting from ear to ear across the apex and/or sectioning horizontally at the occipital area. Horizontal, vertical and pivotal parting patterns are most frequently used to sculpt uniform layers. Partings should be controllable, since partings that are too thick will make it difficult to determine the correct projection angle.

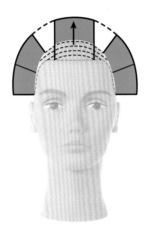  

DISTRIBUTE

To sculpt uniformly layered texture, perpendicular distribution is used from the parting.

PROJECT

When sculpting the uniformly layered form, the hair is always projected 90° from the curve of the head. Establishing a 90° angle to a curved surface such as the head can be difficult. Since inconsistent projection results in uneven lengths, it is essential to frequently check for accuracy while sculpting.

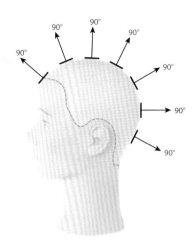

POSITION FINGERS/SHEARS

For uniform layers, the fingers are placed parallel to the partings and to the head. Because uneven lengths can result from inconsistent finger positioning, it is essential that the fingers are also parallel to the head to create totally uniform lengths.

The palm may face up or down, depending on the area of the head being sculpted. This will usually be a matter of comfort.

Depending on the length being sculpted, you may extend your little finger and rest it on the scalp to maintain equal distance throughout.

SCULPT DESIGN LINE

A mobile design line is used to sculpt uniform lengths. Once the design line is sculpted, it is projected to a 90° angle along with the adjacent parting. Then each parting that has been sculpted becomes the new design line for the next parting.

UNIFORMLY LAYERED FORM GUIDELINES
NONPARALLEL FINGER POSITION

Some head shapes may require adapting the technique to create the rounded silhouette. In areas that are flatter, a nonparallel, more curved finger position may be used to compensate.

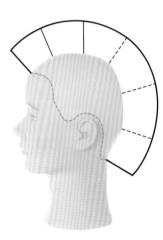 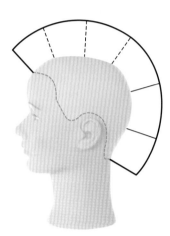

FORM VARIATIONS

A design line may be sculpted in natural fall along the perimeter hairline. This design line can then be used as a guide to sculpt uniform lengths throughout. Sculpting in this manner creates a pure uniformly layered form with no weight line.

 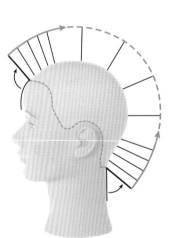 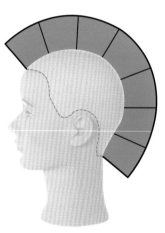

Sculpting a larger section along the perimeter hairline in natural fall establishes more weight. Then the uniformly layered lengths are sculpted using the weight corner as a guide.

 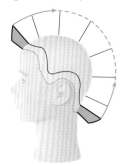 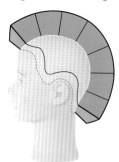

Another way to sculpt this form is to sculpt all lengths at 90° first and then sculpt the perimeter. This adds weight and defines the form line.

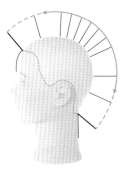  

CURLY TEXTURES

Special caution—sometimes even special techniques, such as freeform sculpting—is needed when sculpting uniform layers on curly texture. The tighter the curls the shorter the hair will appear after sculpting.

 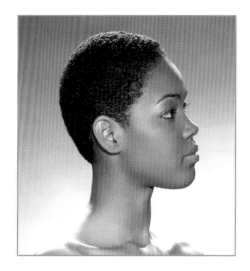

UNIFORMLY LAYERED FORM, HORIZONTAL/ VERTICAL LINE — WORKSHOP

In the salon you'll work with many clients who prefer the ease of shorter hair. Many of these clients can benefit from the uniformly layered form sculpture. Since uniform layers are the same length throughout, the styling options are limitless.

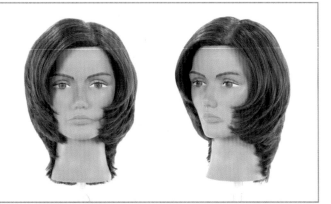

This classic uniformly layered form is sculpted using 90° projection and perpendicular distribution. Lengths are equal throughout the sculpture, resulting in a rounded form. This versatile sculpture can be air formed for a variety of finishes.

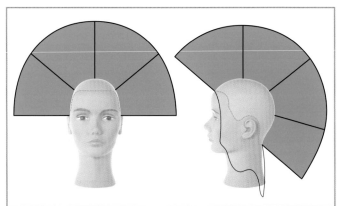

The structure graphics show that lengths are uniform throughout the sculpture.

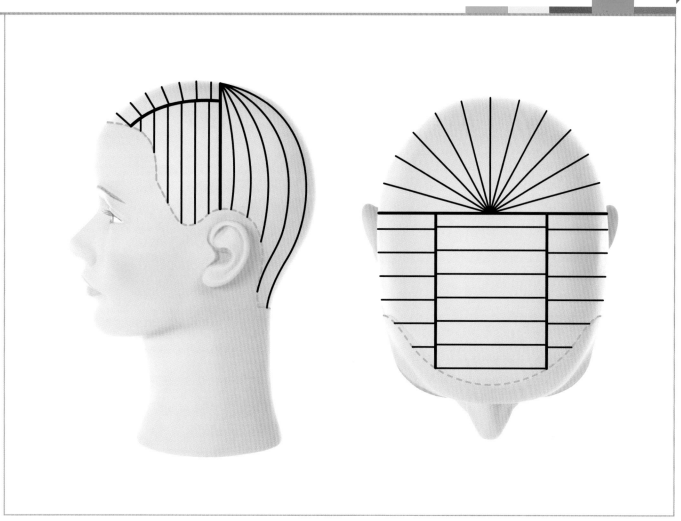

The art shows that the head will be sectioned in five sections. The top is sectioned with a center rectangle that extends to the apex. Horizontal partings are used within this section. The sides are sectioned from the corner of the rectangle to the top of the ear on each side and are sculpted using vertical partings. The back is sectioned from the apex to the center nape and sculpted using pivotal partings.

1

Section the front from the apex to the ears. Then section a rectangle from the front hairline to the apex with the width extending from the center of each eye. Section the back from the apex to the center nape.

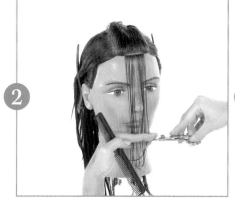

2

Start at the center front hairline. Take a thin horizontal parting and distribute the hair naturally. Establish the length guide to fall below the lips.

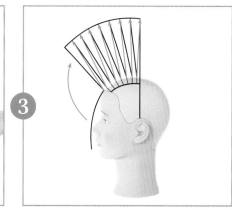

3

The art shows how the length guide will establish the length for the rest of the hair sculpture. A mobile design line is used to sculpt with each parting projected at 90°.

4 After establishing the length guide, release a horizontal parting. Use perpendicular distribution and project the hair 90° from the curve of the head. Position your fingers parallel to the head and sculpt parallel to your fingers.

5 Work from the hairline toward the apex using a mobile design line. Continue using horizontal partings, perpendicular distribution and 90° projection.

6 Continue working to the apex. Use thin partings to ensure an accurate projection at 90° from the curve of the head.

7 The art shows the vertical partings and projection used to sculpt the sides. The hair is projected at 90°.

Release one side and take a vertical parting at the front hairline. Use 90° projection and sculpt parallel to your fingers. Subdivide the parting for control, starting at the top of the section working down.

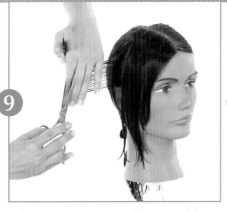

Continue working toward the back of the section using a mobile design line.

Move to the other side and release vertical partings, starting at the front hairline. Project the hair 90° from the curve of the head and sculpt parallel.

90°

Continue to subdivide partings for control. Notice how the change in body position allows you to maintain a consistent finger and sculpting position on either side.

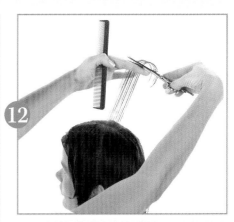

Move to the back and release the left side. Take a thin vertical parting adjacent to the center back. Project the hair 90° from the curve of the head, position your fingers parallel to the head and sculpt.

Subdivide the parting for control, starting at the top of the section working downward. Maintain consistent 90° projection from the curve of the head using a palm-up hand position to sculpt the nape.

Use pivotal partings to work through the remainder of the section. Continue to project at 90° and use perpendicular distribution until you reach the ear.

Release the back right side and take another vertical parting adjacent to the center back. Continue to project 90° from the curve of the head using perpendicular distribution. Use pivotal partings and the same technique to complete this side.

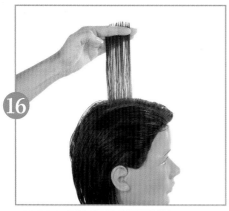

Cross-check the lengths in the opposite direction of the sculpted line. Continue to project lengths at 90° from the curves of the head.

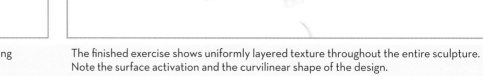

Refine the perimeter form line using low projection.

The finished exercise shows uniformly layered texture throughout the entire sculpture. Note the surface activation and the curvilinear shape of the design.

DESIGN DECISIONS

Draw or fill in the boxes with the appropriate answers.

STRUCTURE:

SHAPE:

TEXTURE:

SECTIONING PATTERN:

TOP: head position	parting	distribution	projection	finger/tool position	design line mobile/stationary

SIDES: head position	parting	distribution	projection	finger/tool position	design line mobile/stationary

BACK: head position	parting	distribution	projection	finger/tool position	design line mobile/stationary

TOOLS:

SCULPTURE DESIGN RUBRIC

Chapter 2: Uniformly Layered Form, Horizontal/Vertical Line

This Rubric is a performance assessment tool designed to measure your ability to **create** Pivot Point sculpture designs.

Name _____ ID Number _____ Date _____

	In Progress Level 1	Getting Better Level 2	Entry-Level Proficiency Level 3
PREPARATION			
• Assemble sculpting essentials	☐	☐	☐
CREATE			
• Section front with a center rectangle that extends to apex; create a vertical part from apex to center nape; section from corner of rectangle to ear on either side	☐	☐	☐
• Position head upright	☐	☐	☐
• Establish length guide at center front hairline	☐	☐	☐
• Part hair horizontally at front hairline within center rectangle section	☐	☐	☐
• Sculpt mobile design line using perpendicular distribution, 90° projection and a parallel finger position; work toward apex	☐	☐	☐
• Part hair vertically at front hairline on side section	☐	☐	☐
• Sculpt mobile design line using perpendicular distribution, 90° projection and a parallel finger position; work toward back of side section	☐	☐	☐
• Sculpt opposite side using same procedures	☐	☐	☐
• Part hair vertically at center back left side and use a portion of top section as a length guide	☐	☐	☐
• Sculpt center back using 90° projection and a parallel finger position to establish mobile design line, sculpting from the top downward	☐	☐	☐
• Sculpt from center toward one side, then from center toward the other side using pivotal partings, perpendicular distribution, 90° projection and a parallel finger position	☐	☐	☐
• Cross-check lengths along opposite line	☐	☐	☐
• Check for totally activated surface texture and curvilinear shape	☐	☐	☐
• Finish sculpture design	☐	☐	☐
• Refine perimeter form line	☐	☐	☐

TOTAL POINTS =   ☐ + ☐ + ☐

TOTAL POINTS _____ ÷ HIGHEST POSSIBLE SCORE 48 = _____ %

Record your time in comparison with the suggested salon speed. _____

To improve my performance on this procedure, I need to: _____
_____

UNIFORMLY LAYERED FORM, PIVOTAL LINE — WORKSHOP

This short uniformly layered sculpture is very popular in the salon. Many clients will ask for this or variations of the design, which can require minimal maintenance, but still look well-put together. Simple education for your clients about styling products can help them create a variety of looks.

This uniformly layered form is sculpted using pivotal partings and perpendicular distribution. All lengths are equal throughout the sculpture, resulting in a rounded form. This versatile sculpture can be finished from any direction, allowing for a wide range of styling options.

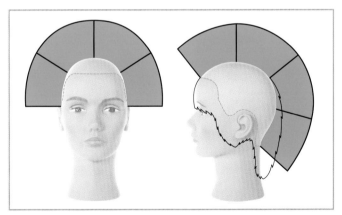

The structure graphic shows that lengths are uniform throughout the sculpture.

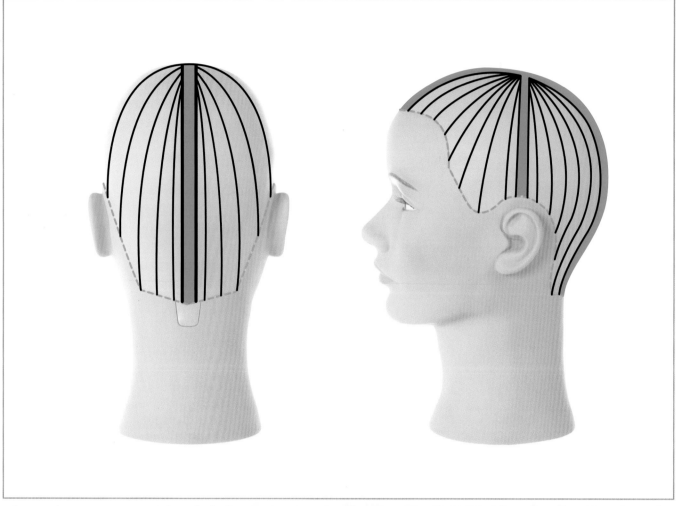

The art indicates a center parting from the forehead to the nape and a parting from the apex to each ear. These partings will serve as length guides while working through this sculpture. The remainder of the sculpture will use pivotal partings.

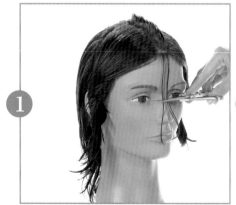

1 Release a center parting from the center forehead to the apex. Release a small section at the hairline and distribute in natural fall. Establish the length guide at the bridge of the nose.

2 Continue establishing the length guide along the center part using perpendicular distribution and projecting at 90°. Position your fingers parallel to the curve of the head and sculpt parallel from the center hairline to the apex.

3 Part and then sculpt from the apex to the occipital area. Note that the projection over the curve of the head is adjusted to remain consistently at 90°.

4 Continue sculpting the length guide from the occipital to the center nape. Note that the hand position is now palm up for comfort and accuracy while sculpting.

5 Now release a parting extending vertically from the apex to each ear. Use perpendicular distribution and project at 90°. Position your fingers parallel to the curve of the head and sculpt parallel to maintain equal lengths.

6

90°

7 Section horizontally at the occipital to separate the entire nape area. Then release a thin pivotal parting in the back left section adjacent to the center guide. Use perpendicular distribution and project at 90° from the curve of the head, using the length guide for reference. Position your fingers parallel to the curve of the head and sculpt parallel starting at the top working down.

8 Continue using pivotal partings, perpendicular distribution, 90° projection and a mobile design line as you complete this section.

9 Move to the back right section and use the center guide as a mobile design line. Use perpendicular distribution and project at 90° from the curve of the head as you sculpt.

10

11

12

Continue to use pivotal partings with perpendicular distribution and project at 90° from the curve of the head. Position your fingers parallel to the curve of the head as you complete the back right section.

Release the nape and part vertically along the left side of the previously sculpted center parting. Distribute the hair perpendicular and project at 90°. Position your fingers palm up and sculpt using the center parting as a length guide. Sculpt first the left then the right side of the nape using a mobile design line.

13

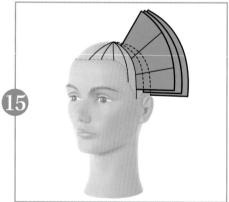

14

Continue to use the same technique with a mobile design line as you work through the section with pivotal partings.

15

Move to the top of the left side section and take a pivotal parting next to the center guide. Continue to use perpendicular distribution while projecting at 90° from the curve of the head. Position your fingers parallel to the head as you sculpt from the apex toward the front hairline. Note how the body position has changed, which helps maintain the same length throughout this section.

The art shows a consistent 90° projection angle used to achieve uniform length.

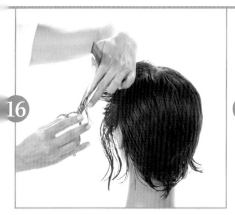

16

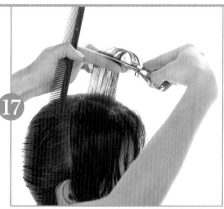

17 · 18

Stand on the right side for more accuracy and better control once the pivotal partings start to extend toward the side. Maintain consistent 90° projection as you work toward the ear.

Move to the top of the right side section and continue to sculpt uniform layers. Take a small piece from the top guide and the mobile design line. Project 90° from the curve of the head, position your fingers parallel to the curve of the head and sculpt.

NOTE: *Stand on the left side to maintain the same finger position for accurate lengths.*

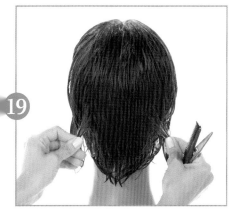

19

Check the entire sculpture for symmetry and equal lengths throughout.

20 · 21

Air form the hair, distribute it naturally and refine the perimeter to build a small amount of weight.

The finished exercise shows a versatile rounded form, which can be finished in any direction allowing a wide range of styling options.

DESIGN DECISIONS

Draw or fill in the boxes with the appropriate answers.

STRUCTURE:

SHAPE:

TEXTURE:

SECTIONING PATTERN:

head position	parting	distribution	projection	finger/tool position	design line mobile/stationary

NAPE:

head position	parting	distribution	projection	finger/tool position	design line mobile/stationary

SIDES:

head position	parting	distribution	projection	finger/tool position	design line mobile/stationary

TOOLS::

SCULPTURE DESIGN RUBRIC

Chapter 2: Uniformly Layered Form, Pivotal Line

This Rubric is a performance assessment tool designed to measure your ability to **create** Pivot Point sculpture designs.

Name _____ ID Number _____ Date _____

	In Progress Level 1	Getting Better Level 2	Entry-Level Proficiency Level 3
PREPARATION			
• Assemble sculpting essentials	☐	☐	☐
CREATE			
• Section from forehead to nape and from apex to each ear	☐	☐	☐
• Release a thin center part from center forehead to apex	☐	☐	☐
• Position head upright	☐	☐	☐
• Establish length guide at center front hairline in natural fall with no tension	☐	☐	☐
• Position fingers parallel to curve of head	☐	☐	☐
• Sculpt length guide from center hairline to apex using perpendicular distribution and 90° projection	☐	☐	☐
• Part hair vertically at center back and use a portion of top section as a length guide	☐	☐	☐
• Sculpt using same technique from apex to nape; change hand position from palm-down to palm-up in nape area	☐	☐	☐
• Release a thin parting from apex to each ear	☐	☐	☐
• Sculpt length guide on both sides using perpendicular distribution and 90° projection	☐	☐	☐
• Section horizontally at occipital to separate entire nape area	☐	☐	☐
• Part in back left section using pivotal partings	☐	☐	☐
• Sculpt using center length guide as mobile design line; use perpendicular distribution and 90° projection	☐	☐	☐
• Sculpt subsequent partings working toward ear using same technique	☐	☐	☐
• Sculpt right section working from center back toward ear using pivotal partings, perpendicular distribution and 90° projection	☐	☐	☐
• Release nape area; part hair vertically on left side of length guide	☐	☐	☐
• Sculpt working toward ear using perpendicular distribution and 90° projection	☐	☐	☐
• Sculpt opposite side using same procedure	☐	☐	☐
• Part front left side using pivotal partings starting at center	☐	☐	☐
• Sculpt using center length guide as mobile design line; use perpendicular distribution and 90° projection working toward ear	☐	☐	☐
• Sculpt opposite side using same procedure	☐	☐	☐
• Check for totally activated surface texture and curvilinear shape	☐	☐	☐
• Finish sculpture design	☐	☐	☐
• Check sculpture for symmetry	☐	☐	☐
• Refine perimeter form line using low projection	☐	☐	☐

TOTAL POINTS = ☐ + ☐ + ☐

TOTAL POINTS _____ ÷ HIGHEST POSSIBLE SCORE 78 = _____ %

Record your time in comparison with the suggested salon speed. _____

To improve my performance on this procedure, I need to: _____

_____

Voices of Success

The Salon Owner:
"WHEN I INTERVIEW A POTENTIAL NEW DESIGNER FOR MY SALON, I LOOK ESPECIALLY FOR STELLAR SKILLS IN SCULPTING CLASSIC DESIGNS, SUCH AS THE SOLID, GRADUATED, INCREASE-LAYERED AND UNIFORMLY LAYERED FORMS. I KNOW THAT WHEN A NEW DESIGNER CAN DO THESE SCULPTURES WELL, HE OR SHE WILL BE ABLE TO MASTER PRETTY MUCH ANY HAIR SCULPTURE A CLIENT MAY ASK FOR."

The Educator:
"MANY STUDENTS ARE NERVOUS AND EVEN INTIMIDATED BY THE THOUGHT OF SCULPTING THEIR FIRST CLIENT'S HAIR. I'M GLAD I CAN GIVE THEM A STRONG FOUNDATION BY TEACHING THE FOUR BASIC FORMS AND PREDICTABLE SCULPTING RESULTS."

The Client:
"MY STYLIST IS REALLY AMAZING! I CAN TELL SHE USES A VERY METHODICAL APPROACH WHEN SHE CUTS MY HAIR, AND IT ALWAYS TURNS OUT EXACTLY THE WAY WE DISCUSSED."

IN OTHER WORDS:

With a proven set of sculpting procedures and techniques under your belt, you will be able to create nearly any hair sculpture for your clients accurately and efficiently.

Learning Challenge

This challenge contains a combination of multiple-choice and short-answer items. For multiple-choice items, circle the letter corresponding to the correct answer. For short-answer items, write the correct answer in the space provided.

1. Section, position head, part, distribute, project, position fingers/shears, and sculpt design line comprise the:
   a. structure
   b. four basic forms
   c. design principles
   d. Seven Sculpting Procedures

2. Natural, perpendicular, shifted and directional are all different types of:
   a. sectioning
   b. distribution
   c. length guides
   d. parting patterns

3. The type of design line that establishes more weight is known as:
   a. mobile
   b. vertical
   c. stationary
   d. directional

4. In natural fall, all lengths in the solid form fall to the same:
   a. level
   b. angle
   c. length
   d. texture

5. The distribution used to sculpt solid forms is:
   a. 45°
   b. natural
   c. directional
   d. perpendicular

6. Graduation can be created by using a vertical parting pattern and positioning your fingers along the intended _____ of _____.

7. The design line for a graduated form may be stationary, mobile or a combination of the two, depending on the _____ of _____ desired in a given area.

8. In the increase-layered form the projection angle of the stationary design line is most important since it establishes the _____ to which all other lengths are _____.

9. The most common increase-layering technique is _____ _____.

10. To sculpt uniformly layered texture, _____ distribution is used from the parting.

Lessons Learned

The seven steps that will produce predictable sculpting results are: section, position head, part, distribute, project, position fingers/shears and sculpt design line.

The solid form is a true classic and is characterized by its smooth, unactivated texture and concentrated weight at the perimeter.

The graduated form features a triangular shape, with weight above the perimeter, and a combination of unactivated texture in the interior and activated texture in the exterior.

The increase-layered form is an ideal choice for clients who want volume and movement in the interior but want to maintain their lengths in the exterior.

The uniformly layered form distributes weight and texture activation evenly throughout the sculpted area.

a designer's approach to
ADVANCED SCULPTING

- Combination form
- Proportion
- Texturizing
- Slide cutting
- Notching
- Razor etching
- Pressure graduation
- Point cutting
- Peeling
- Freehand sculpting

Sculpting combination forms and using specialized techniques increase your creative options.

Following this lesson on A Designer's Approach to Advanced Sculpting, you will be able to:

☐ List what each basic form adds when incorporated into a combination form

☐ Describe the surface texture of various combination forms

☐ List criteria to consider when determining the position of weight within a combination form

☐ Describe various specialized sculpting techniques and the specific results they create

☐ State in your own words the client-centered guidelines for advanced sculpting

☐ Demonstrate the knowledge and ability to perform combination form sculptures using various specialized sculpting techniques

ESSENTIAL QUESTIONS FOR THIS CHAPTER:

Does following an advanced sculpting approach exclude applying what you know about the four basic forms?

Why is it important to learn advanced sculpting techniques when only a few clients really want to experiment with different hair sculptures?

If a sculpture looks great on one client, could you recreate it exactly the same way on another client and achieve a successful result?

At this point in your education in sculpture, you are probably starting to feel more confident about your skills and are able to create more accurate results. This means that it is time for you to take the leap to advanced sculpting. In a previous chapter, you learned about sculpting the four basic forms: solid, graduated, increase-layered and uniformly layered. Advanced sculpting mainly involves combining two or more of these basic forms into one sculpture and often incorporates advanced sculpting techniques to produce special effects.

Advanced sculpting naturally builds upon what you already know about sculpting overall. Designers are always aware of the results these techniques and combination forms will produce. These results become just as predictable as the ones achieved using basic sculpting techniques.

In *Chapter 3, A Designer's Approach to Advanced Sculpting*, you will learn about and put into practice various combination forms and specialized sculpting techniques, broadening your sculpting repertoire to satisfy a wider range of client needs.

ADVANCED SCULPTING TECHNIQUES

Several times during the course of this program, you have read that nearly any sculpture can be created by combining two or more of the four basic forms. Now you will further explore how such combinations can be created. In addition, you will take a closer look at the most commonly used specialized sculpting techniques, which produce a variety of effects, such as softer end texture or more mobility.

COMBINING FORMS

Most often, you will combine forms to create the look that your client desires. This means that you may sculpt one form in one component area and another form elsewhere in the design.

When combining forms, be aware of the qualities of each form or texture and what each one adds to the overall design. The options to choose from are limited only by your creativity and your client's expectations.

SHAPE/STRUCTURE
The shape and structure of a combination form can change dramatically, depending on the proportions used and the length at which the design is sculpted. The head is sectioned into components relative to the desired changes in line, shape and structure. On the following page we will have a look at just a few examples.

INCREASE/SOLID COMBINATION

While the solid exterior of a form can add weight to the perimeter line, increase layers add volume to the interior and soften the otherwise angular shape of a solid form.

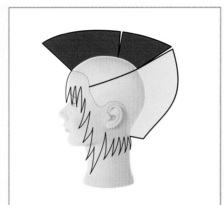

INCREASE/GRADUATED COMBINATION

High graduation sculpted in the exterior and throughout much of the crest area pushes the weight into the interior, where increase layers disperse this weight and add texture.

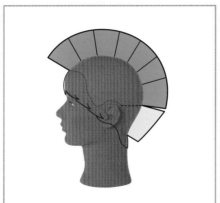

UNIFORM/GRADUATED COMBINATION

A graduated exterior reveals an angular shape along the line of inclination, while uniform interior lengths evenly distribute the weight, creating a rounded silhouette.

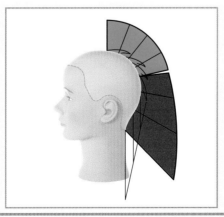

UNIFORM/INCREASE COMBINATION FORM

The increased exterior and uniform interior combination has a rounded shape. However, the silhouette parallels the curve of the head in the interior while the exterior is elongated without showing a discernible build-up of weight.

TEXTURE

When combining forms, the surface texture most evident in the final result is usually based on the form sculpted in the interior of the style. Many clients will ask for "movement" and "texture" when they consult with their designer. Keep in mind that most combination forms apply increase or uniform layers in the interior because they add movement and volume and offer styling versatility. Depending on the length of these interior layers, the surface texture can appear to be totally or partially activated. Studying these examples will help sharpen your observation skills when assessing the surface texture of a combination form sculpture.

INCREASE/SOLID COMBINATION

When increase layers are sculpted over a solid form, the overall texture is activated. This is ideal for clients who want maximum exterior length and weight with internal movement and texture.

INCREASE/GRADUATED COMBINATION

Increase/graduated combination forms have an overall activated surface texture. The ends of the increase-layered portion appear to spread out while the graduated ends stack closely to one another.

UNIFORM/INCREASE COMBINATION

Generally, the increase-layered portion of an uniform/increase design has a more spread out appearance than the surface texture of the uniformly layered portion.

Does following an advanced sculpting approach exclude applying what you know about the four basic forms?

Courtesy of DF 281.

PROPORTIONS

When combining two or more forms within a design, you must carefully plan their proportional relationship. This relationship affects the amount and position of weight within a form as well as its surface texture. Be aware of the placement of the weight area relative to the client's head shape and facial features, as well as the proportion of the textures. The client's hair type and density will also help determine the best proportional relationships between the basic forms that are being considered.

INCREASE/SOLID

The proportions of solid to increase-layered lengths will be determined by the desired result and density of the client's hair. Depending on the shortest lengths and the amount of perimeter weight desired, you may choose from various methods to sculpt the interior layers.

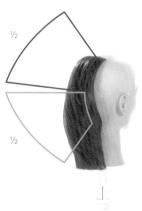

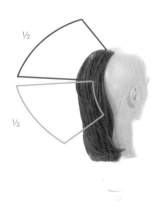

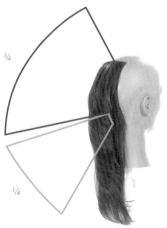

Longer interior layers add soft texture while maintaining the characteristics of the solid form exterior.

Shorter interior layers create volume and a higher degree of surface activation while reducing more perimeter weight.

Sculpting only a small amount of solid lengths at the perimeter to refine an increase-layered form achieves minimal weight.

Sculpture · 169

INCREASE/GRADUATION

When combining increase-layering with graduated forms, proportional planning is especially important. This is because the resulting weight area will be evident, creating an illusion of width within a specific area of the form.

The line of inclination will affect the placement of the weight area within a design. A higher line of inclination will position the weight area higher in the combination form. At the same time the length of these layers and the rate of the length increase determine the amount of weight retained.

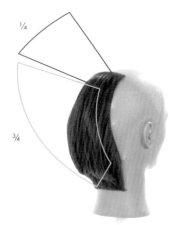 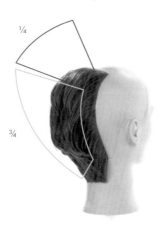 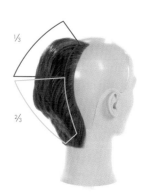

The examples below may help you to better understand the use of proportion within combinations of increase-layered and graduated forms.

Note that the way clients style their hair may change the appearance and position of a weight area.

GRADUATION/INCREASE

Although not as common, the reverse combination of graduation over increase-layered texture can also be sculpted. Here, interior weight contrasts with longer, close-fitting exterior lengths. Graduation is usually sculpted first in this combination form.

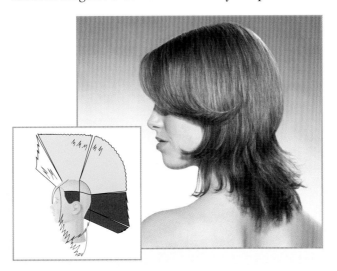

UNIFORM/GRADUATION

When combining uniformly layered and graduated forms, be especially aware of the weight area that occurs and where it falls relative to the client's features.

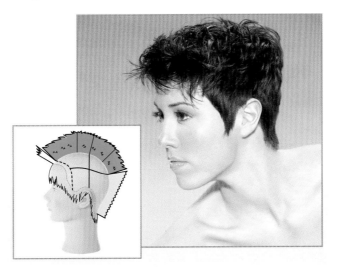

Generally, graduation is positioned within the combination to create a weight area that accentuates the bone structure or highlights the eyes. This occurs partially because of the added expansion and directional capabilities of the combination form.

In some cases, you may position graduated texture only at the perimeter to add definition to that area.

UNIFORM/INCREASE

The results of combining uniformly layered and increase-layered textures will be largely influenced by the proportions of one structure to the other. The sectioning will be directly related to this proportional relationship. If proportionately more of the form is uniform, the sculpture will take on the more rounded qualities of the uniformly layered form.

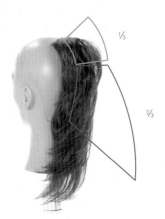 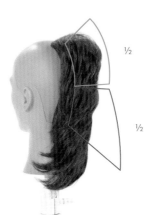 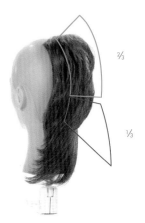

Sculpting proportionately less uniformly layered texture will create a more elongated combination form with increase-layered texture dominating the overall design.

IDENTIFYING FORMS

Review the images below. Study each one closely, then use a pencil to draw along the silhouette or shape of the design. Further trace along the lines within the surface texture of each of the designs to identify broken or unbroken lines.

Write in the space provided which combinations of forms you have identified, then draw a structure graphic that illustrates the length arrangement of the combination forms featured.

combination   structure

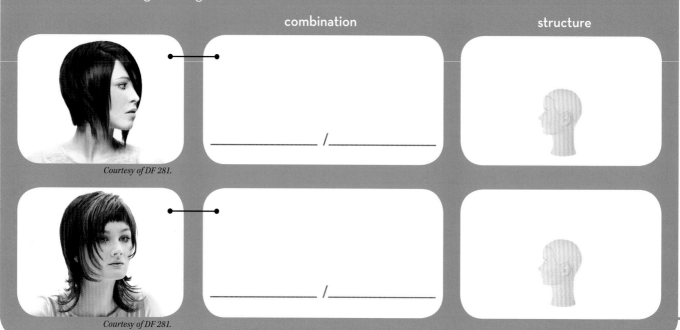

Courtesy of DF 281.

_____ / _____

Courtesy of DF 281.

_____ / _____

Practice Makes Perfect INCREASE/SOLID COMBINATION FORM

The focus of this exercise is to provide practice in using a stationary design line from multiple areas to create an increase/solid combination form. The result will be an activated texture throughout with solid perimeter weight.

Practice this exercise to build skill and accuracy using an upright head position, horizontal partings, natural and perpendicular distribution, 0° and 90° projection, parallel finger/shear position and two stationary design lines—one positioned in the exterior and another in the interior.

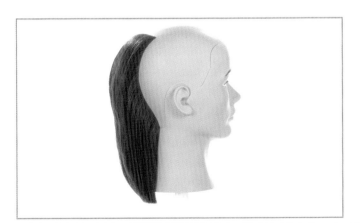

The finish shows increase layers over solid perimeter lengths. An activated surface texture is achieved while maintaining perimeter weight.

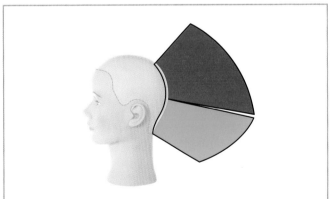

The structure graphic shows the combination of increase-layered lengths over a solid form, using approximately 50/50 proportions.

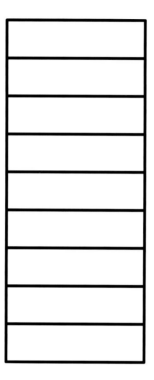

The art shows horizontal partings used to sculpt this combination form.

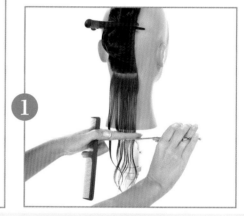

Release a horizontal parting in the nape. Use natural distribution and no projection. Position your fingers parallel to the part and sculpt. This will now serve as a stationary design line.

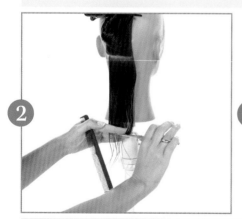

Continue to use horizontal partings, natural distribution and no projection. Sculpt parallel to the stationary design line.

Maintain natural distribution as you work over the curve of the head. Sculpt parallel to the stationary design line.

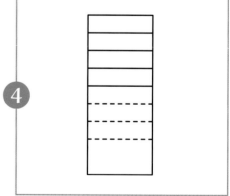

The art shows that horizontal partings will also be used to sculpt interior layers.

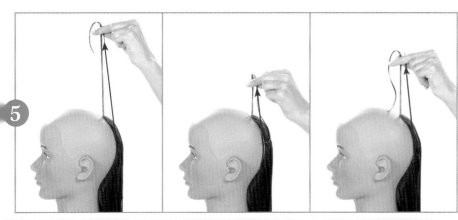

Compare interior lengths with lengths from various areas of the previously sculpted solid form to determine the length of the interior stationary design line and the proportions in which the two forms will be combined.

Sculpt a length guide using the length at the crest. This will create a 50/50 proportion.

Standing opposite the intended length increase, release a horizontal parting at the top. Project the hair straight up, position your fingers horizontally and sculpt to create the stationary design line. Project subsequent horizontal partings to the stationary design line, which is projected straight up. Continue sculpting parallel. Work until lengths no longer reach the design line.

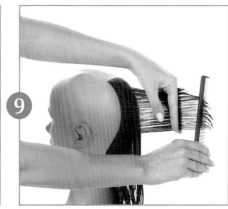

Here we see the weight corner that is created when increase and solid forms are combined.

Practice Makes Perfect INCREASE/GRADUATED COMBINATION FORM

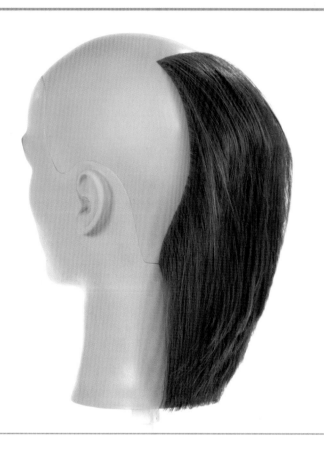

The focus of this exercise is to provide practice in using a mobile design line to create a graduated form combined with increase layers. Depending on the proportion of increase-layered versus graduated lengths, results will vary.

Practice this exercise to build skill and accuracy using an upright head position, horizontal partings, perpendicular distribution, 45° projection, parallel finger/shear position and a mobile design line.

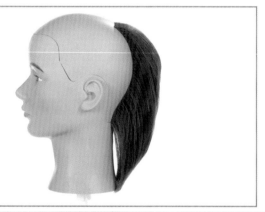

The finish shows a combination of increase and graduated textures with a diminished weight area.

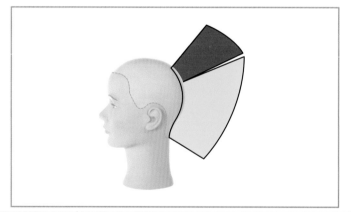

The structure graphic shows the combination of increase layers over a graduated form in approximately ⅓ increase - ⅔ graduation proportions.

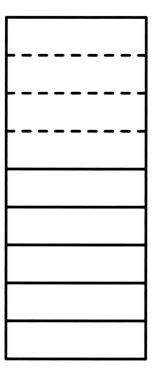

The art shows horizontal partings used to sculpt the exterior. The horizontal pattern is extended upward to ensure blending.

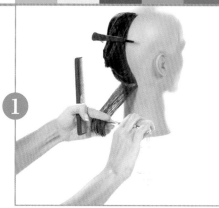

1 Release a horizontal parting in the nape. Use perpendicular distribution and 45° projection. Position your fingers parallel to the part and sculpt.

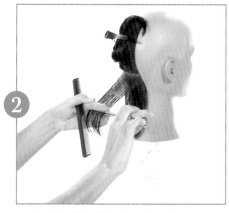
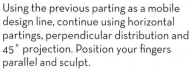

2 Using the previous parting as a mobile design line, continue using horizontal partings, perpendicular distribution and 45° projection. Position your fingers parallel and sculpt.

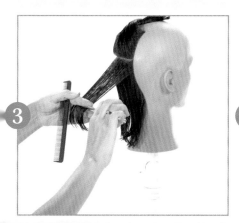

3 Continue to use the same techniques as you work upward.

4 Continue to sculpt with the same technique until lengths no longer reach. Extend the partings to ensure blending.

5 Distribute the lengths straight out to observe the position of the weight area.

Practice Makes Perfect

UNIFORM/GRADUATED COMBINATION FORM

The focus of this exercise is to provide practice in using a mobile design line to create a rounded shape of the uniformly layered form combined with the texture of the graduated form. The result will be a totally activated texture.

Practice this exercise to build skill and accuracy using an upright head position, vertical partings, perpendicular distribution, 90° projection, parallel finger/shear position and a mobile design line.

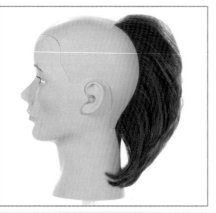

The finish shows the combination of graduated and uniformly layered textures.

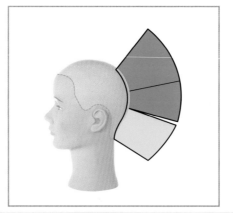

The structure graphic shows uniform lengths through the interior and graduated texture below the crest.

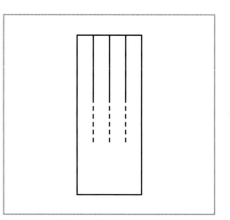

The art shows that vertical partings will be used to sculpt uniform layers. These partings will be extended into the graduated form to ensure blending.

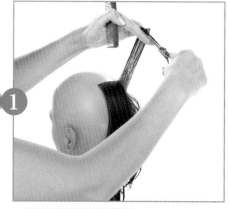

Begin with the head in an upright position. Release a thin vertical parting starting on the right side. Use 90° projection, position your fingers parallel to the curve of the head and sculpt parallel. Work downward. Maintain 90° projection while working over the curve of the head. As the parting extends, sculpt until lengths no longer reach the design line.

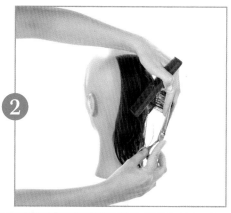

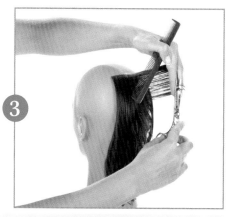

Take the next vertical parting and use a portion of the previous parting as a mobile design line. Project at 90° and position your fingers parallel to sculpt.

Continue using the same technique as you work toward the opposite side of the rectangle component. Maintain the 90° projection and a parallel finger position.

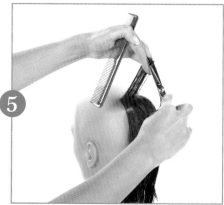

Work to the opposite side using the same technique.

Observe the subtle weight area that is created where the two forms connect.

Why is it important to learn advanced sculpting techniques when only a few clients really want to experiment with different hair sculptures?

SPECIALIZED TECHNIQUES

One important aspect of advanced hair sculpting is the personalization of a design to suit a specific client. Once the overall sculpture has been determined according to the client's features, head shape and desired result, specialized sculpting techniques can be chosen to make the final design fit the client just right. Specialized techniques can be applied as a designer proceeds through the sculpture, as a final phase of the sculpture service, or even after the sculpted hair has been air formed, before using styling products. Many of these specialized techniques are often referred to as "texturizing techniques" and involve sculpting shorter lengths within the form.

This kind of "texturizing" can be performed at the base, the midstrand, and the ends of the hair strands or any combination of the three.

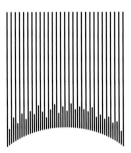

The base is usually texturized in short to mid-length forms to create lift and volume.

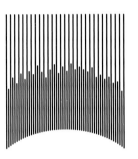

The midstrand can be texturized on any length to create mobility and reduce bulk.

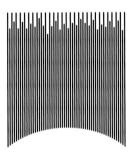

The ends are commonly texturized to add a specific end texture, such as chunky or soft. This can be used on any

Specialized sculpting techniques can be performed with a variety of tools, such as the shears, a razor, texturizing shears (also known as tapering or thinning shears) or clippers, depending on the desired effect.

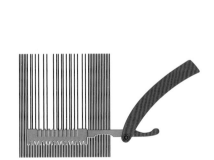

Following is a brief overview of the ways in which the specialized sculpting techniques can be applied, as shown later in this program.

NOTCHING

In this example the notching technique is used to create chunky, irregular end texture.

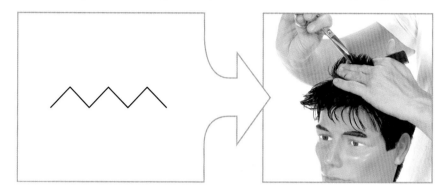 

POINT CUTTING

In this example the point cutting technique is used to add irregular lengths to blend between component areas.

SLIDE CUTTING

In this example slide cutting is used to add texture and mobility to longer lengths.

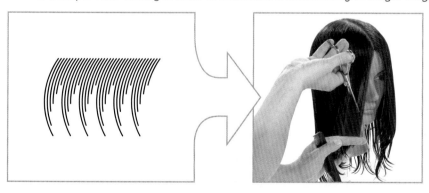 

TAPERING

In this example tapering is used to blend short lengths along the crest.

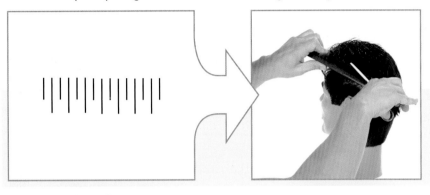

RAZOR ETCHING

In this example razor etching is used to create texture and a rapid length increase for a long, disconnected fringe.

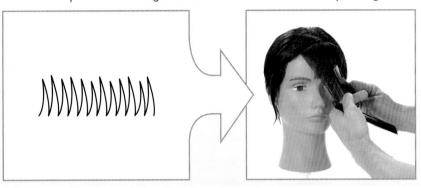

RAZOR PEELING

In this example razor peeling is used to create soft, irregular end texture.

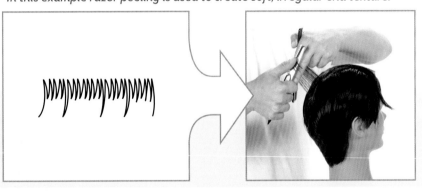

RAZOR ROTATION

In this example razor rotation is used to create soft end texture and mobility.

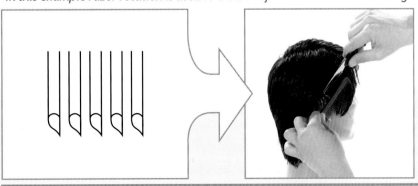

MATCHMAKER

Draw lines to appropriately connect the individual technical images shown with the name of the specialized sculpting technique used. In the spaces provided, describe the special effect each technique creates.

NOTCHING

POINT CUTTING

RAZOR ETCHING

RAZOR PEELING

CLIENT-CENTERED GUIDELINES FOR ADVANCED SCULPTING

Client-centered guidelines are designed to help you do everything possible to enhance your client's comfort during the service and satisfaction after the service. Combining your experience with advanced sculpting techniques and client-centered guidelines will not only broaden your creative options but also help you grow and maintain a loyal clientele.

ADVANCED SCULPTING TECHNIQUE TIPS

POINT CUTTING
- Keep hair evenly moist
- Do not open shears all the way while slide or point cutting
- Do not use shears with serrated blades, which would cause pulling and client discomfort when slicing

PRESSURE GRADUATION
- Assess the client's curl pattern prior to shampooing and beginning the sculpture
- Check for areas with looser or tighter curl patterns and adjust tension while sculpting if needed

FREEFORM SCULPTING
- Position client in front of a light-colored background to better see the shape of the hair sculpture while creating it
- Take a couple steps back frequently to judge the shape from a distance and at varying angles when sculpting

NOTCHING
- Choose deeper or shallower notching strokes, depending on how evident the chunky end texture should be
- Be sure to let the design line extend through your fingers, at least equal to the depth of your notching stroke, to assure that lengths don't gradually increase with each parting
- When choosing a deep notching stroke, be sure to alter the angle between both sides of the head to assure symmetric flow in the end texture

RAZOR ETCHING
- Ensure hair is evenly moist
- Use a sharp razor and change the blade frequently
- Ensure that the blade of the razor touches the hair at a slight angle; use even, fluid strokes to remove the hair
- Choose longer or shorter strokes, depending on the amount of end texture desired

RAZOR PEELING
- Ensure hair is evenly moist
- Use a razor with a guard
- If less end texture is desired, use more pressure with the razor against the thumb
- For more end texture, use less pressure with razor against the thumb and position the blade closer to the midstrand and farther away from the ends

3.2 ADVANCED SCULPTURES

If a sculpture looks great on one client, could you recreate it exactly the same way on another client and achieve a successful result?

There are a few haircuts in a client's life that are more memorable than others. Most definitely the first haircut is one, but then there is also the worst haircut as well as the best haircut. Which do you want your clients to remember you by? The best haircut, of course.

But what are the ingredients that make the "best haircut ever"? From a client's perspective, this hair sculpture makes the most of a person's hair; is flattering and easy to style; helps control frizz; gives volume in the right areas; hides a receding hairline, and more.

Good hair designers know how to address each individual client's sculpture needs and accomplish all that the client asks for and then some. The key to this success is in knowing how and why to combine forms and structures and knowing when to use which specialized sculpting technique. This knowledge doesn't come overnight, and a good part of it needs to be acquired over time and through experience. However, the sculptures you are about to learn will give you a good head start. The looks chosen are some of the most commonly requested by clients. Once you master them, you will be able to take parts of each and create your own designs.

SOLID/INCREASE COMBINATION FORM— SLIDE CUTTING/ NOTCHING — WORKSHOP

Long layers frame the face and contrast with primarily solid lengths in the back. The layers are sculpted to maintain a heavier feeling and weight is reduced slightly along the surface of the solid form.

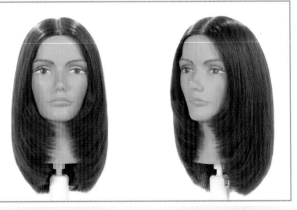

This combination of increase layers and solid lengths creates soft texture around the face and weight in the back of the design.

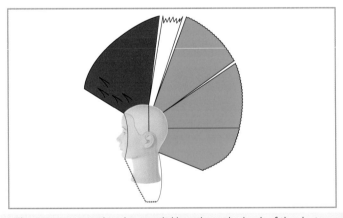

The structure graphic shows solid lengths in the back of the design, contrasted by increase layers in the front. Subtle blending connects the two forms, and the solid form becomes slightly rounded to reduce the appearance of weight.

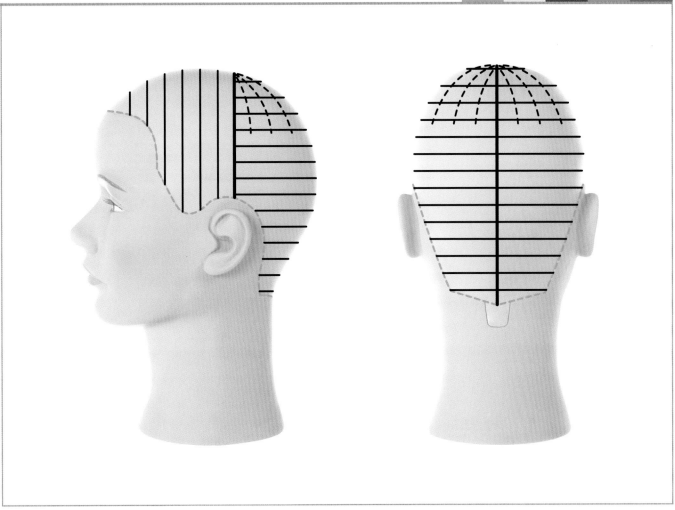

The art shows that the head will be sectioned with a center part from the forehead to the nape and from the apex to each ear. Horizontal partings will be used to sculpt the back, and vertical partings will be used to sculpt the front. Pivotal partings in the crown are used to soften the weight of the solid form.

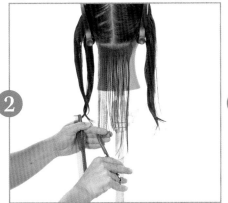

1 Section with a center part from the forehead to the nape. Then use the center of the ear as a guide to section the front from the back on either side.

2 With the head upright, release a horizontal parting at the nape. Use natural distribution with no projection and position your fingers horizontally. Sculpt parallel using the notching technique, first from the center to one side and then to the other side. Continue working up the back section. Maintain consistent horizontal partings, natural distribution and no projection as you work toward the top of the head.

4

In the crown area, carefully maintain natural distribution. Sculpt horizontally with no projection and no tension.

5

The art shows pivotal partings that will be used to sculpt the upper back to reduce weight. Depending on the amount of weight to be reduced, these partings can be extended farther.

6

Release a pivotal parting at the center back of the crown. Project the lengths straight out, position your fingers vertically and sculpt with the notching technique.

7

Work toward one side, sculpting each pivotal parting individually. Work to the sectioning line at the ear. Then repeat the same technique on the opposite side.

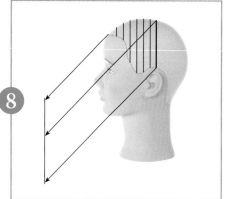

8

Vertical partings will be used to sculpt the front of the design. Each parting will be distributed forward at approximately 45°.

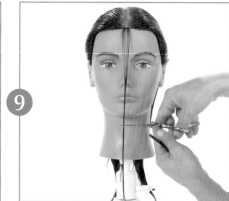

9

Release a small section at the center front hairline and establish the length guide just below the chin.

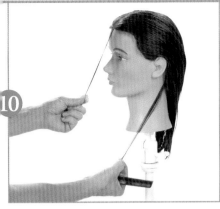

Then compare lengths at the sideburn and nape with the length guide. This will help to accurately predict your results and make modifications if necessary.

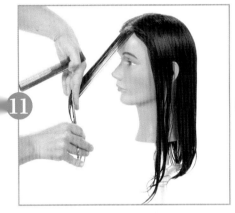

Begin on one side. Take a vertical parting, and distribute the hair forward at approximately 45°. Position your fingers vertically and sculpt parallel, creating a stationary design line.

Distribute subsequent vertical partings to the stationary design line in the same manner. Continue sculpting vertically.

Work toward the ear, converging subsequent vertical partings forward. Continue sculpting vertically, working from the top of each parting to the bottom.

Continue working toward the center back if lengths reach the design line. Use pivotal partings and the same sculpting technique.

Move to the other side and continue to take partings beyond the sectioning line to ensure blending with the back.

16 Continue to use the same sculpting technique while working toward the center back.

17 Converge the hair from the front to the center and check for symmetry. If needed, blend the two sides using natural fall, slightly refining the line.

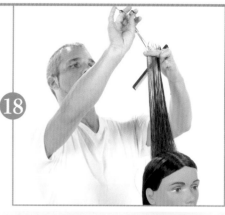

18 Take a small section at the apex and project straight up. Notch to create a subtle blend between the front and the back lengths.

19 Tilt the head slightly and distribute close to the intended finished direction. Position your fingers near the ends and slide cut with the shears through the midstrand along the front to add mobility.

20

21

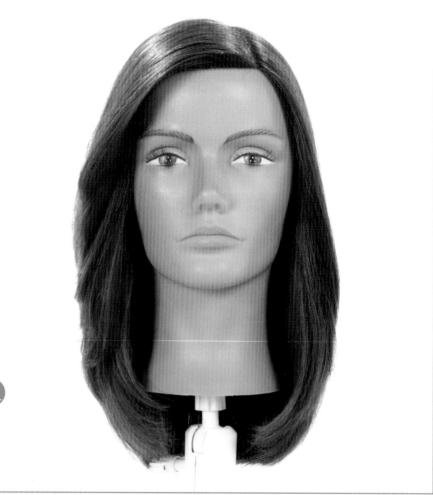

The completed sculpture shows solid perimeter lengths in the back, with a reduction of weight through the crown for a softer finish. Layers frame the face and can be worn toward or away from the face.

DESIGN DECISIONS
Draw or fill in the boxes with the appropriate answers.

STRUCTURE:

SHAPE:

TEXTURE:

SECTIONING PATTERN:

NAPE:

head position	parting	distribution	projection	finger/tool position	design line mobile/stationary

CROWN:

head position	parting	distribution	projection	finger/tool position	design line mobile/stationary

SIDES:

head position	parting	distribution	projection	finger/tool position	design line mobile/stationary

TOOLS:

SCULPTURE DESIGN RUBRIC

Chapter 3: Solid/Increase Combination Form-Slide Cutting/Notching

This Rubric is a performance assessment tool designed to measure your ability to **create** Pivot Point sculpture designs.

Name _____ ID Number _____ Date _____

	In Progress Level 1	Getting Better Level 2	Entry-Level Proficiency Level 3
PREPARATION			
• Assemble sculpting essentials	☐	☐	☐
CREATE			
• Section with center part from forehead to nape and from apex to each ear	☐	☐	☐
• Position head upright and part horizontally in nape	☐	☐	☐
• Sculpt a horizontal stationary design line using natural distribution, no projection, parallel finger position and the notching technique; work from center of one side and then the other to top of back sections	☐	☐	☐
• Part in center back of upper crown, project straight out and position fingers vertically	☐	☐	☐
• Sculpt parallel using notching technique	☐	☐	☐
• Sculpt each pivotal parting separately using the notching technique; work from center to one side then repeat techniques on other side	☐	☐	☐
• Release a small section in center of front hairline, distribute straight down	☐	☐	☐
• Sculpt length guide below chin using no projection and no tension; compare lengths at sideburns and nape to length guide	☐	☐	☐
• Part vertically on one side; distribute hair forward and project at approximately 45°	☐	☐	☐
• Sculpt stationary design line using a vertical finger position and sculpting parallel; work toward ear using pivotal partings in back if lengths reach design line	☐	☐	☐
• Repeat same sculpting techniques on opposite side	☐	☐	☐
• Check for symmetry by converging front lengths to center front; blend using natural fall and the notching technique as necessary	☐	☐	☐
• Section at apex and project lengths straight up	☐	☐	☐
• Sculpt using the notching technique to blend front and back	☐	☐	☐
• Slide cut through the midstrand and ends of the front interior lengths to texturize	☐	☐	☐
• Finish sculpture design	☐	☐	☐

TOTAL POINTS = ☐ + ☐ + ☐

TOTAL POINTS _____ ÷ HIGHEST POSSIBLE SCORE 51 = _____ %

Record your time in comparison with the suggested salon speed. _____
To improve my performance on this procedure, I need to: _____
_____

GRADUATED/INCREASE COMBINATION FORM— RAZOR ETCHING
— WORKSHOP

This soft and feminine sculpture beautifully blends graduated texture in the interior, creating a subtle contrast in the shape, with increase layers in the exterior, allowing for length and added mobility. This design provides versatility and functionality for clients with various hair textures.

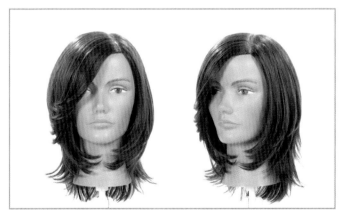

This combination of graduated and increase-layered lengths creates a totally activated texture and a versatile shape. This sculpture is a great example of a longer form that still achieves a great shape.

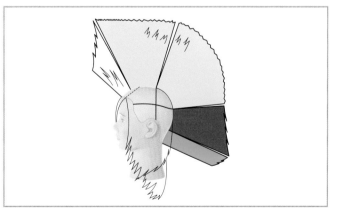

The structure graphic shows graduated lengths in the crown, sculpted with the planar sculpting and notching techniques. Through the upper sides, graduated lengths increase in length toward the face. Exterior lengths are razor-sculpted in increase layers. The nape perimeter is refined with the razor.

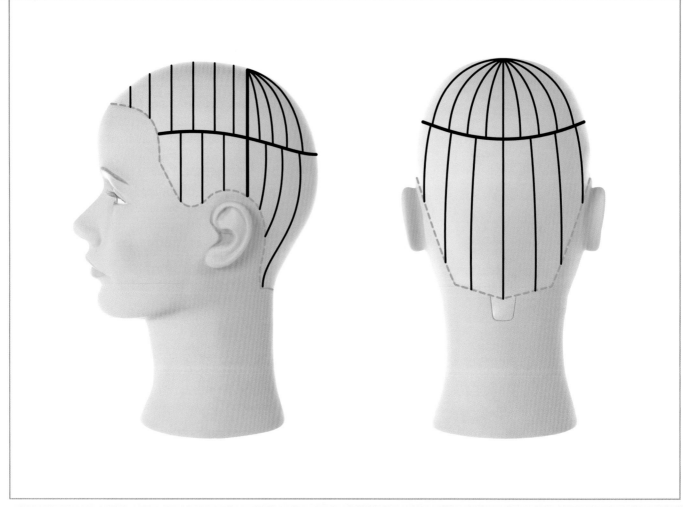

The art shows the sectioning and parting pattern used to sculpt this design. The front is sectioned from behind the apex to the back of each ear. The interior is sectioned from the exterior at the crest. Pivotal partings are used through the crown and vertical partings are used to sculpt the remainder of the design.

1

Section the front from the back with a vertical line from behind the apex to the back of each ear and section the interior from the exterior at the crest. Subsection the front of the interior with a center part.

2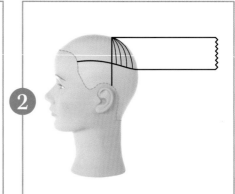

The art shows pivotal partings used with the planar sculpting technique in the back interior. Lengths are projected straight out from the curve of the head.

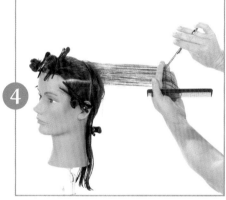

3 Release a pivotal parting in the center back of the interior. Project straight out, position your fingers vertically and sculpt with the notching technique.

4 Work toward one side using a mobile design line. Project each parting straight out, position your fingers vertically and continue sculpting with the notching technique.

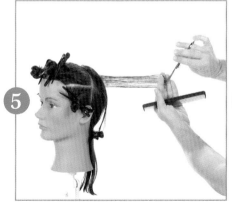

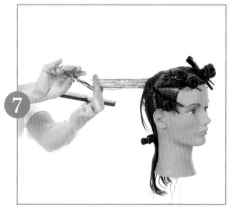

5 When you reach the last parting behind the ear, shift the lengths back to the previously sculpted parting, which is projected straight out. This creates a slight length increase.

6 Then work from the center toward the opposite side, continuing to use the planar and notching techniques.

7 Again shift the last parting behind the ear back to the previously sculpted parting to create a subtle length increase.

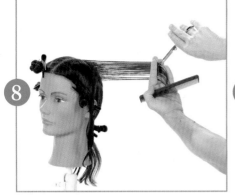

Starting on one side of the interior section, release a vertical parting at the ear. Project the parting behind the ear straight out and use it as a stationary design line. Converge the new parting back to the stationary design line, position your fingers vertically and continue sculpting with the notching technique. Work toward the front using the same technique.

Work to the front hairline taking vertical partings, converging lengths back to the stationary design line and sculpting with the same technique.

Use the same technique to sculpt the opposite side, projecting the parting behind the ear straight out and using it as a stationary design line.

Work to the front hairline converging subsequent vertical partings to the stationary design line and sculpting with the same technique.

Move to the back exterior and take a vertical parting at the center. Using the perimeter of the interior section as a length guide, project at a medium-high angle and position your fingers vertically. Sculpt with the razor, using medium etching strokes, creating a subtle length increase toward the exterior lengths.

Then work from the center to the opposite side of the nape, using the same technique. Continue using a medium-high projection angle.

Use the same sculpting techniques to complete this side of the nape.

Work toward one side, taking vertical partings and using the same technique to sculpt each parting individually.

Move to one side. Use vertical partings and shift the lengths back to the last sculpted parting behind the ear. Continue to use the razor-etching technique to create a length increase toward the exterior. Work to the front hairline using this technique.

Then use the same technique to sculpt the opposite side.

20

Create a side part over the left eye and distribute the hair in the intended finished direction. Begin below the tip of the nose on the heavier side, position your fingers along a diagonal-back line and razor etch.

21

Then use a guide from the heavier side and perform the same technique on the lighter side. Position your fingers along a steep diagonal-back line and razor etch toward the perimeter.

22

Then distribute the lengths with no projection and etch with the razor to refine the perimeter lengths, maintaining a softer form line.

23

To add more mobility, project the crown lengths at 90° and converge the front top lengths toward the crown. Use the notching technique to remove lengths that extend beyond the stationary design line.

24

The completed sculpture shows a beautiful shape accentuated by soft texture. This versatile design can be adapted for many clients.

DESIGN DECISIONS

Draw or fill in the boxes with the appropriate answers.

SHAPE:

TEXTURE:

STRUCTURE:

SECTIONING PATTERN:

BACK INTERIOR:	head position	parting	distribution	projection	finger/tool position	design line mobile/stationary

SIDES INTERIOR:	head position	parting	distribution	projection	finger/tool position	design line mobile/stationary

BACK EXTERIOR:	head position	parting	distribution	projection	finger/tool position	design line mobile/stationary

SIDES EXTERIOR:	head position	parting	distribution	projection	finger/tool position	design line mobile/stationary

TOOLS:

SCULPTURE DESIGN RUBRIC

Chapter 3: Graduated/Increase Combination Form–Razor Etching

This Rubric is a performance assessment tool designed to measure your ability to **create** Pivot Point sculpture designs.

Name _____ ID Number _____ Date _____

	In Progress Level 1	Getting Better Level 2	Entry-Level Proficiency Level 3
PREPARATION			
• Assemble sculpting essentials	☐	☐	☐
CREATE			
• Section interior from exterior just above crest using horseshoe-shaped parting and from behind apex to back of each ear	☐	☐	☐
• Position head upright	☐	☐	☐
• Part in center of back interior using pivotal partings; project lengths straight out	☐	☐	☐
• Sculpt mobile design line using a vertical finger position and the notching technique; work toward one side	☐	☐	☐
• Distribute last parting behind ear shifting back to previously sculpted parting	☐	☐	☐
• Repeat same techniques on other side	☐	☐	☐
• Part vertically on one side of interior	☐	☐	☐
• Project parting behind ear straight out and use as stationary design line	☐	☐	☐
• Sculpt using vertical finger position and the notching technique converging lengths back to stationary design line; work through section to hairline	☐	☐	☐
• Repeat using same techniques on opposite side	☐	☐	☐
• Part vertically in center back exterior using interior perimeter as length guide	☐	☐	☐
• Sculpt using medium-high projection, vertical finger position and the razor-etching technique	☐	☐	☐
• Sculpt each parting individually working from center to one side, then to other side	☐	☐	☐
• Part horizontally on one side of nape; converge lengths back to last sculpted parting behind ear	☐	☐	☐
• Sculpt stationary design line using the razor-etching technique and vertical finger position; work to front hairline	☐	☐	☐
• Repeat using same techniques on other side	☐	☐	☐
• Release side part over eye in the interior; distribute in direction of intended finish	☐	☐	☐
• Sculpt starting below tip of nose on heavy side using a diagonal-back finger position and the razor-etching technique	☐	☐	☐
• Sculpt lighter side using guide from heavy side, steep diagonal-back finger position and the etching technique	☐	☐	☐
• Refine perimeter using the razor-etching technique	☐	☐	☐
• Finish sculpture design	☐	☐	☐
• Project crown lengths at 90° and converge top lengths toward crown	☐	☐	☐
• Sculpt using the notching technique to add mobility and remove lengths that extend beyond stationary design line	☐	☐	☐

TOTAL POINTS = ☐ + ☐ + ☐

TOTAL POINTS _____ ÷ HIGHEST POSSIBLE SCORE 72 = _____ %

Record your time in comparison with the suggested salon speed. _____

To improve my performance on this procedure, I need to: _____

_____

GRADUATED FORM— PRESSURE GRADUATION — WORKSHOP

When sculpting a graduated form on curlier textures, it is essential that length reduction and expansion of the form be taken into consideration. The pressure graduation technique is ideal when a minimal amount of graduation is desired on wavy to curly textures.

This graduated form was sculpted using a stationary design line with tension placed on the hair. While the pressure graduation technique will produce less graduation than sculpting with projection, the results will depend largely on the amount of curl texture present in the hair.

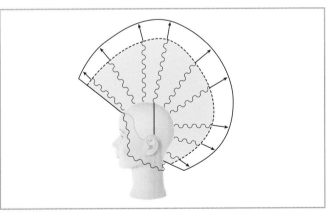

The structure graphic shows the length progression from the shorter exterior to the longer interior. This allows lengths to stack upon one another to create the graduated texture.

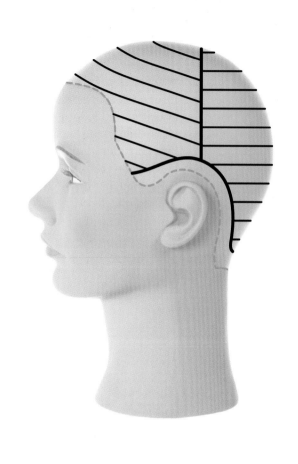
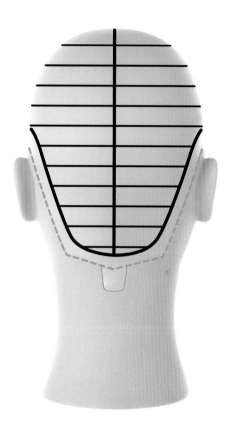

The art shows that the head will be sectioned with a center part from the forehead to the nape and from behind the apex to the back of each ear. Horizontal partings will be used to sculpt the back, and diagonal-back partings will be used to sculpt the front. A hairline parting will be used to create the initial design line.

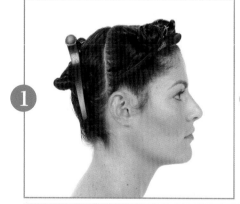

1 Section with a center part from the forehead to the nape. Then section from behind the apex to the back of each ear.

2 Release a ½" (1.25 cm) parting parallel to the perimeter hairline.

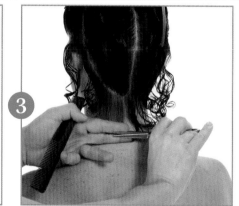

3 Begin at the center back. Distribute naturally applying tension to straighten the hair. Use one-finger projection, position your fingers horizontally and sculpt parallel. Work toward the side.

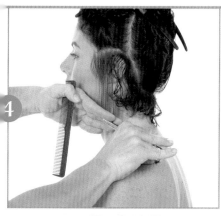

When you reach the side, use natural distribution with tension, and position your fingers along a low diagonal-back line. Sculpt parallel to your fingers.

Then sculpt from the center to the opposite side, creating a symmetrical perimeter line that will serve as a stationary design line.

Move to the back and release a horizontal parting. Use natural distribution with tension and 1-finger projection. Position your fingers parallel to the horizontal perimeter and sculpt parallel.

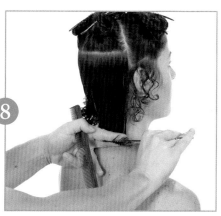

Sculpt subsequent horizontal partings using the same technique. Work from the center to either side to maintain balance.

Work to the top of the back section using the same sculpting technique.

10 Move to the left side and release a low diagonal-back parting that extends into the back section. Use natural distribution with tension and sculpt parallel to the stationary design line.

11 As the partings extend into the fringe area, shift the lengths back slightly. Continue sculpting parallel to the stationary design line using tension and 1-finger projection.

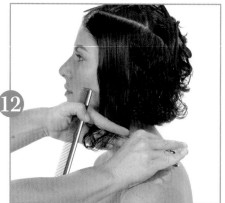

Work to the top of the side using the same techniques. Continue shifting the lengths from the fringe back slightly to retain length around the face.

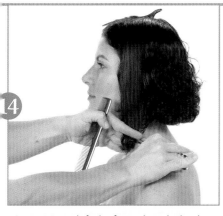

Continue to shift the fringe lengths back and use tension while completing this side.

Sculpt the opposite side using the same techniques.

Distribute the fringe lengths forward with low projection. Position your fingers horizontally and sculpt to blend the two sides, removing minimal length.

This graduated sculpture has been adapted to suit clients with curly hair. The finished design shows a graduated form that makes great use of the curly texture. The line of inclination will depend on the amount of curl texture and the amount of tension used.

DESIGN DECISIONS

Draw or fill in the boxes with the appropriate answers.

STRUCTURE:

SHAPE:

TEXTURE:

SECTIONING PATTERN:

BACK:

head position	parting	distribution	projection	finger/tool position	design line mobile/stationary

SIDES:

head position	parting	distribution	projection	finger/tool position	design line mobile/stationary

TOOLS:

SCULPTURE DESIGN RUBRIC

Chapter 3: Graduated Form–Pressure Graduation

This Rubric is a performance assessment tool designed to measure your ability to **create** Pivot Point sculpture designs.

Name _____ ID Number _____ Date _____

	In Progress Level 1	Getting Better Level 2	Entry-Level Proficiency Level 3
PREPARATION			
• Assemble sculpting essentials	☐	☐	☐
CREATE			
• Section hair with center part from forehead to nape and from behind apex to back of each ear	☐	☐	☐
• Position head upright	☐	☐	☐
• Part a ½" (1.25 cm) perimeter hairline parting and distribute in natural fall	☐	☐	☐
• Sculpt horizontal stationary design line starting in center back using parallel finger position, tension and one-finger projection; work toward ear	☐	☐	☐
• Sculpt area in front of ear using a low diagonal-back line, natural distribution and tension	☐	☐	☐
• Repeat techniques on other side sculpting horizontally in back and sculpting diagonal back in front of ear to create a symmetrical stationary design line	☐	☐	☐
• Part horizontally in nape and use perpendicular distribution	☐	☐	☐
• Sculpt graduated lengths using tension, 1-finger projection and parallel finger position working from center toward ear through back sections	☐	☐	☐
• Release low, diagonal-back parting parallel to design line that extends into back section on left side	☐	☐	☐
• Sculpt using natural distribution, tension and a parallel diagonal-back finger position working toward center part	☐	☐	☐
• Shift lengths slightly back in fringe area to retain length; continue using same techniques to complete section	☐	☐	☐
• Sculpt right side using same techniques	☐	☐	☐
• Distribute fringe lengths forward, use low projection, position fingers horizontally and sculpt to blend	☐	☐	☐
• Check for symmetrical balance	☐	☐	☐
• Finish sculpture design	☐	☐	☐

TOTAL POINTS = ☐ + ☐ + ☐

TOTAL POINTS _____ ÷ HIGHEST POSSIBLE SCORE 48 = _____ %

Record your time in comparison with the suggested salon speed. _____

To improve my performance on this procedure, I need to: _____

_____

UNIFORM/INCREASE/ GRADUATED/SOLID COMBINATION FORM— POINT CUTTING — WORKSHOP

This medium-length sculpture reaps the benefits of each of the four basic forms: a solid perimeter adds weight and definition, while graduation shifts volume toward the interior, where it is evenly distributed through uniform layering. Increase layers at the front interior add texture and versatility.

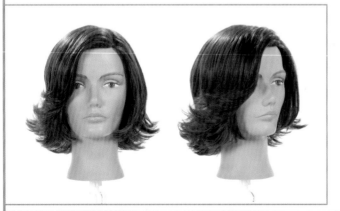

This combination of sculpted forms creates a highly activated appearance without becoming wispy or undefined.

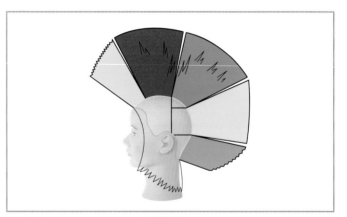

The structure graphic shows a combination of solid, graduated, uniform and increase-layered lengths.

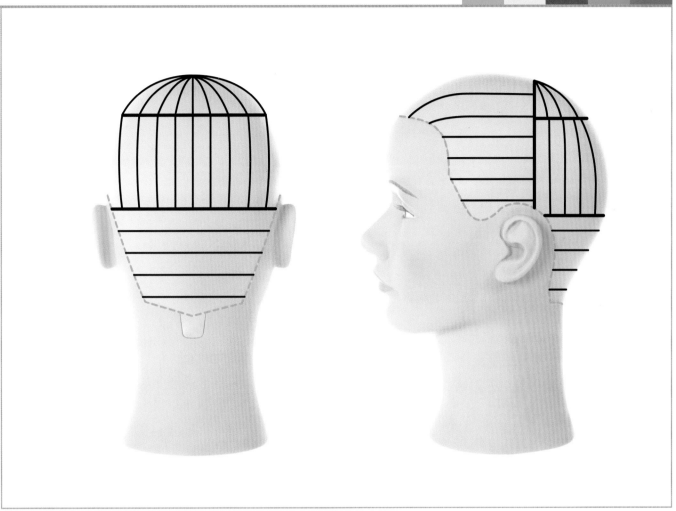

The art shows the sectioning and parting patterns used to sculpt this design. The front is sectioned from the back vertically, from the back of each ear, over the crown. The front is sectioned with a center part for control. The back is subsectioned horizontally at the top of the ear and at the lower crown.

1

2

3

After sectioning, release a horizontal parting at the nape. Use natural distribution with no projection. Position your fingers horizontally and sculpt with the notching technique. Sculpt from the center to one side and then to the other. Check for symmetry before proceeding.

Continue using horizontal partings, natural distribution, no projection and the notching technique, working to the top of this section.

4. Move to the next horizontal section and release a vertical parting at the center back. Project the lengths straight out, use a length guide from the nape and position your fingers diagonally at a high angle. Sculpt parallel to your fingers to create graduation.

5. Work toward one side, using a mobile design line and the same sculpting technique.

6. Consistently project straight out from the curve of the head and maintain the same diagonal finger position as you work.

7. 8. Then work from the center to the opposite side using the same sculpting technique.

9

Move to the crown section and release a pivotal parting at the center back. Use perpendicular distribution and 90° projection. Use a length guide from the previously sculpted section, position your fingers parallel to the head and sculpt uniform layers.

10

Use a mobile design line and work from the center to one side using the same sculpting technique. Maintain consistent projection and finger position as you work.

11

Use the same technique to sculpt the other side of the section.

12

Move to the front interior and release a center parting. Project straight up and position your fingers horizontally. Use the crown as a guide. Sculpt horizontally to create a stationary design line.

13

14

Then work toward one side, taking horizontal partings. Use perpendicular distribution and converge the lengths to the stationary design line, which is projected straight up. Sculpt parallel. Continue using the same technique, working to the exterior or until lengths no longer reach the stationary design line. Note that the designer stands opposite the length increase.

15

16

Then use the same technique to sculpt the opposite side. Continue to project the stationary design line straight up and sculpt with the conversion layering technique.

The art shows the diagonal-back parting pattern that will now be used on the sides of the design.

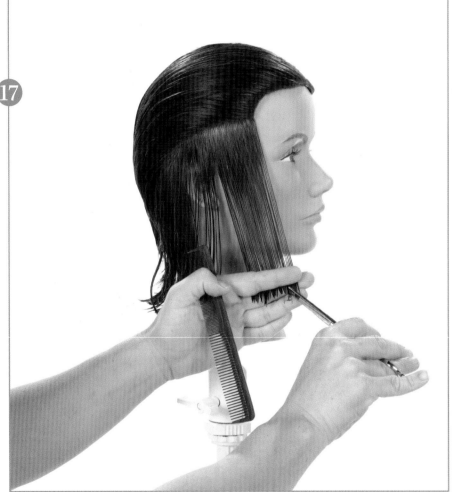

17

18

Use the same technique on the opposite side then check for symmetry before continuing.

19

Release a diagonal-back parting on one side at approximately 30°. Extend the parting to the back to ensure blending. Use perpendicular distribution with low projection, and position your fingers parallel to the diagonal-back parting. Sculpt parallel to your fingers using the notching technique.

Work up the first side. Use diagonal-back partings, perpendicular distribution, low projection, a mobile design line and the notching technique. Work until no lengths reach the design line.

20 Use the same technique to sculpt the other side. Note that some lengths may not reach the design line depending on the previous hair sculpture.

21 The art shows a wide vertical section that will be used to create a visual blend between the back and front lengths.

22 Project the hair at 90° from the center of the wide vertical parting and point cut to blend. Lengths at the center top already blend, so work from the crown toward one side.

23 Then work from the crown to the other side using the same technique.

24 Use the same point-cutting technique to texturize the midstrand and ends as needed or desired.

25 The finished sculpture features highly activated textures while maintaining some weight and definition around the perimeter.

DESIGN DECISIONS
Draw or fill in the boxes with the appropriate answers.

SHAPE:

TEXTURE:

STRUCTURE:

SECTIONING PATTERN:

NAPE:	head position	parting	distribution	projection	finger/tool position	design line mobile/stationary

CREST:	head position	parting	distribution	projection	finger/tool position	design line mobile/stationary

CROWN:	head position	parting	distribution	projection	finger/tool position	design line mobile/stationary

TOP:	head position	parting	distribution	projection	finger/tool position	design line mobile/stationary

SIDES:	head position	parting	distribution	projection	finger/tool position	design line mobile/stationary

TOOLS:

SCULPTURE DESIGN RUBRIC

Chapter 3: Uniform/Increase/Graduated/Solid Combination Form–Point Cutting

This Rubric is a performance assessment tool designed to measure your ability to **create** Pivot Point sculpture designs.

Name _____ ID Number _____ Date _____

	In Progress Level 1	Getting Better Level 2	Entry-Level Proficiency Level 3

PREPARATION
- Assemble sculpting essentials ☐ ☐ ☐

CREATE
- Section from behind apex to back of each ear and section front with center part; subsection back horizontally at top of ears and at lower crown ☐ ☐ ☐
- Position head upright and part horizontally in nape ☐ ☐ ☐
- Sculpt a horizontal stationary design line beginning in center using natural distribution, no projection, parallel finger position with the notching technique; work to top of section ☐ ☐ ☐
- Part vertically in center of next horizontal section, distribute lengths straight out and use a length guide from the previously sculpted section ☐ ☐ ☐
- Sculpt mobile design line; position fingers diagonally for high line of inclination ☐ ☐ ☐
- Work from center to one side then repeat techniques on other side ☐ ☐ ☐
- Part in center of crown section using pivotal partings and a guide from previously sculpted section ☐ ☐ ☐
- Sculpt a mobile design line using perpendicular distribution, 90° projection and parallel finger position; work to one side then the other ☐ ☐ ☐
- Part vertically in center of interior section, project straight up and position fingers horizontally ☐ ☐ ☐
- Sculpt stationary design line parallel using hair at crown as length guide ☐ ☐ ☐
- Part horizontally on one side and use perpendicular distribution ☐ ☐ ☐
- Sculpt interior by converging hair to stationary design line; stand opposite the length increase ☐ ☐ ☐
- Repeat same sculpting techniques on opposite side ☐ ☐ ☐
- Release diagonal-back parting at approximately 30° extending parting into back on one side ☐ ☐ ☐
- Sculpt mobile design line using perpendicular distribution, low projection, parallel finger position and the notching technique ☐ ☐ ☐
- Sculpt mobile design line on other side using same techniques; check for symmetry before continuing ☐ ☐ ☐
- Work through first side using perpendicular distribution, low projection, parallel finger position and the notching technique until lengths no longer reach design line ☐ ☐ ☐
- Repeat same techniques on opposite side ☐ ☐ ☐
- Section a wide vertical section on one side of crown ☐ ☐ ☐
- Sculpt using the point-cutting technique to blend the front and back ☐ ☐ ☐
- Repeat same blending technique on opposite side ☐ ☐ ☐
- Texturize using the point-cutting technique through midstrand and ends as desired ☐ ☐ ☐
- Finish sculpture design ☐ ☐ ☐

TOTAL POINTS = ☐ + ☐ + ☐

TOTAL POINTS _____ ÷ HIGHEST POSSIBLE SCORE 72 = _____ %

Record your time in comparison with the suggested salon speed. _____

To improve my performance on this procedure, I need to: _____

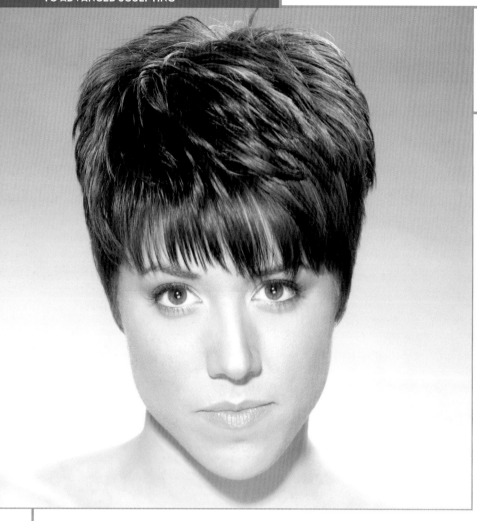

UNIFORM/GRADUATED COMBINATION FORM— NOTCHING/PEELING — WORKSHOP

This combination of uniform layers and graduation is enhanced by the use of the notching and razor-peeling techniques. Changes in the proportions used can adapt the form to suit a variety of clients and hair textures.

In this exercise you will sculpt a combination of uniformly layered and graduated textures. The notching technique is used to sculpt the graduated texture and the uniform layers are sculpted with the razor-peeling technique.

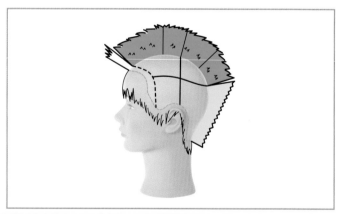

The structure graphic shows uniform lengths in the interior, from the upper crest to the top and high graduation in the remainder of the head. A parting along the front hairline features irregular, personalized lengths.

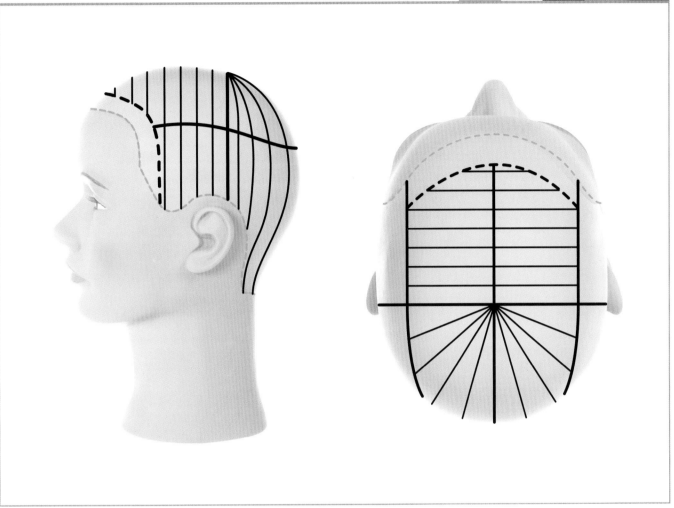

The art shows the sectioning and parting patterns used to sculpt this exercise. The interior and exterior are divided slightly above the upper crest and each of these areas is sectioned with a center part from the front hairline to the nape. In the exterior, vertical partings will be used to sculpt high graduation. The interior section is sculpted with horizontal and pivotal partings. A parting along the front hairline is isolated and sculpted later for personalizing.

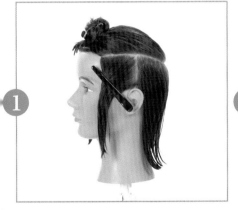

1

Section with a center part from the front hairline to the nape. Then section the interior from the exterior with a horseshoe-shaped parting slightly above the upper crest. Subsection the exterior vertically at each ear.

2

3

Begin sculpting at the center back of the exterior. Release a vertical parting, use high projection and position your fingers for a high line of inclination. Sculpt with the notching technique using small notching strokes. Work from the center to one side using a mobile design line.

4 Continue taking vertical partings and work to the ear using the same sculpting technique.

5 Then sculpt from the center back toward the opposite side, using the same sculpting technique. Continue using high projection and a nonparallel finger position. Work to the ear.

6

7 Move to one side. Take a vertical parting at the ear. Use the parting behind the ear as a mobile design line and sculpt with the same technique.

8 Work toward the front using the same high projection angle and nonparallel finger position.

9 When you reach the front hairline, shift the parting back to the previously sculpted parting, then sculpt. This results in a subtle length increase toward the face.

Work to the front of the other side, checking for symmetry.

Project the top lengths of the exterior straight out and notch any lengths that protrude. These lengths will now serve as the stationary design line. Then section the interior with a center part and release a parting parallel to the exterior sectioning line. Distribute lengths to the stationary design line, which is projected straight out. Sculpt with the notching technique.

Continue using the same technique to sculpt subsequent parallel partings. Work up to the center part.

Sculpt the other side of the interior using the same technique.

Isolate a parting at the front hairline before proceeding. Next, release a thin center parting from behind the front hairline to the back of the interior. Use perpendicular distribution and 90° projection. Position your fingers parallel to the curve of the head using the exterior as a length guide. Sculpt with the razor-peeling technique. Work up to the isolated front hairline using the same technique.

Work toward one side using pivotal partings from the crown with 90° projection and a mobile design line. Continue using the razor-peeling technique.

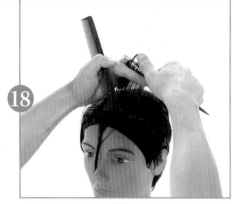

(18) Work toward the front of the section using horizontal partings and the same sculpting technique.

(19) Move to the other side and use the same technique to sculpt, beginning in the back of the section with pivotal partings.

(20) Work to the front of the section using the same sculpting technique.

(21) Use the razor to personalize the front hairline and the perimeter of the form as needed.

(22) To texturize, lift the midstrand and ends with the comb and close the taper shears at the midstrand working from underneath.

(23) The finished design shows soft, activated texture with a fuller, rounded shape in the interior and more tapered lengths in the exterior.

DESIGN DECISIONS

Draw or fill in the boxes with the appropriate answers.

SHAPE:

TEXTURE:

STRUCTURE:

SECTIONING PATTERN:

BACK EXTERIOR:	head position	parting	distribution	projection	finger/tool position	design line mobile/stationary

SIDES:	head position	parting	distribution	projection	finger/tool position	design line mobile/stationary

INTERIOR-GRADUATION:	head position	parting	distribution	projection	finger/tool position	design line mobile/stationary

INTERIOR-UNIFORM:	head position	parting	distribution	projection	finger/tool position	design line mobile/stationary

TOOLS:

variation
UNIFORM/GRADUATED
COMBINATION FORM

As a hair designer you will work with various head and face shapes in the salon. Fringes can be sculpted and styled to accentuate clients' facial features and bone structure. Depending on your clients' needs and desires you can create soft flicks framing the face or bold, dramatic focus points within a hair design.

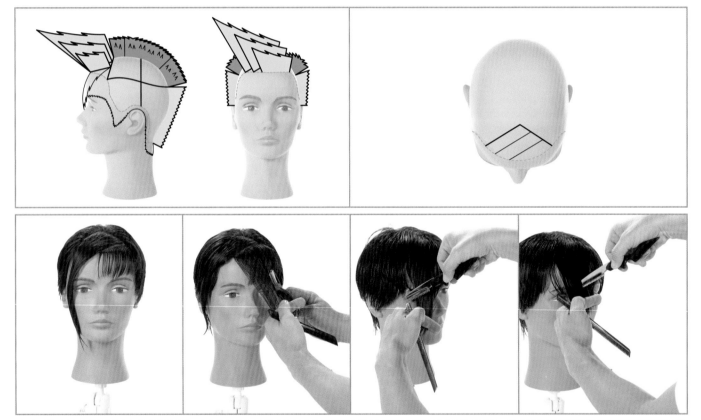

This combination of uniform layers and graduation is accentuated by an asymmetric, disconnected fringe. Diagonal partings were used within the triangular fringe, which is sectioned from in front of the apex to the outside corner of each eye. Each parting was sculpted using perpendicular distribution, low projection, a parallel sculpting position and the razor-etching technique. Sculpting each parting individually with an independent, overlapping design line creates a more dramatic length increase toward one side. The initial length guide is taken from lengths at the front hairline adjacent to the fringe. The longest fringe lengths are visually connected to the shortest lengths using the razor-etching technique. Texturizing within the shape creates more mobility while reducing weight in this personalized, face-framing variation.

SCULPTURE DESIGN RUBRIC

Chapter 3: Uniform/Graduated Combination Form–Notching/Peeling

This Rubric is a performance assessment tool designed to measure your ability to **create** Pivot Point sculpture designs.

Name _____ ID Number _____ Date _____

	In Progress Level 1	Getting Better Level 2	Entry-Level Proficiency Level 3
PREPARATION			
• Assemble sculpting essentials	☐	☐	☐
CREATE			
• Section with center part from forehead to nape, interior from exterior using a horseshoe-shaped parting and subsection exterior vertically at each ear	☐	☐	☐
• Position head upright	☐	☐	☐
• Part hair vertically at center back of exterior	☐	☐	☐
• Project hair at high angle and position fingers along a high line of inclination and sculpt with notching technique to establish the mobile design line; work from center to one side then the other to complete section	☐	☐	☐
• Part hair vertically on one side at ear; use mobile design line from previously sculpted section as length guide	☐	☐	☐
• Sculpt using same sculpting techniques working toward front hairline	☐	☐	☐
• Shift last parting at front hairline back to previous parting to retain length	☐	☐	☐
• Sculpt opposite side using same procedures	☐	☐	☐
• Project top exterior lengths straight out; notch protruding lengths to establish the stationary design line for interior lengths	☐	☐	☐
• Section interior with a center part; then part parallel to horseshoe-shaped section	☐	☐	☐
• Distribute hair to stationary design line projected straight out and sculpt with notching technique; work toward center and repeat using same techniques on other side	☐	☐	☐
• Release thin center parting from back of interior section to front isolating front hairline	☐	☐	☐
• Sculpt beginning in back using exterior as length guide, perpendicular distribution, 90° projection and the razor-peeling technique working toward front hairline; isolate parting at front hairline	☐	☐	☐
• Sculpt on one side of back interior guide using pivotal partings, mobile design line, 90° projection and parallel finger position working toward front	☐	☐	☐
• Part horizontally and use same sculpting technique up to side section; work through section toward fringe area	☐	☐	☐
• Repeat on opposite side using same sculpting techniques	☐	☐	☐
• Sculpt front hairline and perimeter lengths using razor etching to personalize	☐	☐	☐
• Texturize by lifting lengths with comb and drawing tip of razor through lengths from underneath	☐	☐	☐
• Finish sculpture design	☐	☐	☐
TOTAL POINTS =	☐ +	☐ +	☐

TOTAL POINTS _____ ÷ HIGHEST POSSIBLE SCORE 60 = _____ %

Record your time in comparison with the suggested salon speed. _____

To improve my performance on this procedure, I need to: _____

_____

UNIFORM/GRADATED COMBINATION FORM— FREEHAND SCULPTING — WORKSHOP

Sculpting short, curly forms requires patience and a keen eye. A freehand sculpting technique is used in this exercise because much of the hair is too short to comfortably hold with the fingers. Shears or clippers can be used to sculpt these lengths. Keep in mind that short, curly hair can be especially challenging because lengths can "shrink" immediately after combing or picking.

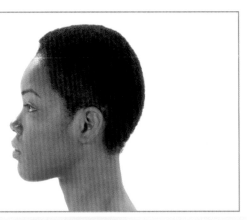

This combination of uniform layers and gradation at the sides and nape creates a rounded shape that emphasizes the contour of the head. This low-maintenance hair sculpture is great for both women and men.

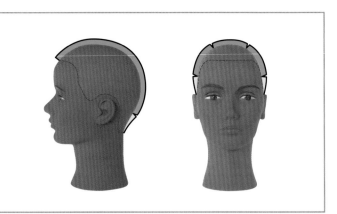

The structure graphics show that lengths are uniform in the interior and exterior with gradation at the perimeter sides and nape.

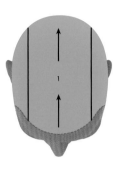  

The art shows that the head will be sculpted in four zonal areas. Although the lengths are too short to section effectively, a sequential pattern is followed. The first zone (Zone 1) encompasses the center of the head, from the front hairline to the occipital area. The second and third zones (Zones 2 and 3) encompass either side. The fourth zone (Zone 4) ecompasses the perimeter hairline area.

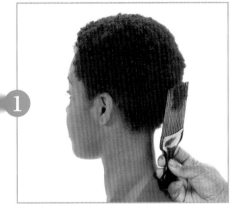

1 Pick the hair from base to ends using a scooping motion. Start in the nape and work toward the crown. A blow dryer may also be used to expand the form.

2 Move to one side and pick the hair starting at the hairline and work toward the crown. Repeat on the other side.

3 Next, pick from the front hairline toward the crown. Continue picking the hair until the existing sculpture is fully expanded.

4 Position the head upright and begin sculpting at the center front (Zone 1). Position the shears parallel to the head and sculpt uniform lengths. To sculpt accurately, pick the area again and continue sculpting. Note that you will continue to pick then sculpt alternately until the center zone is even and rounded in shape.

5

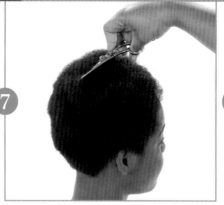

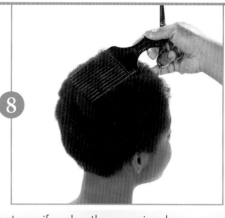

Continue to sculpt Zone 1, working toward the crown. While sculpting freehand, step back or look in the mirror from time to time to help you assess the rounded shape.

Work through the crown area. Continue picking to see if any lengths were missed or unevenly expanded prior to sculpting. Sculpt again if necessary. Note that the lengths may need to be adjusted due to irregularities in the shape of the head. Continue working for a uniform, rounded appearance.

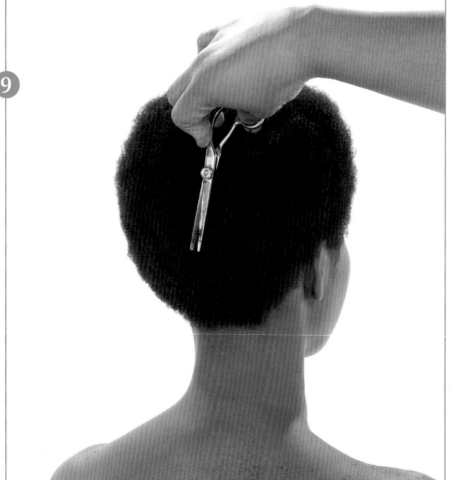

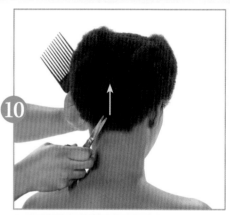

When you reach the nape (Zone 4), tilt the head forward slightly. Sculpt gradation, blending from the hairline up to the previously sculpted lengths.

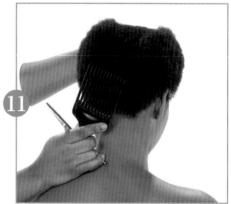

Continue to sculpt Zone 1 working toward the occipital. Be careful to not sculpt the hair too close to the scalp near the occipital bone. Make sure to pick the lengths after sculpting to check for accuracy.

Continue to pick the lengths up and out, checking each area for accuracy.

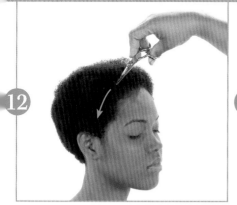

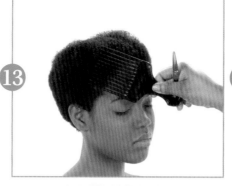

Next, move to one side (Zone 2). Stand in front and position the head upright. Sculpt lengths vertically, parallel to the head, starting at the top. Use the previously sculpted lengths as a guide. Work toward the bottom, leaving the perimeter hairline untouched. After sculpting, pick up and out, also starting at the top.

Check to make sure that Zones 1 and 2 are evenly connected.

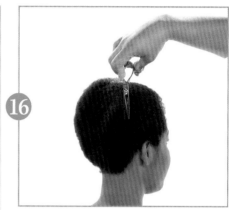

Continue to sculpt Zone 2 using the same sculpting techniques. As you work behind the ear, adjust your body position. Be sure to thoroughly blend Zone 2 with the previously sculpted lengths in Zone 1.

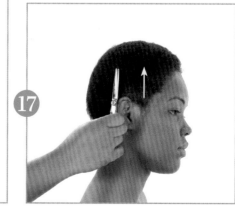

Next, sculpt gradation at the perimeter (Zone 4) starting at the front hairline. Sculpt vertically from the hairline, working upward.

As you work toward the back, check the rounded shape for accuracy. Remember to stand back or look into the mirror to help gain perspective on the rounded shape. Make sure you view the shape from various angles.

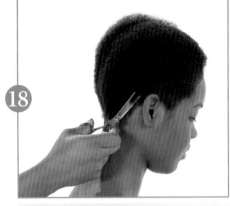

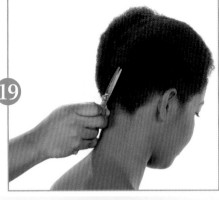

Continue to use the same sculpting techniques as you work behind the ear toward the back. As you complete this section, be sure to thoroughly blend to the center zone. Notice that the head can be tilted forward and the shear position can be altered for comfort, ease and accuracy.

Move to the opposite side (Zone 3), and use the same techniques. Start at the front hairline and sculpt from the top toward the perimeter using the lengths in Zone 1 as a guide.

Next, sculpt gradation along the perimeter. Note that you can begin sculpting at the nape, working from the hairline to the previously sculpted lengths.

Continue to use the same sculpting techniques as you work toward the back. Remember to step back to view the rounded shape from various angles.

Continue to sculpt gradation to complete the side. Note that the ear can be moved forward for ease.

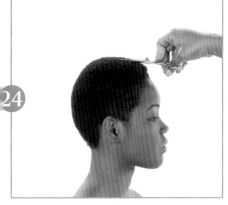

To refine the form, pick the lengths thoroughly. Trim any uneven lengths, following the same sequential pattern used to sculpt the combination form.

Next, outline the lengths around the ear. Bend the ear back and use the tips of the shears to sculpt from the top of the ear toward the front. Then, bend the ear forward and sculpt from the bottom of the ear toward the top. Note that the head can be tilted to facilitate sculpting around the ear.

Repeat the same sculpting techniques on the opposite side to complete the sculpture.

The completed design displays beautiful, short uniform and gradated curly lengths that are easy to maintain.

DESIGN DECISIONS

Draw or fill in the boxes with the appropriate answers.

STRUCTURE:

SHAPE:	TEXTURE:		ZONAL PATTERN:

CENTER (ZONE 1):
head position

picking direction	sculpting direction	picking direction	sculpting direction

SIDES (ZONE 2 & 3):
head position

picking direction	sculpting direction	picking direction	sculpting direction

---

PERIMETER (ZONE 4):
head position

picking direction	sculpting direction

TOOLS:

SCULPTURE DESIGN RUBRIC

Chapter 3: Uniform/Gradated Combination Form–Freehand Sculpting

This Rubric is a performance assessment tool designed to measure your ability to **create** Pivot Point sculpture designs.

Name _____ ID Number _____ Date _____

	In Progress Level 1	Getting Better Level 2	Entry-Level Proficiency Level 3
PREPARATION			
• Assemble sculpting essentials	☐	☐	☐
CREATE			
• Position head upright	☐	☐	☐
• Identify zonal patterns consisting of center of head from front hairline to occipital (Zone 1), remaining areas on sides (Zones 2 and 3) and perimeter (Zone 4)	☐	☐	☐
• Pick hair starting in center nape from base to ends using a scooping motion working toward crown, then from sides and front hairline toward crown until existing sculpture is fully expanded	☐	☐	☐
• Sculpt beginning at center front with shears positioned parallel to head; pick sculpted area	☐	☐	☐
• Pick and sculpt alternately until center front of Zone 1 is even and rounded	☐	☐	☐
• Sculpt toward center crown in Zone 1 using same techniques	☐	☐	☐
• Assess rounded shape by stepping back or using mirror often while freehand sculpting	☐	☐	☐
• Sculpt from crown toward occipital picking and sculpting alternately; adjust lengths as necessary due to irregularities in the shape of head making sure not to sculpt too short near occipital bone	☐	☐	☐
• Position head slightly forward in nape (Zone 4) and sculpt gradation blending from hairline to previously sculpted lengths	☐	☐	☐
• Pick lengths up and out to check accuracy	☐	☐	☐
• Position head upright, stand in front and beginning at top of Zone 2, sculpt vertically parallel to head using previously sculpted lengths as guide; leave perimeter hairline untouched	☐	☐	☐
• Pick and sculpt alternately making sure Zones 1 and 2 are evenly connected; work to ear blending Zones 1 and 2	☐	☐	☐
• Assess rounded shape by stepping back or using mirror often while freehand sculpting and view shape from various angles	☐	☐	☐
• Sculpt area behind ear using same techniques adjusting your body position as needed to assess shape	☐	☐	☐
• Sculpt gradation at perimeter (Zone 4) starting at front hairline with shears held vertically; work upward using the same techniques	☐	☐	☐
• Sculpt using the same techniques toward the back to complete section and blend with center zone; tilt head forward; alter shear position for comfort, ease and accuracy	☐	☐	☐
• Repeat the same techniques on the opposite side (Zone 3 and 4)	☐	☐	☐
• Pick and trim uneven lengths using sequential pattern to refine form	☐	☐	☐
• Sculpt lengths around the ear to outline; bend ear back and use tips of shears sculpting from top of ear to front; bend ear forward and sculpt from bottom of ear to top; tilt head if necessary	☐	☐	☐
• Repeat same techniques on opposite side	☐	☐	☐
• Finish sculpture design	☐	☐	☐
TOTAL POINTS =	☐	+ ☐ +	☐

TOTAL POINTS _____ ÷ HIGHEST POSSIBLE SCORE 66 = _____ %

Record your time in comparison with the suggested salon speed. _____

To improve my performance on this procedure, I need to: _____

_____

Voices of Success

The Salon Owner:

"MANY OF OUR REGULAR CLIENTS AREN'T LOOKING FOR THE LATEST OUTRAGEOUS TRENDS, BUT STILL WANT SUBTLE CHANGES AND UPDATING. MANY OF THESE CLIENTS CAN RECEIVE A 'NEW LOOK' WHEN THE DESIGNERS IN MY SALON DECIDE TO CREATE A STYLE WITH THE RAZOR VERSUS THE SHEARS. THIS ALLOWS OUR CLIENTS TO FEEL LIKE THEY HAVE A NEW, CUSTOMIZED STYLE AND SPORT SOME OF THE LATEST HAIR FASHIONS, WITHOUT GIVING THEM INAPPROPRIATE DESIGNS."

The Educator:

"I LIKE TO EXPLAIN TO MY STUDENTS THAT USING AN ADVANCED SCULPTING APPROACH IS MUCH LIKE CUSTOM-TAILORING A HAIR DESIGN FOR A CLIENT. WHEN DESIGNERS JUST ENTERING THE INDUSTRY ARE ABLE TO COMBINE FORMS AND APPLY ADVANCED SCULPTING TECHNIQUES, THEY CAN IMMEDIATELY SET THEMSELVES APART FROM MANY OTHER SALON PROFESSIONALS, WHO FOLLOW A MORE-OR-LESS 'COOKIE-CUTTER' APPROACH."

The Client:

"I USED TO THINK WHEN I NEEDED A QUICK TRIM THAT I COULD GO AND SEE A STYLIST AT A CHEAPER SALON. WHAT A MISTAKE. MY HAIR JUST DIDN'T LAY RIGHT—DIDN'T HAVE A GOOD SHAPE—AND WAS REALLY HARD TO WORK WITH. I FINALLY FOUND A STYLIST WHO CAN CUT MY HAIR IN A WAY NO ONE ELSE EVER HAS BEFORE. IT'S LIKE WATCHING AN ARTIST AT WORK AND WOULDN'T YOU BELIEVE IT, EVERY MORNING I CAN STYLE MY HAIR EASILY AND LOOK GREAT THROUGHOUT THE DAY. "

IN OTHER WORDS:

Knowing how to create advanced sculptures gives you the power to be more versatile and custom-design each client's hair sculpture.

Learning Challenge

This challenge contains a combination of multiple-choice and short-answer items. For multiple-choice items, circle the letter corresponding to the correct answer. For short-answer items, write the correct answer in the space provided.

1. Sculpting one form in one component area and another form elsewhere in the design refers to sculpting a:
    a. *basic form*
    b. *long sculpture*
    c. *combination form*
    d. *a similar structure throughout*

2. In combination forms, the head is sectioned relative to the desired changes in line, shape and:
    a. *angle*
    b. *structure*
    c. *length guides*
    d. *finishing direction*

3. When increase layers are sculpted over a solid form, the overall texture is:
   a. short
   b. rounded
   c. activated
   d. unactivated

4. The base is usually texturized in short- to mid-length forms to create:
   a. mobility
   b. lift and volume
   c. soft end texture
   d. chunky end texture

5. Razor etching should be done on hair that is:
   a. dry
   b. layered
   c. very fine
   d. evenly damp

6. The shape and structure of a combination form can change dramatically, depending on the _____ and _____ at which the hair is sculpted.

7. The proportional relationship between individual forms that are combined in one design affects the _____ and _____ of weight.

8. Combining an increase-layered form with a graduated form creates an illusion of _____ within the form.

9. Specialized sculpting techniques can be applied while proceeding through the sculpture or as the _____ _____ of the sculpture service.

10. When sculpting pressure graduation, it is important to assess the client's curl pattern prior to _____ and _____ the sculpture.

Lessons Learned

Each form's specific qualities are more or less evident in a combination form.

Various criteria, such as the placement of the weight area in relation to the client's head shape and facial features as well as the proportion of the textures, must be considered when combining forms.

Specialized sculpting techniques can be performed with a variety of tools, such as shears, a razor, texturizing shears (also known as tapering or thinning shears) or clippers, and can be performed at the base, the midstrand, along the ends of the strand or a combination of the three depending on the desired effect.

a designer's approach to
MEN'S SCULPTING

- Planar
- Directional distribution
- Gradation
- Shear-over-comb
- Clipper-over-comb
- Fade

Adding planar and gradation techniques to your repertoire will help you create more masculine designs and build a strong male clientele.

Following this lesson on A Designer's Approach to Men's Sculpting, you will be able to:

☐ Explain the guidelines for ensuring client satisfaction with the result of the sculpture
☐ Describe planar sculpting techniques
☐ List techniques used to achieve gradation
☐ Demonstrate the knowledge and ability to sculpt longer forms for male clients
☐ Demonstrate the knowledge and ability to sculpt mid-length forms for male clients
☐ Demonstrate the knowledge and ability to sculpt short forms for male clients

ESSENTIAL QUESTIONS FOR THIS CHAPTER:

Are planar and overcomb techniques only appropriate for the male client or can they be adapted to suit female clients?

What is the difference between gradation and graduation?

What can you recommend to male clients who do not want the more angular designs traditionally associated with men's sculpture?

As you continue to improve upon your skills in sculpting the basic forms and expand your repertoire by adding advanced sculpting techniques, have you begun to wonder: What could possibly be different when sculpting a male client's hair? For starters, male clients often wear their hair shorter than female clients. In many cases a male client's design requires lengths too short to be controlled with your fingers while sculpting. Additional factors that need to play into your design plan are that male features are generally more angular; thus, male hair designs require special attention to enhance these more masculine characteristics. What you may find surprising is that most of the "typically male" sculpting techniques can also be applied to female clients.

In *Chapter 4, A Designer's Approach to Men's Sculpting*, you will learn about and put into practice techniques that are specifically geared toward creating sculpted forms in a variety of lengths that most reflect the masculine sensibility.

ESSENTIAL SCULPTING TECHNIQUES

In this portion of the chapter you will learn about and practice essential techniques and skills needed to perform planar and gradation sculpting techniques. Both are required for every successful hair designer's repertoire.

You have already worked with the idea of combining sculpted forms within a sculpture. Generally, the forms are sculpted one at a time and joined or blended. You will now learn about a technique that allows you to create a combination form automatically as you sculpt. Later in this section of the chapter, you will also look at sculpting techniques that are used to create designs that fit closely to the exterior of the head for a tapered look.

Are planar and overcomb techniques only appropriate for the male client or can they be adapted to suit female clients?

PLANAR SCULPTING

While all sculpting techniques can be adapted to suit both male and female clients, there are certain styles or forms that will work better for one or the other. Many male clients will want to avoid a look that is too soft or that may appear feminine, while many female clients will desire exactly that look. Since the male body and face tend to be more angular than the female's, hair sculptures that reflect that angularity, or help create the illusion of angularity, are usually considered most complimentary for the male client. The planar sculpting technique, which results in a more square or rectilinear form with weight corners, is used to create this more masculine effect. The "squared-off" effect of the planar form may be more or less apparent, based on the sculpted length, hair type and any variations that are done while sculpting.

LENGTH VARIATIONS

 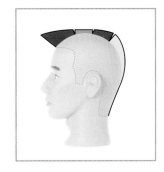

When sculpted quite short, as in this flat-top style, lengths stand away from the head and make the corners of the rectilinear form more obvious. The sculpted form becomes almost an exaggeration of the angularity that is the hallmark of masculine style.

Sculpted at longer lengths that fall and lay closer to the head, the planar form is used more for ease of sculpting than to create a squared shape. The overall effect is still more masculine because areas of weight are created within the form.

Sculpted at medium lengths, the planar form can be at its most versatile. Altering the styling direction can make the angularity of the form more or less apparent. To take advantage of this, it is important that your client knows how to work with his own hair.

Sculpted at medium to longer lengths in the interior, the planar form can be incorporated into a female hair design. In the first example, the exterior features longer lengths. In the second example, the exterior is shorter but features soft end texture at the perimeter.

PLANAR COMBINATIONS

As styles in both hair and clothing change, the degree of angularity or "boxiness" that is desired in a hair sculpture changes as well. The planar form can be very effectively combined with other sculpted forms. Generally, either the interior or the exterior is sculpted using the planar sculpting technique and the remainder of the hair is sculpted using other sculpting techniques.

Most commonly, the planar sculpting technique is used in the interior and shorter lengths are sculpted in the exterior.

The planar sculpting technique can also be used in the exterior to create layers without too much volume for the client.

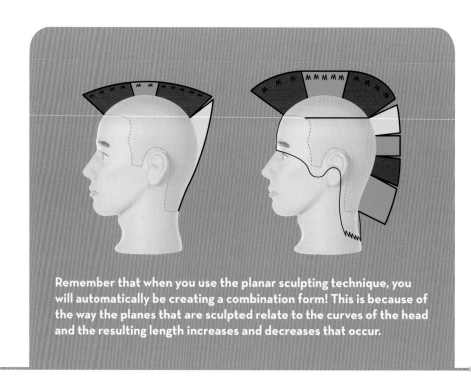

Remember that when you use the planar sculpting technique, you will automatically be creating a combination form! This is because of the way the planes that are sculpted relate to the curves of the head and the resulting length increases and decreases that occur.

GRADATION

Gradation and graduation are similar—*there is only one letter difference between the two*. Both create a length progression from the exterior toward the interior, and both can be described by referring to the line of inclination. The key difference between the two is that gradation is always quite short—so short that the hair cannot be easily controlled between the fingers, as with graduation. Gradation requires the use of a comb to control the hair while sculpting. Depending on the client's hair density and type, these short lengths created by gradation can also allow the scalp to be seen, creating a degree of transparency.

What is the difference between gradation and graduation?

OVERCOMB TECHNIQUES

When sculpting lengths that are too short to control between your fingers, the overcomb sculpting techniques can be used. These techniques require patience and practice to build skill and accuracy. Through practice and experience, designers often develop preferences for the types of tools and combs they choose to work with. So you may also find that you work more effectively with specific combs, or you may find a particular length of shears to work better for you. Sculpting movements need to be fluid during the overcomb techniques, so it is essential to be guided by tools that are most comfortable for you to use.

SHEAR-OVER-COMB TECHNIQUE

You may use the shear-over-comb technique to sculpt the majority of a hair sculpture or you may use it only to refine and taper the perimeter. The techniques that you will use are the same, no matter where on the head you are applying them.

Remember that larger combs are used initially, then smaller combs are used as the form becomes more refined. For instance, a taper comb may be used to refine the perimeter for a completely tapered effect. A larger comb is too thick to achieve this.

Generally, the taper shear-over-comb technique is used for blending purposes. This may create a softer effect to blend areas that are not as smoothly blended as you would like them to be. Some hair textures, such as fine, straight hair, can benefit from additional blending to create a more finished look.

Practice Makes Perfect

MEDIUM GRADATION

The focus of this exercise is to provide practice in sculpting medium gradation using the shear-over-comb technique. The result will be short activated lengths that progress from shorter at the perimeter to longer near the occipital.

Practice this exercise to build skill and accuracy using an upright head position, 90° projection, horizontal comb and shear position, and the shear-over-comb technique.

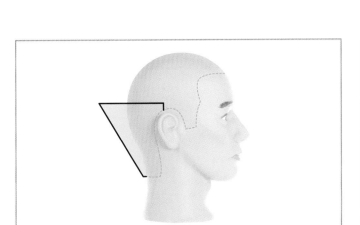

The structure graphic shows a progression of lengths from the nape hairline toward the occipital, resulting in transparency that extends into the occipital area.

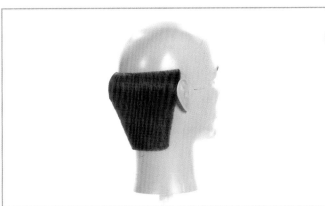

The finish shows medium gradation. The amount of transparency will also depend on a client's hair type and density.

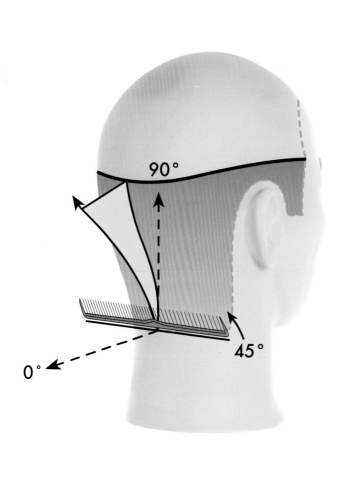

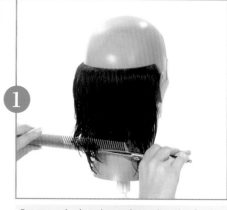

1 Position the head upright and sculpt from the perimeter upward. Use the large teeth of a large comb and project the lengths at 90° to remove initial length starting at the center.

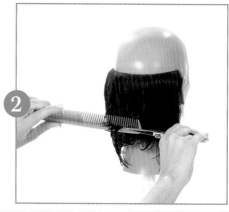

2 Work upward in one continuous movement. Sculpt the protruding lengths.

The angle of your comb and the distance between the comb and the head will control the length progression and resulting line of inclination.

3 Redistribute lengths downward before combing upward again.

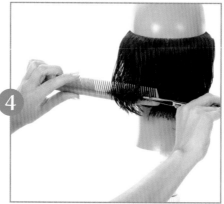

4 Work from the center to the left side using the same shear-over-comb technique. Follow the same line of inclination.

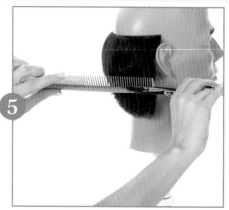

5 Repeat the same sculpting technique as you work from the center to the right side.

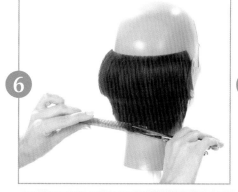

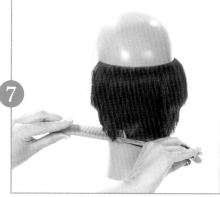

Switch to the sculpting comb, and sculpt lengths closer to the head and refine the line of inclination. Again, use the shear-over-comb technique starting at the center. Work from the center to the left side using the same sculpting technique.

NOTE: *Depending on hair density, you may work with the wider teeth or finer teeth of the comb.*

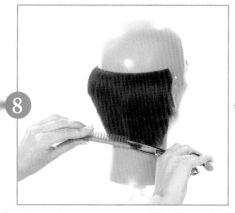

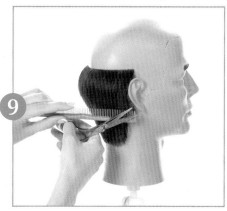

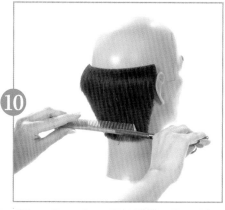

Then, repeat this technique on the right side, working from the center.

Alter your palm and shear position as you move toward the far right for control behind the ear and to maintain a consistent line of inclination.

Next, use taper shears with the shear-over-comb technique to blend lengths along the line of inclination. Use a smooth, continuous movement working up from the perimeter.

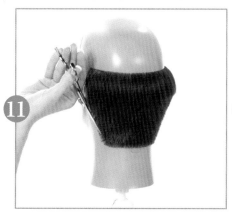

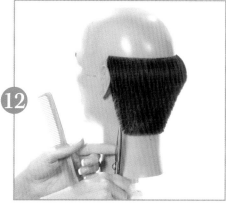

Outline the perimeter using the tips of the shears. Work from the top to the bottom.

Then, outline the perimeter in the opposite direction, working toward the top to refine the line.

The finish shows the subtle illusion of a color progression due to the exposure of the scalp at the perimeter.

CLIPPER-OVER-COMB TECHNIQUE

Once perfected, your clipper-over-comb skills can be used to great advantage in the salon. You may find that you and your client save time using clipper-over-comb techniques, versus the shear-over-comb technique.

 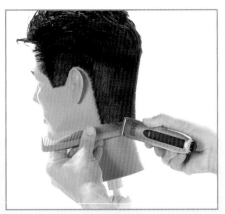

Just as in shear-over-comb techniques, you will change combs according to the specific work that you are doing. When working with the smaller combs, especially the taper comb, you may need to use trimmers, which are smaller than the clippers.

Practice Makes Perfect

HIGH GRADATION

The focus of this exercise is to provide practice in sculpting high gradation using the clipper-over-comb technique. The result will be short, activated lengths that progress from shorter to longer lengths starting at the perimeter nape with transparency that extends above the occipital area.

Practice this exercise to build skill and accuracy using an upright head position, 90° projection, horizontal comb and clipper position, and the clipper-over-comb sculpting technique.

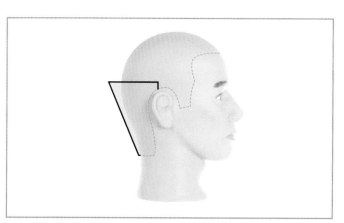

The structure graphic shows a progression of shorter lengths toward longer lengths, which results in transparency that extends above the occipital area.

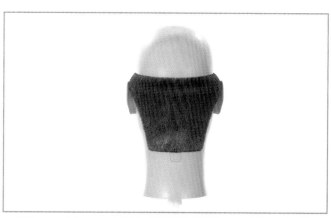

The finish shows high gradation. Client hair type and density will affect the degree of transparency that is evident.

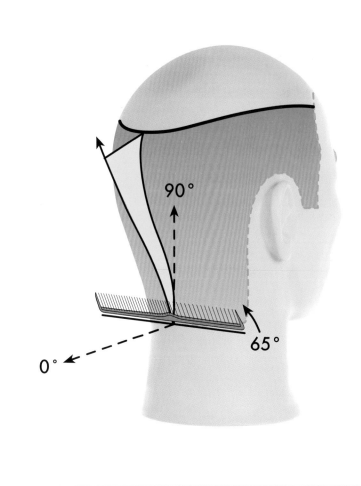

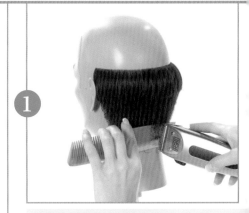

1

With the head upright, begin sculpting at the center perimeter nape. Use the finer teeth of a large comb and 90° projection. Move the clippers across the comb to sculpt.

2

As you move up the center, maintain 90° projection. Hold the comb along the intended high line of inclination and sculpt across the comb to remove protruding lengths.

The angle of your comb and the distance between the comb and the head will control the length progression and resulting line of inclination.

3

Move to the left and use the same clipper-over-comb technique to sculpt. Use the center as a length guide and follow the line of inclination.

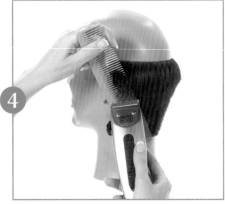

4

Change your hand position as you work behind the ear. Hold the comb on a steep diagonal and move the clippers up along the comb.

5

Repeat the same clipper-over-comb technique as you sculpt the right side.

6 To refine the gradation, switch to the sculpting comb and use the clipper-over-comb technique positioning the clippers parallel to the comb. Work from the center upward, then toward the left side.

7 Angle the sculpting comb on a steep diagonal behind the ear, and move the clippers upward along the comb to remove any protruding lengths.

8 Move to the right side and sculpt with the same clipper-over-comb techniques.

9

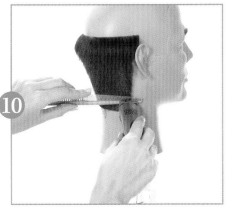

10 Refine the perimeter using a taper comb to sculpt closer to the scalp. Position the comb against the head to control the lengths and protect the scalp. Position the trimmers parallel to the comb. Work around the hairline using the same technique.

11 Outline the perimeter hairline with the trimmers. Starting in the center, position the trimmers against the skin horizontally.

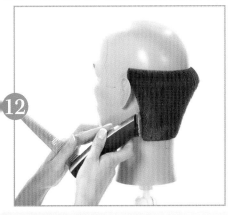

12 Move to the sides and outline the perimeter using the tip of the trimmers working upward. Remove any uneven lengths.

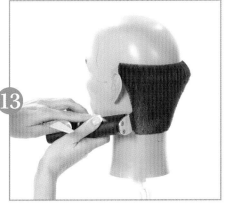

13 Then position the trimmers against the skin for a clean, accurate line.

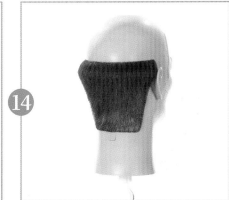

14 The finish shows activated texture throughout the nape with a well-blended progression of lengths.

FADES

Various versions of a hairstyle known as a "fade" have been popular for decades. It gains its name from the fact that the hair appears to be "fading away" the closer it is to the perimeter hairline. This type of hair sculpture is really a very, very short version of gradation. In many instances areas of the head are sculpted to the skin, resulting in a "bald fade." This type of sculpture is almost always done with clippers and requires careful blending and leaves little room for error. After years of practice, some designers can execute this hair design easily. Many designers will approach the sculpture by sculpting different zones of the head to the desired lengths and then blending them to create smooth transitions. This blending may be sculpted freehand by arcing the clippers away from the head where zones meet. Blending may also be facilitated by the use of various attachments or guards.

When designing a fade hair sculpture, the placement of each of the zones should be predetermined so that the design is well-balanced and flattering to the client. Too much or too little skin showing can look unattractive, no matter how well the sculpture is performed technically. In general the lowest zone in the design is sculpted the shortest while the zones gradually get longer toward the interior. Depending on the amount of transparency or baldness desired, zones may vary in numbers and size.

FEWER ZONES, LESS TRANSPARENCY

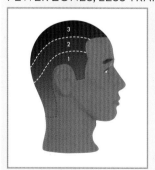

MORE ZONES, HIGHER TRANSPARENCY

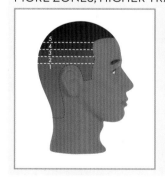

What can you recommend to male clients who do not want the more angular designs traditionally associated with men's sculpture?

It is also important to look at how the perimeter of a design is defined or lined. Make sure the lines that are chosen work with the client's hairline, density and facial features.

 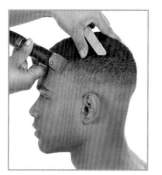

GUIDELINES FOR CLIENT-CENTERED MEN'S SCULPTING

Client-centered guidelines are designed to help you do everything possible to enhance your client's comfort during the service and satisfaction after the service. Combining your experience with essential sculpting techniques for male clients with client-centered guidelines will ensure that you build a loyal male customer base.

PROCEDURAL GUIDELINES FOR PLANAR FORMS

The following chart will help ensure the most predictable and desirable results when creating planar form sculptures.

- Ensure the client's head is perfectly upright when using planar sculpting techniques. If the head is tilted, it becomes near to impossible to judge whether partings, distribution and finger position are correct while sculpting.

- Check the directional distribution while sculpting by turning the client so that you can use the mirror to watch how you are distributing the hair. Often this mirror perspective helps reveal inconsistencies.

- Use the mirror to carefully gauge your finger position to make sure that you are sculpting horizontally in the interior and vertically in the exterior. Check frequently to avoid errors.

- Sculpting a planar form first, then modifying it by softening or removing the weight corners, can be an effective way of maintaining the symmetrical balance of a form as well as creating a desired shape for male clients who prefer to wear a less traditional hair sculpture.

GRADATION CONSIDERATIONS

The following chart will help ensure the most predictable and desirable gradation results when creating short hair sculptures for men.

- In many cases it is advisable to change the sculpting direction while using shear-over-comb techniques to sculpt against the "grain" of the hair, meaning against the growth pattern. This helps assure that all the hair is picked up and controlled by the comb, thus ensuring more accurate lengths.

- Carefully assess the density of the hair. Use the taper-shear-over-comb technique to increase transparency in higher density areas to achieve the appearance of consistent lengths and even transparency throughout the gradated area.

- Be sure your client's head position remains consistent while using overcomb techniques. If the head position changes, the resulting line of inclination may not accurately reflect the angle of the comb used while sculpting.

- Only move the thumb of your sculpting hand during shear-over-comb techniques so that the still blade of the shears can rest gently against the teeth of the comb, and both tools can travel in unison.

GOT A MATCH?

Review the images of the various hair designs below and match them to the sculpting techniques indicated by the technical photographs.

A

B

C

D

4.2 LONGER FORMS

You can probably name at least one male musician, actor or model who looked more or less attractive with longer hair. What's important to remember as a designer is that whether hair is considered long, medium or short is somewhat subjective. In general, however, these categories differ between male and female clients. In other words, what is considered mid-length for a male client would probably be considered short for a female client. Because of these different and individual perceptions, it is advisable to use images as a reference when consulting with a client.

One of the challenges of sculpting longer forms on male clients is making sure that the finished result still has a masculine feeling. In addition to the physical considerations that go into your design decisions, you will have to consider the client's lifestyle and personality to determine what length is appropriate and how long is too long. Remember that longer forms on male clients still shouldn't have too much volume, which is especially challenging if the client has wavy or curly hair.

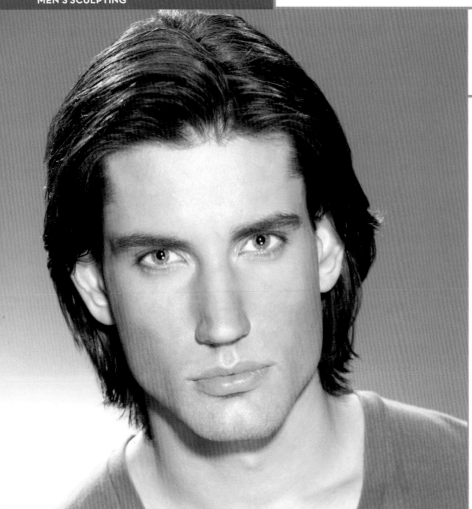

GRADUATED/HORIZONTAL/ DIAGONAL-BACK FORM — WORKSHOP

Graduated forms are popular with men because of their versatility. This sculpture can be worn off the face when sculpted with a longer fringe.

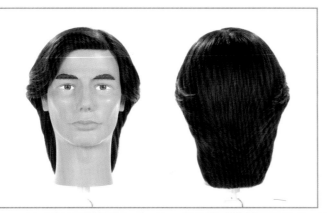

In this exercise, graduated lengths are sculpted along a horizontal line in the back and blend into diagonal-back graduated lengths at the sides. The graduated fringe is sculpted horizontally.

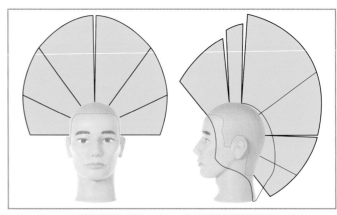

The structure graphics show diagonal-back graduated lengths on the sides that blend to the horizontal graduation in the back and in the fringe.

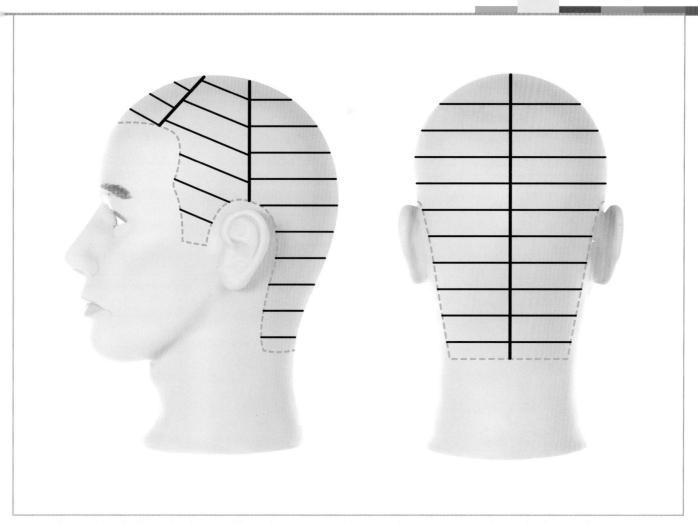

Section the hair from the back of each ear, and from the center front hairline to the nape. The art indicates that horizontal partings are used for the back, and diagonal-back partings are used for the sides. Horizontal partings are used in the fringe.

1

2

3

With the head upright, begin at the back nape and release a horizontal parting. Use natural distribution and 1-finger projection. Position fingers horizontally and sculpt parallel to establish a mobile design line. Sculpt from the center to one side, then to the other side.

On the next horizontal parting, use perpendicular distribution with a medium projection angle. Use a mobile design line and sculpt parallel to the horizontal parting.

4

Continue to use perpendicular distribution and medium projection until you reach the crest area.

5

Once you reach the crest area, lower the projection angle to create weight.

6

Continue working upward distributing each subsequent horizontal parting to the stationary design line to complete the section.

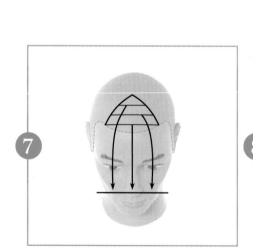

7

Section the fringe from in front of the apex to the end of the eyebrow on each side. Natural distribution and horizontal partings will be used to sculpt the fringe.

8

In the fringe area, release a parting parallel to the hairline. Use natural distribution, 1-finger projection and sculpt horizontally using the tip of the nose as a length guide. Sculpt from the center to one side, then to the other side. Check for symmetry before proceeding.

9 Direct subsequent horizontal partings to the stationary design line and sculpt horizontally.

10 Use the comb to determine the angle of the diagonal-back line that will be used to connect the fringe and the back. Then, release a small parting parallel to the hairline. Position your fingers along the diagonal-back line and sculpt in natural fall to create the diagonal-back mobile design line. Avoid using tension over the ear as you blend lengths to the back.

11

12 Move to the opposite side and use the same techniques to establish the diagonal-back line. Check for symmetry before continuing.

13 Return to the right side, take a diagonal-back parting and sculpt using perpendicular distribution, medium projection and a mobile design line.

14　At the crest, lower the projection angle and distribute the remaining partings to the stationary design line.

15　Work to the top of the section using the same techniques.

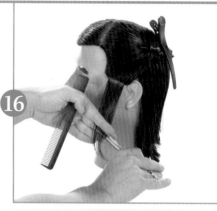

16　Move to the opposite side and release a diagonal-back parting.

17　Use perpendicular distribution, medium projection and a mobile design line to sculpt. Continue using the same techniques until you reach the crest.

18　Work to the top, distributing subsequent diagonal-back partings to the stationary design line at the crest.

19　This completed exercise shows medium graduation along a horizontal line in the back, blending into diagonal-back graduation on the sides.

DESIGN DECISIONS
Draw or fill in the boxes with the appropriate answers.

STRUCTURE:

SHAPE:

TEXTURE:

SECTIONING PATTERN:

BACK:				finger/tool	design line
head position	parting	distribution	projection	position	mobile/stationary

FRINGE:				finger/tool	design line
head position	parting	distribution	projection	position	mobile/stationary

SIDES:				finger/tool	design line
head position	parting	distribution	projection	position	mobile/stationary

TOOLS:

SCULPTURE DESIGN RUBRIC

Chapter 4: Graduated/Horizontal/Diagonal-Back Form

This Rubric is a performance assessment tool designed to measure your ability to **create** Pivot Point sculpture designs.

Name _____ ID Number _____ Date _____

	In Progress Level 1	Getting Better Level 2	Entry-Level Proficiency Level 3
PREPARATION			
• Assemble sculpting essentials	☐	☐	☐
CREATE			
• Section hair from back of each ear and from center front hairline to center nape	☐	☐	☐
• Position head upright	☐	☐	☐
• Release horizontal parting in the nape	☐	☐	☐
• Distribute in natural fall, use 1-finger projection; position fingers horizontally and sculpt parallel from center to one side and then to the other	☐	☐	☐
• Release next horizontal parting, distribute perpendicular, project at a medium angle and sculpt parallel; work up to the crest area using a mobile design line	☐	☐	☐
• Project at a lower angle in the crest area and work upward, distributing subsequent horizontal partings to a stationary design line	☐	☐	☐
• Section fringe from in front of apex to end of eyebrow on each side; release parting parallel to hairline; use natural distribution, 1-finger projection and sculpt horizontally using the tip of the nose as a guide	☐	☐	☐
• Sculpt remaining fringe area using horizontal partings, natural distribution and stationary design line	☐	☐	☐
• Position comb to determine diagonal-back line at right side	☐	☐	☐
• Release parting parallel to hairline; position fingers along diagonal-back line; use natural fall to sculpt a diagonal-back design line; repeat on left side	☐	☐	☐
• Sculpt a diagonal-back parting on right side using perpendicular distribution, medium projection and a mobile design line	☐	☐	☐
• Project at a lower angle at the crest and distribute remaining partings to the stationary design line; work to top of section using same techniques	☐	☐	☐
• Sculpt a diagonal-back parting on the left side using perpendicular distribution, medium projection and a mobile design line	☐	☐	☐
• Project at a lower angle at the crest and distribute remaining partings to the stationary design line; work to top of section using same techniques	☐	☐	☐
• Finish sculpture design	☐	☐	☐

TOTAL POINTS = ☐ + ☐ + ☐

TOTAL POINTS _____ ÷ HIGHEST POSSIBLE SCORE 48 = _____ %

Record your time in comparison with the suggested salon speed. _____

To improve my performance on this procedure, I need to: _____

_____

UNIFORM/INCREASE/ SOLID COMBINATION FORM – WORKSHOP

This sculpture is well-suited for men who want longer lengths and a variety of styling options. Texturizing throughout the interior and sides removes weight and adds mobility. The notching technique will be used throughout the design for blending and textural interest.

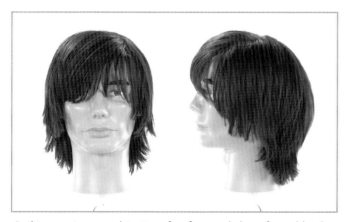

In this exercise, a combination of uniform and planar forms blend with the solid perimeter lengths.

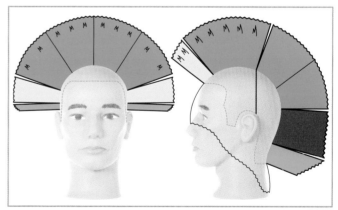

The structure graphics show a solid perimeter in the nape and graduated lengths in the fringe. Uniform interior layers blend to a planar from in the exterior.

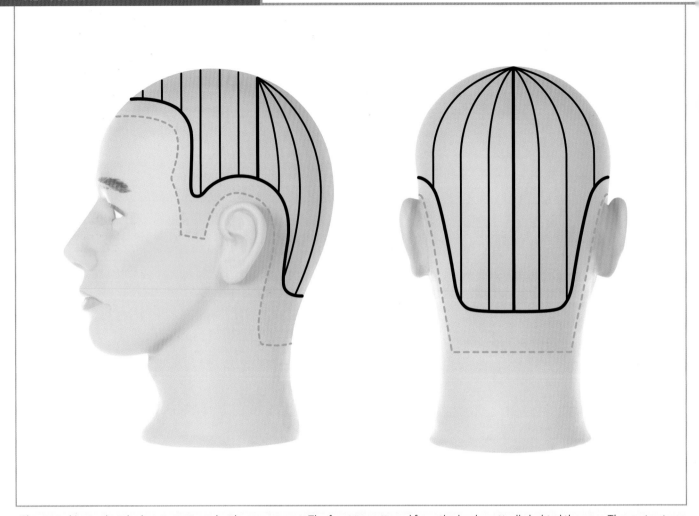

The art indicates that the hair is sectioned with a center part. The front is sectioned from the back vertically behind the ears. The perimeter is sectioned parallel to the hairline at the front and sides. At the back the perimeter section is thicker, extending to just below the occipital. Pivotal partings will be used to sculpt the back and vertical partings will be used to sculpt the front.

1

Section the hair and check sectioning for symmetry.

2

3

Begin at the center front hairline, use natural distribution, position your fingers horizontally at the tip of the nose and notch a horizontal line. Work toward one side, positioning your fingers along a diagonal-back line. Sculpt parallel with the notching technique working to the recession area. Then sculpt from the center to the recession area on the opposite side. Check for symmetry and balance before proceeding.

4 Work toward one side, continuing to use natural distribution and no projection. Extend the diagonal-back line and sculpt with the notching technique.

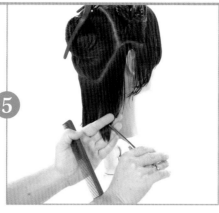

5 Work toward the center nape sculpting a steep diagonal-back line.

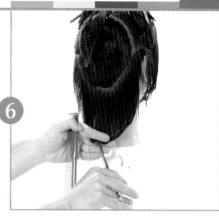

6 At the center back, notch to sculpt a horizontal line that blends into the diagonal-back lines at the sides.

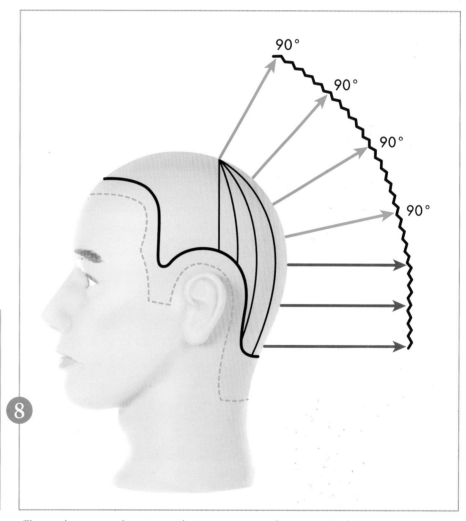

7 Repeat the same techniques on the opposite side, working from the fringe to the center nape.

8 The art shows pivotal partings with 90° projection in the interior. Each parting is sculpted from the top to the bottom. Below the crest, directional distribution is used to sculpt a planar form.

Take a pivotal parting at the center back. Project at 90°, position your fingers parallel to the curve of the head and notch to create uniform lengths in the interior. Continue toward the exterior, projecting the hair straight out at the crest. Position your fingers vertically and sculpt with the notching technique. Work to the bottom, blending to the perimeter weight.

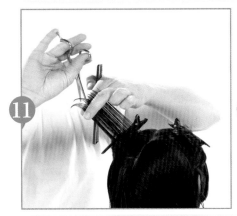

Work toward one side using pivotal partings. Use a mobile design line to sculpt uniform layers in the interior and a planar form in the exterior. Work to the sectioning line behind the ear.

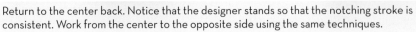

Return to the center back. Notice that the designer stands so that the notching stroke is consistent. Work from the center to the opposite side using the same techniques.

Use the same techniques, working up to the sectioning line on this side.

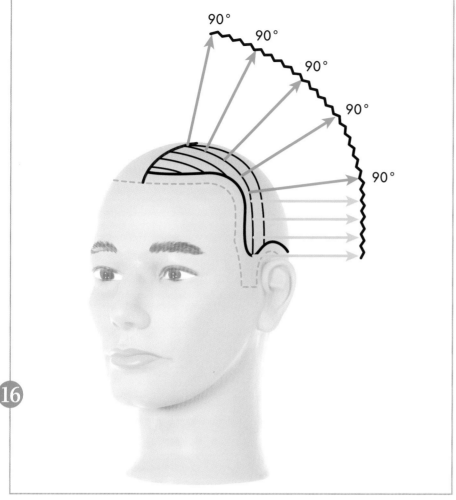

The art shows the projection angles and sculpting direction that will be used to sculpt the front. Use 90° projection to sculpt uniform layers in the interior. The sides are projected straight out and sculpted vertically.

Move to the left side. Take a vertical parting and project at 90°. Position your fingers parallel to the head and sculpt uniform lengths. Work toward the bottom of the parting. Below the crest, project straight out and sculpt vertically. Work to the front of this side using the same techniques with a mobile design line.

Use the same techniques on the opposite side. Continue to stand in a position to ensure that the notching direction is consistent.

20

Next, take random, horizontal partings along the center part and project straight up. Position your fingers horizontally and notch to ensure blending between the two sides.

21

To texturize the interior, use diagonal-back partings and draw the tip of the razor through the midstrand. Work through one side of the interior, then repeat on the opposite side.

22

Move to the front hairline and use horizontal partings with low projection. Continue texturizing the midstrand with the razor.

23

Work to the crown using the same techniques to complete the sculpture.

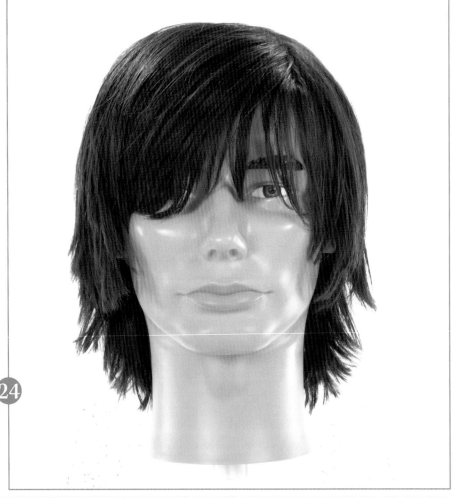

24

The finished design features planar layers, which create some activation while maintaining weight at the perimeter.

DESIGN DECISIONS

Draw or fill in the boxes with the appropriate answers.

STRUCTURE:

SHAPE:

TEXTURE:

SECTIONING PATTERN:

PERIMETER: head position	parting	distribution	projection	finger/tool position	design line mobile/stationary

BACK: head position	parting	distribution	projection	finger/tool position	design line mobile/stationary

SIDES: head position	parting	distribution	projection	finger/tool position	design line mobile/stationary

TOOLS:

SCULPTURE DESIGN RUBRIC

Chapter 4: Uniform/Increase/Solid Combination Form

This Rubric is a performance assessment tool designed to measure your ability to **create** Pivot Point sculpture designs.

Name _____ ID Number _____ Date _____

	In Progress Level 1	Getting Better Level 2	Entry-Level Proficiency Level 3
PREPARATION			
• Assemble sculpting essentials	☐	☐	☐
CREATE			
• Position head upright	☐	☐	☐
• Section hair with center part; section front from back vertically from ear to ear; section perimeter parallel to hairline	☐	☐	☐
• Sculpt beginning at center front hairline with hair in natural distribution, fingers positioned horizontally using the notching technique and the tip of the nose as a length guide	☐	☐	☐
• Position fingers along diagonal-back line toward one side and sculpt parallel using notching technique; work toward recession area	☐	☐	☐
• Sculpt from center toward opposite side using same technique; check for symmetry and balance	☐	☐	☐
• Sculpt toward one side using same techniques to extend diagonal-back line; work toward center nape along a steep diagonal-back line	☐	☐	☐
• Sculpt a horizontal line at the center back using notching technique	☐	☐	☐
• Repeat on opposite side working from fringe to center nape	☐	☐	☐
• Release pivotal parting at center back, project at 90°, position fingers parallel to curve of head and notch to sculpt; work toward exterior	☐	☐	☐
• Project straight out at crest, position fingers vertically and notch to sculpt, working toward the bottom	☐	☐	☐
• Sculpt toward one side using pivotal partings and mobile design line; work to sectioning line	☐	☐	☐
• Sculpt from center back to opposite side using the same techniques; stand so notching stroke is consistent	☐	☐	☐
• Part vertically on left side, project at 90°, position fingers parallel to head and sculpt; work toward bottom of parting	☐	☐	☐
• Project straight out below crest and sculpt vertically, working to front of section using same techniques	☐	☐	☐
• Repeat on opposite side; stand so notching direction is consistent	☐	☐	☐
• Part horizontally along center part, project straight up, position fingers horizontally and notch to blend	☐	☐	☐
• Texturize interior using diagonal-back partings, drawing razor through midstrand	☐	☐	☐
• Texturize through midstrand, at the front hairline using horizontal partings and low projection; work toward the crown	☐	☐	☐
• Finish sculpture design	☐	☐	☐

TOTAL POINTS = ☐ + ☐ + ☐

TOTAL POINTS _____ ÷ HIGHEST POSSIBLE SCORE 60 = _____ %

Record your time in comparison with the suggested salon speed. _____

To improve my performance on this procedure, I need to: _____

_____

4.3 MID-LENGTH FORMS

As mentioned earlier, mid-length forms can be among the most versatile hair sculptures to offer the male client. Lengths are short enough to showcase a great shape and texture yet often allow for styling versatility and ease. Mid-length sculptures can tend to appear "grown-out" unless they are well-maintained. If that is not the look that you and your client are going for, make sure you book regular appointments to maintain the shape and texture to the best advantage.

The classic mid-length designs for male clients feature a planar form in the interior. Depending on the desired look the exterior may be sculpted in various ways—ranging from planar form to uniform lengths—even to low and medium gradations.

After considering the client's hair texture and density, advanced sculpting and texturizing techniques are often incorporated to adapt the design for the individual client.

PLANAR FORM —
WORKSHOP

This combination of increase, uniform and graduated forms—the result of planar sculpting —creates a defined look without being too conservative. The use of texturizing shears helps add mobility and versatility.

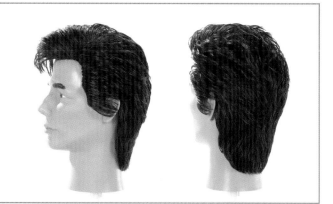

The square form is a classic yet contemporary sculpture that appeals to many clients. The majority of this sculpture is created using the planar sculpting technique with uniform nape lengths. End tapering increases mobility.

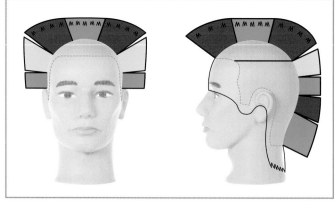

The structure graphics show an angular form that is a combination of graduated, increase-layered and uniformly layered lengths, which result from planar sculpting. The form is adapted to include uniform layers at the nape.

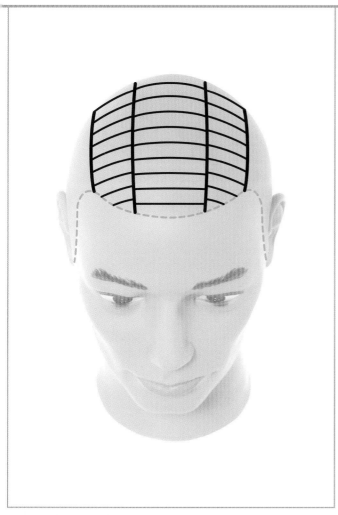

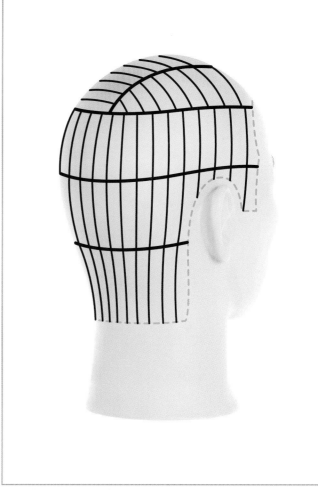

The art shows three sections in the interior and that horizontal partings are used.

The exterior is also sculpted using three sections, although the hair is not sectioned prior to sculpting. Vertical partings are used to sculpt the exterior.

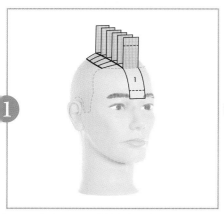

1

2

3

Design line lengths for the first section can be determined by various anatomical features.

After sectioning, release a thin horizontal parting at the front hairline. Sculpt the horizontal length guide at the bridge of the nose using minimal tension and no projection. With the head upright, part horizontally at the front hairline. Distribute the lengths straight up, position your fingers horizontally and sculpt parallel.

4 Work toward the back of the section using a mobile design line and the planar sculpting technique. Consistently project straight up and position your fingers horizontally.

5 Continue to use the same sculpting technique as you work to the back of the crown. It is important to maintain consistent projection while sculpting, since altering it will result in a more rounded form.

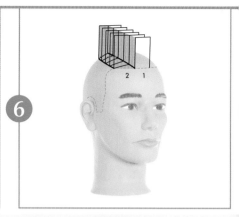

6 The middle panel will be used as a guide to sculpt the right panel.

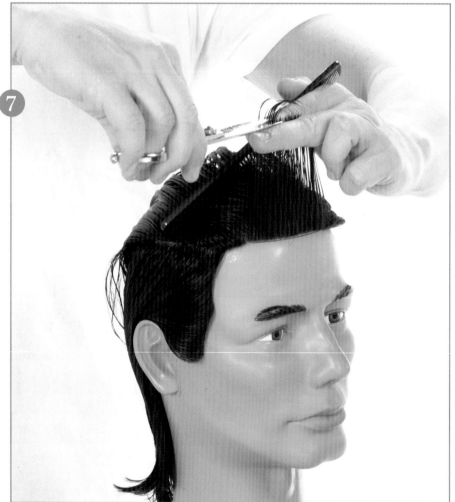

7 Move to the right panel. Release a horizontal parting at the front hairline and use a portion of the previously sculpted panel as a length guide. Project the hair straight up and position your fingers and shears horizontally and sculpt.

8 Continue to work toward the back using a mobile design line and projecting the lengths straight up. Position your fingers and shears parallel to the floor and sculpt.

9 Use the same techniques as you work to the back of this panel.

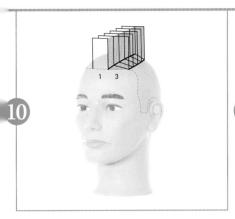

10

The middle panel is also used as a length guide for the left panel.

11

Move to the left panel. Distribute each horizontal parting straight up, position your fingers parallel to the floor and sculpt using a mobile design line.

12

Then, cross-check the lengths, parting in the opposite direction. Project the hair straight up to cross-check.

13

Release a small amount of hair from the perimeter of the interior section to use as a length guide to sculpt the sides.

14

The exterior will be sculpted in three sections. Arrows indicate the sculpting direction for each section. Each section corresponds to the length of your finger, up to the second knuckle.

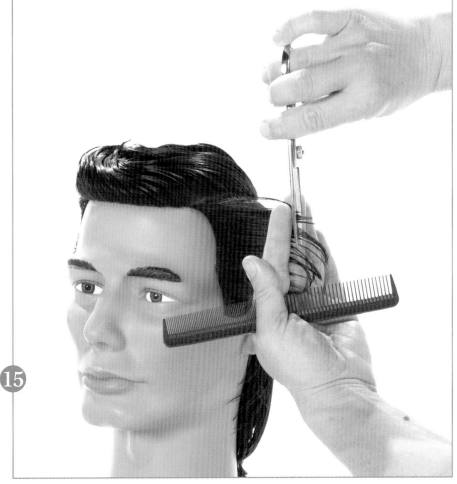

15

Release a vertical parting at the front hairline on the left side. Position your fingers vertically with your palm facing away from the head. Sculpt parallel, only to your second knuckle. Work from the front to the center back, using vertical partings.

Work toward the ear using a mobile design line. Continue to project the lengths straight out, positioning your fingers and shears perpendicular to the floor to sculpt.

Continue to use the same sculpting techniques with a mobile design line as you work to the center back. Sculpt only up to your second knuckle.

Move to the front of the opposite side and release a vertical parting. Project straight out, position your fingers and shears vertically and sculpt to your second knuckle.

Use a mobile design line and the same sculpting techniques as you work from the front toward the ear.

Then work from the ear to the center back. Continue using vertical partings and a mobile design line.

Continue to project lengths straight out as you work toward the ear using a mobile design line. Position your fingers vertically and sculpt parallel.

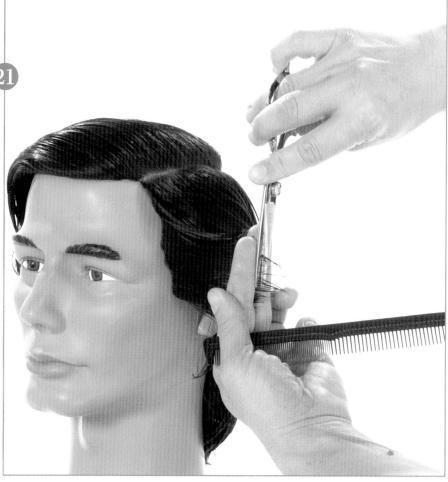

21 Return to the left front hairline, release a vertical parting and project straight out. Use a portion of the previously sculpted section as a guide, position your fingers vertically and sculpt. Depending on the length of your fingers, these partings may reach the hairline. If not, you may choose to extend partings to the hairline at this point.

Then work to the center back using the same sculpting techniques. Use the mobile design line, as well as the guide from the previously sculpted section.

24 Use the same techniques to sculpt the opposite side, starting at the front hairline.

25 Work from the hairline toward the ear using a mobile design line.

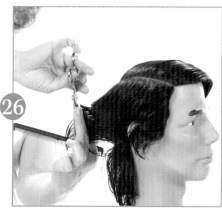

26 Continue working to the center back, projecting straight out and sculpting vertically.

In the nape, release a vertical center parting. Project at 90° and position your fingers parallel to the head, using a length guide from the previously sculpted section. Sculpt parallel to create uniform layers.

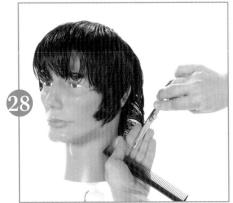

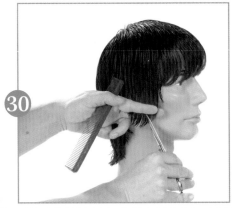

Work from the center to one side and then the other. Use a mobile design line, 90° projection and a parallel finger position to sculpt the entire nape section.

Define the perimeter line at the sides using natural distribution and minimal projection. Position your fingers horizontally and sculpt with the notching technique.

31 Use the same technique to define the nape. Use natural fall with a horizontal finger position. Sculpt with the notching technique.

32 **33** To texturize, use the same partings, projection and sculpting position used earlier. Sculpt using the texturizing shears near the ends of the hair to increase mobility in the sculpture.

34 **35** The finished sculpture can be worn with a classic square form or casually styled for a more modern, contemporary feel.

DESIGN DECISIONS

Draw or fill in the boxes with the appropriate answers.

STRUCTURE:

SHAPE:

TEXTURE:

SECTIONING PATTERN:

INTERIOR: head position	parting	distribution	projection	finger/tool position	design line mobile/stationary

EXTERIOR/CREST: head position	parting	distribution	projection	finger/tool position	design line mobile/stationary

EXTERIOR/NAPE: head position	parting	distribution	projection	finger/tool position	design line mobile/stationary

TOOLS:

SCULPTURE DESIGN RUBRIC

Chapter 4: Planar Form

This Rubric is a performance assessment tool designed to measure your ability to **create** Pivot Point sculpture designs.

Name _____ ID Number _____ Date _____

	In Progress Level 1	Getting Better Level 2	Entry-Level Proficiency Level 3
PREPARATION			
• Assemble sculpting essentials	☐	☐	☐
CREATE			
• Section interior into three sections; exterior is not sectioned prior to sculpting	☐	☐	☐
• Position head upright	☐	☐	☐
• Establish interior length guide using anatomical features as reference; sculpt horizontal length guide at front hairline using minimal tension and no projection	☐	☐	☐
• Distribute horizontal front hairline parting straight up; position fingers horizontally and sculpt parallel	☐	☐	☐
• Sculpt using a mobile design line and planar sculpting technique; sculpt toward the crown	☐	☐	☐
• Part horizontally at front hairline on right side of interior; use middle panel as length guide; position fingers and shears horizontally and sculpt; repeat same techniques on the left panel to complete interior	☐	☐	☐
• Part interior lengths in opposite direction and project hair straight up to cross-check	☐	☐	☐
• Release small parting from perimeter of interior to use as length guide on sides; sculpt exterior using three sections	☐	☐	☐
• Sculpt with vertical mobile design line starting at left front side hairline; distribute hair straight out and position fingers vertically with palm facing away from head	☐	☐	☐
• Sculpt parallel, only up to second knuckle, using interior as length guide; work toward ear	☐	☐	☐
• Sculpt using same techniques to center back; then sculpt from other side hairline toward ear and from ear to center back	☐	☐	☐
• Sculpt second exterior section using planar technique, beginning at left front hairline; working to center back, sculpt opposite side of section using same techniques	☐	☐	☐
• Sculpt vertical center parting in nape, projecting at 90°, positioning fingers parallel to head	☐	☐	☐
• Use a length guide from previously sculpted section; sculpt from center to one side and then the other using a mobile design line, 90° projection and parallel finger position	☐	☐	☐
• Distribute side perimeter naturally, use minimal projection, position fingers horizontally and notch to define side perimeter	☐	☐	☐
• Notch nape perimeter in natural fall with fingers positioned horizontally	☐	☐	☐
• Texturize ends using texturizing shears and planar sculpting techniques throughout	☐	☐	☐
• Finish sculpture design	☐	☐	☐

TOTAL POINTS =   ☐ + ☐ + ☐

TOTAL POINTS _____ ÷ HIGHEST POSSIBLE SCORE 57 = _____ %

Record your time in comparison with the suggested salon speed. _____

To improve my performance on this procedure, I need to: _____

_____

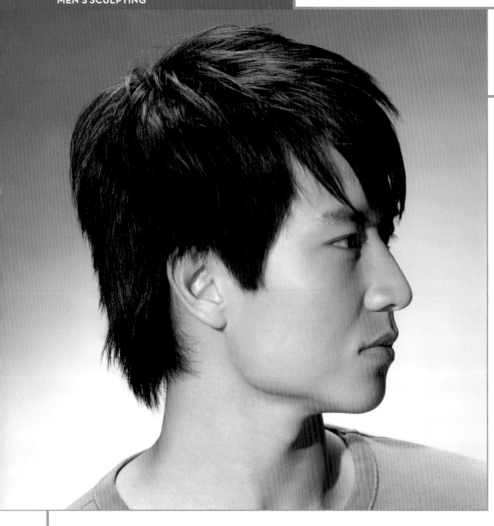

PLANAR/UNIFORM COMBINATION FORM —
WORKSHOP

This sculpture is worn well by men who want to express a strong classic style, but also have the versatility to wear more trendy looks. The razor rotation technique will be used to increase blending and mobility. The notching technique will be used in the interior for blending and textural interest.

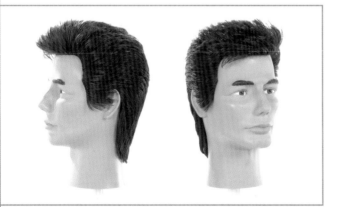

The interior of the design is created using the planar sculpting technique with uniform layers in the occipital and nape to create closeness. Razor rotation through the sides and back creates additional blending while increasing mobility.

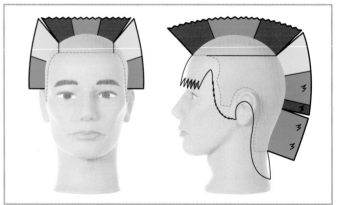

This angular form has a combination of increase, uniformly layered and graduated components with uniform layers in the occipital and nape.

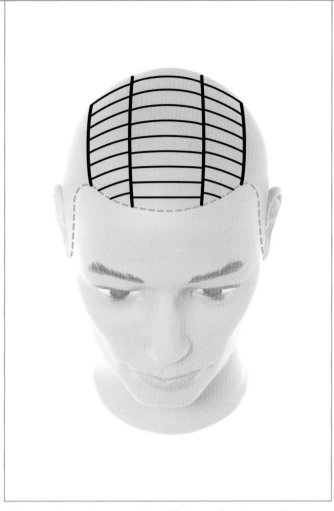

The art indicates three panels with horizontal partings in the interior.

Vertical partings are used in the exterior.

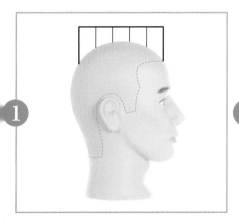

1 When planar sculpting, hair is distributed straight up vertically and sculpted horizontally. This achieves longer lengths in the front and back due to the curves of the head.

2 Take a small center section at the front hairline and sculpt to establish a length guide above the bridge of the nose.

3 Then take a parting through the center and distribute the hair straight up. Position your fingers parallel to the floor and sculpt.

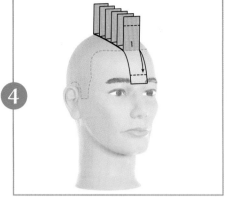

4

Horizontal partings and the planar sculpting technique are used throughout the interior, which will be sculpted in three panels.

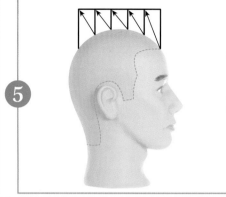

5

Within these panels, each previously sculpted horizontal parting is used as a mobile length guide.

6

With the head upright, start at the center front. Release a horizontal parting, distribute the hair straight up, position your fingers horizontally and sculpt parallel to the floor.

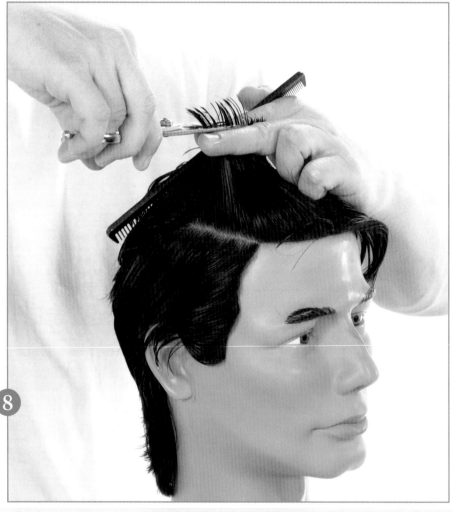

7

Continue to use the planar sculpting technique and a mobile design line as you work toward the back of this center panel.

8

Then move to the next panel. Distribute the hair straight up and sculpt parallel to the floor. Use a mobile design line and the previously sculpted panel as a guide. Work to the back of the panel, then use the same technique to sculpt the third panel.

9

Next, drop a thin parting at the perimeter of the interior section. This parting will be used as a length guide to sculpt the side and back lengths.

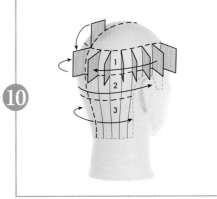

10

The exterior will be sculpted in three panels. Vertical partings are used throughout. The arrows indicate sculpting directions.

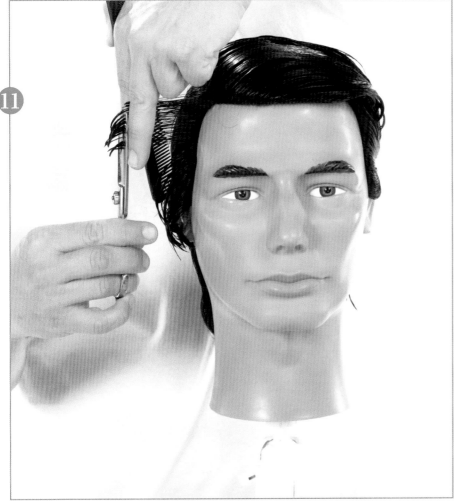

11

Begin sculpting the exterior at the front hairline on the right side, using the planar sculpting technique. Part vertically and distribute straight out. Position your fingers vertically and sculpt only up to the second knuckle. Be sure that your fingers are perpendicular to the floor as you sculpt. This will serve as a mobile design line. Sculpt from the right side to the left side.

12

Continue using the planar sculpting technique. Be sure to maintain thin partings and a visible mobile design line as you work toward the back.

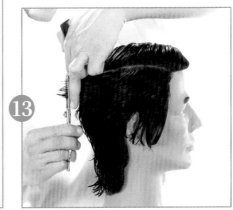

13

Continue working to the center back using the same technique.

14

Then, work from the back to the other side. Adapt your body position to maintain a parallel finger and shear position.

15

Work to the front hairline to complete the first panel on the left side.

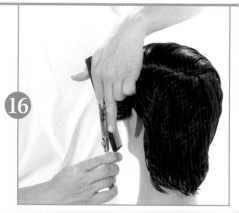

16

Then, use a portion of the first panel as a length guide for the second panel. Sculpt the second panel starting on the left side. Use the same planar sculpting technique, working toward the back.

17

Continue to use a mobile design line, projecting straight out and sculpting vertically. Avoid sculpting past the second knuckle.

18

Continue to use the same sculpting techniques on the right side working to the front hairline to complete the second panel.

19

To sculpt the nape (3rd panel), tilt the head forward and release a vertical parting at the center. Use a portion from the second panel as a length guide for this panel, which will be sculpted in uniform layers. Use perpendicular distribution and 90° projection. Position your fingers parallel to the head and sculpt uniform lengths.

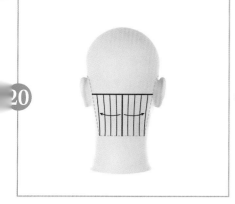

Note that the nape will be sculpted from the center to one side and then to the other side.

Work toward one side using vertical partings, 90° projection and a mobile design line. Then work from the center to the opposite side.

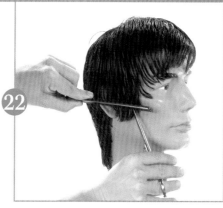

Refine the side perimeter using comb control with no projection. Use the tips of the shears to notch a horizontal line.

Refine the perimeter of the nape using a freehand technique. Notch into the lengths using the tips of the shears. You may choose to tilt the head forward. Notch a horizontal line to refine the back of the nape. Work from the center to either side.

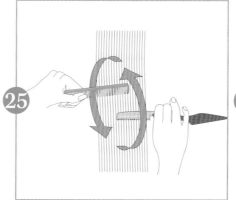

Next, perform the razor rotation technique through the sides and back. Rotate the razor and the sculpting comb in a circular motion lightly over the surface to blend the lengths and increase mobility. Begin performing the razor rotation technique starting on the right side. Distribute the hair diagonally to facilitate the technique.

27 Continue using the razor rotation technique as you work around the back of the head, toward the left side.

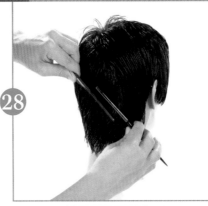

28 Then work from the opposite side using the same technique. Note that the comb and razor are positioned along the opposite diagonal line.

29 To complete the sculpture, project interior lengths straight up. Position your fingers horizontally and notch to blend and create textural interest.

31

30

The finish displays a masculine angular form that conforms to the curve of the head in the nape.

DESIGN DECISIONS
Draw or fill in the boxes with the appropriate answers.

STRUCTURE:

SHAPE:

TEXTURE:

SECTIONING PATTERN:

INTERIOR:

head position	parting	distribution	projection	finger/tool position	design line mobile/stationary

EXTERIOR/CREST:

head position	parting	distribution	projection	finger/tool position	design line mobile/stationary

EXTERIOR/NAPE:

head position	parting	distribution	projection	finger/tool position	design line mobile/stationary

TOOLS:

SCULPTURE DESIGN RUBRIC

Chapter 4: Planar/Uniform Combination Form

This Rubric is a performance assessment tool designed to measure your ability to **create** Pivot Point sculpture designs.

Name _____ ID Number _____ Date _____

	In Progress Level 1	Getting Better Level 2	Entry-Level Proficiency Level 3
PREPARATION			
• Assemble sculpting essentials	☐	☐	☐
CREATE			
• Position head upright	☐	☐	☐
• Establish interior length guide using anatomical features as reference; sculpt length guide at front hairline above bridge of nose	☐	☐	☐
• Release center parting in interior, distribute straight up, position fingers parallel to floor and sculpt	☐	☐	☐
• Part horizontally at center front hairline, distribute straight up, position fingers horizontally and sculpt parallel to floor using mobile design line; work to back of center panel	☐	☐	☐
• Part horizontally at front hairline on right side of interior; using middle panel as length guide, position fingers and shears horizontally and sculpt	☐	☐	☐
• Use a mobile design line and work to back of panel; repeat same techniques on the left panel to complete interior	☐	☐	☐
• Release small parting at perimeter of interior to use as exterior length guide to sculpt the first panel	☐	☐	☐
• Part vertically at right side hairline, distribute straight out, position fingers vertically and sculpt up to second knuckle; sculpt from right side to left using mobile design line and thin partings	☐	☐	☐
• Sculpt the second panel using the same planar sculpting technique; work from the left front hairline to the right front hairline	☐	☐	☐
• Tilt the head forward to sculpt third panel; release vertical parting in center nape; use length guide from second panel; distribute perpendicular, project at 90°, position fingers parallel to head and sculpt uniform lengths	☐	☐	☐
• Sculpt from center to one side and then center to the other side using vertical partings, 90° projection and a mobile design line	☐	☐	☐
• Sculpt to refine side perimeter using comb control with no projection; notch with tips of shears along a horizontal line; sculpt to refine nape perimeter using freehand technique to notch horizontal line working from center to one side and then center to the other side	☐	☐	☐
• Texturize the sides and back using razor rotation technique with hair distributed diagonally	☐	☐	☐
• Project interior lengths straight up, position fingers horizontally and notch with shears to blend	☐	☐	☐
• Finish sculpture design	☐	☐	☐

TOTAL POINTS = ☐ + ☐ + ☐

TOTAL POINTS _____ ÷ HIGHEST POSSIBLE SCORE 48 = _____ %

Record your time in comparison with the suggested salon speed. _____

To improve my performance on this procedure, I need to: _____

_____

PLANAR/MEDIUM GRADATION COMBINATION FORM – WORKSHOP

This combination of planar form and medium gradation is ideal for male clients who want a strong masculine image. The shear-over-comb technique will be used to create medium gradation. Notching will be performed in the interior for blending and textural interest.

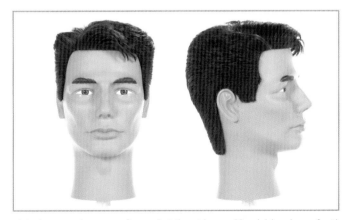

Medium gradation performed at the sides and back blends perfectly with the previously sculpted short interior planar lengths.

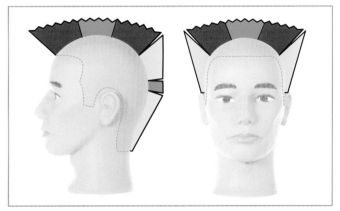

The structure graphics show medium gradation in the exterior, which blends to the planar form in the interior.

1 The previous sculpture consists of a planar form over uniform lengths in the nape.

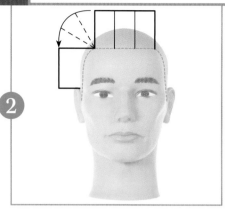

2 The sides and back are sculpted using the planar sculpting technique with the top as a length guide.

NOTE: *In this exercise, a wide version of a sculpting comb, with larger spaces between the teeth, is used to remove initial length. Then a standard sculpting comb is used to refine the gradation.*

3

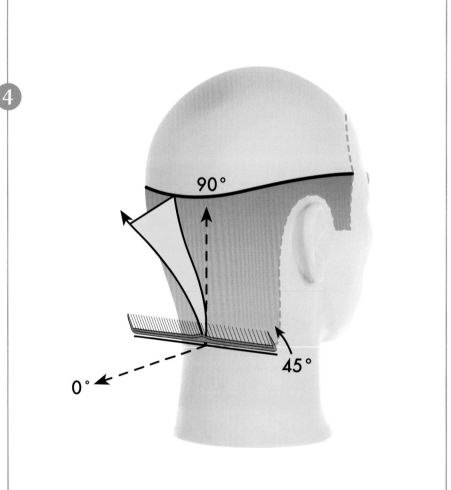

4 The angle of the comb and the distance between the comb and the head will control the length progression and the line of inclination.

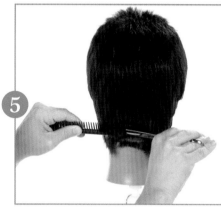

5 Begin at the center nape. Use the wider teeth of the wide sculpting comb, perpendicular distribution and 90° projection. Position the shears parallel to the comb and sculpt upward toward the occipital area.

6 Gradually remove length at the sides of the nape to maintain consistency.

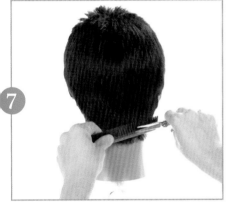

(7) Continue the shear-over-comb technique on the other side. Continue sculpting parallel to the comb, working upward from the hairline to the occipital area.

(8) Work from the back to the sides using the back lengths as a guide. Position the comb diagonally back while angling it away from the head to create medium gradation. Continue sculpting parallel to the comb.

(9) Position the comb horizontally and continue to sculpt the sides, maintaining a medium line of inclination.

(10) Use the same technique to sculpt medium gradation on the opposite side.

(11) Using the fine teeth of the standard sculpting comb, refine the gradation in the back using the same shear-over-comb technique. Note that this will produce more transparency in the occipital area.

12 Work toward the side using a diagonal-back comb position near the ear. Gradually turn the comb in a pivotal motion and continue sculpting parallel to the comb.

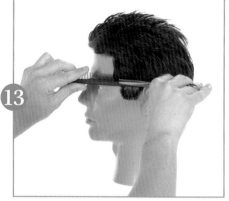

13 Move to the sideburn area and position the sculpting comb horizontally. Maintain a consistent angle while working upward to the temple. Repeat the same sculpting techniques on the opposite side.

14 Now outline the perimeter front hairline and sideburn area along a horizontal line.

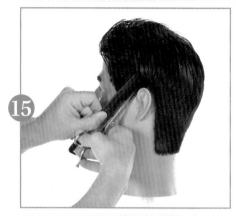

15 Move to the area in front of the ear, directing the hair back with the sculpting comb. Sculpt the protruding lengths using the tips of the shears.

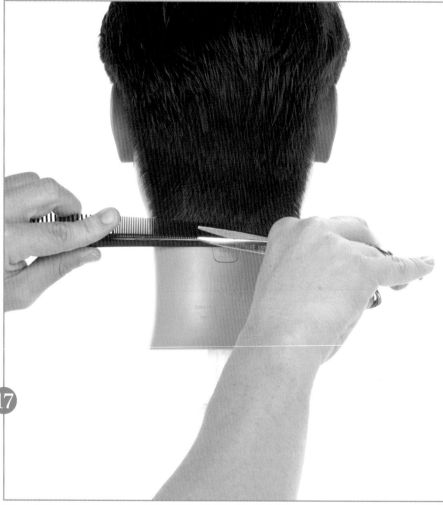

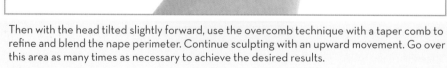

16 Outline carefully around the ear using the tips of the shears. Bend the ear forward to allow greater freedom and movement.

17 Then with the head tilted slightly forward, use the overcomb technique with a taper comb to refine and blend the nape perimeter. Continue sculpting with an upward movement. Go over this area as many times as necessary to achieve the desired results.

18

To blend and texturize the ends, use a taper shear-over-comb technique throughout the weight area. Repeat on the opposite side.

19

In the interior, take wide horizontal partings, project straight up and position your fingers horizontally. Notch to texturize without reducing length. Work from the front hairline to the crown.

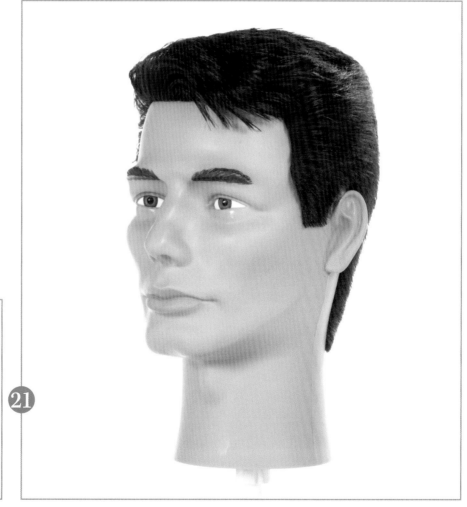

20

21

The finish shows a short square form with perimeter gradation. This masculine design complements the angular lines of the face.

DESIGN DECISIONS

Draw or fill in the boxes with the appropriate answers.

STRUCTURE:

SHAPE:

TEXTURE:

SECTIONING PATTERN:

NAPE: head position	parting	distribution	projection	finger/tool position	line of inclination
	N/A				

SIDES: head position	parting	distribution	projection	finger/tool position	line of inclination
	N/A				

TOOLS:

variation
PLANAR/MEDIUM GRADATION

This planar form with high graduation is very popular with male clients. The strong angular shape of the planar form produces a very masculine look while the wavy texture adds softness. The high graduation through the nape and sides blends to medium gradation at the perimeter for minimal styling time with great results.

The interior is sculpted in three zones, using the planar sculpting technique in combination with a notching technique. The sides are sculpted using diagonal-back partings with medium projection and a nonparallel finger position. In the back and nape, vertical partings are used with a nonparallel finger position to achieve a high line of inclination. Interior lengths are blended to each side using low projection and the notching technique. The perimeter is refined using the shear-over-comb technique to produce medium gradation. To remove weight and encourage movement in the interior, the point-cutting technique is used.

SCULPTURE DESIGN RUBRIC

Chapter 4: Planar/Medium Gradation Combination Form

This Rubric is a performance assessment tool designed to measure your ability to **create** Pivot Point sculpture designs.

Name _____ ID Number _____ Date _____

	In Progress Level 1	Getting Better Level 2	Entry-Level Proficiency Level 3
PREPARATION			
• Assemble sculpting essentials	☐	☐	☐
CREATE			
• Position head upright	☐	☐	☐
• Sculpt medium gradation in exterior starting at center nape using perpendicular distribution and 90° projection; use shear-over-comb technique with wider teeth of wide sculpting comb; position shears parallel to comb while sculpting toward occipital area	☐	☐	☐
• Repeat same shear-over-comb technique on side nape areas	☐	☐	☐
• Sculpt sides using back lengths as a guide, angling comb away from head to blend side lengths to back lengths; sculpt medium gradation on one side, then the other side	☐	☐	☐
• Refine gradation using shear-over-comb technique with fine teeth of standard sculpting comb; sculpt nape to either side; use diagonal-back comb position near ear; gradually pivot comb around ear and continue to sculpt parallel	☐	☐	☐
• Sculpt sides using same technique	☐	☐	☐
• Sculpt to define sideburn area; refine hair in front of ear and outline around ear using comb and tips of shears	☐	☐	☐
• Sculpt to refine nape perimeter with head tilted slightly forward; use shear-over-comb technique with a taper comb and upward movements	☐	☐	☐
• Texturize and blend ends using taper-shear-over-comb technique throughout weight area	☐	☐	☐
• Texturize interior taking wide horizontal partings; position fingers parallel and notch with tips of shears	☐	☐	☐
• Finish sculpture design	☐	☐	☐

TOTAL POINTS = ☐ + ☐ + ☐

TOTAL POINTS _____ ÷ HIGHEST POSSIBLE SCORE 36 = _____ %

Record your time in comparison with the suggested salon speed. _____
To improve my performance on this procedure, I need to: _____

SHORT FORMS

Short forms tend to be the most popular with the male client because they are often low-maintenance and easy to care for. This is not to say that the short sculpture cannot be groomed to make as strong a fashion statement as your client may want to make. These short designs feature an exposed hairline and require frequent and regular upkeep, which makes these sculptures popular among designers who have mastered the skills to create them successfully. Short forms, especially those with high gradation or fades, really allow the shape of the client's head to be seen, so consider this when making your design decisions. Also, consider how well your client's hair texture and hairline will support a shorter shape, and adapt the design accordingly.

PLANAR/HIGH GRADATION COMBINATION FORM—CLIPPERS — WORKSHOP

This combination of an interior planar form and high gradation expresses a freedom of style that many men like. A short, planar form will be sculpted in the interior and the clipper-over-comb technique will be used at the sides and back to create high gradation. The notching technique will be performed in the interior for blending and to create textural interest.

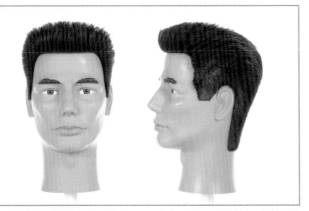

The short planar form in the interior is complemented by the high gradation at the sides and back.

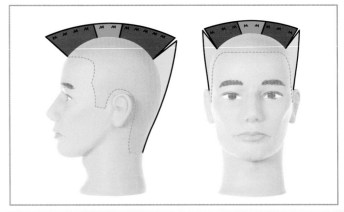

The structure graphics show high gradation in the exterior, which blends to the planar form in the interior.

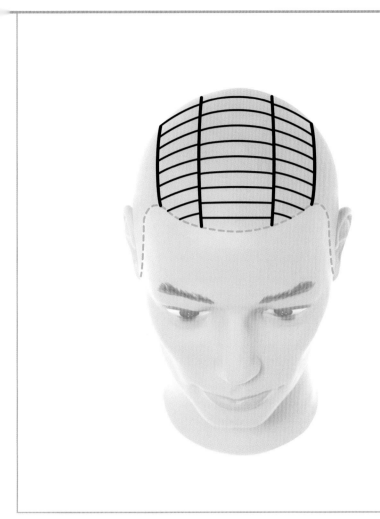

The art indicates three panels with horizontal partings in the interior. The center panel will be used as a guide to sculpt the panels at either side.

1 Starting at the front of the center panel, distribute the lengths straight up and position your fingers horizontally. Sculpt parallel to the floor.

2 Continue to use the planar sculpting technique and a mobile design line as you work toward the back of the center panel.

3 Continue to sculpt parallel to the floor as you complete the center panel.

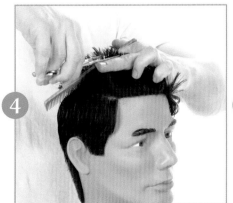

4 Then move to the right panel. Starting at the front, use a mobile design line and a portion of the center panel as a length guide. Sculpt using the planar sculpting techniques.

5 Continue using the planar sculpting technique as you complete this panel.

6 Now move to the left panel and continue using the planar sculpting technique.

7 Work to the back of this panel using the same techniques.

8 Cross-check the interior along the opposite line. Work from one side to the other sculpting any protruding lengths.

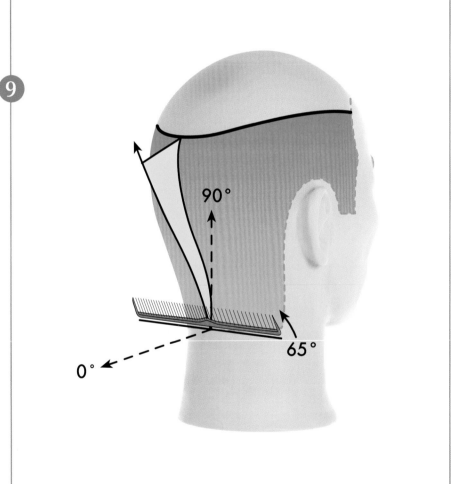

9 The angle of the comb and the distance between the comb and the head will control the length progression and the line of inclination.

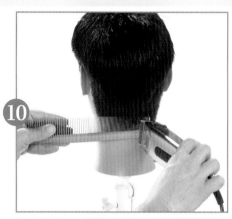

10 With the head upright, begin sculpting the exterior at the center nape. Use the finer teeth of a large comb and 90° projection. Move the clippers across the comb to sculpt.

11 As you move upward, maintain 90° projection. Hold the comb along the intended line of inclination and sculpt across the comb.

Work toward the left side using the same technique.

Continue working toward the left side using the same clipper-over-comb technique. Angle the comb and follow the line of inclination from the center section.

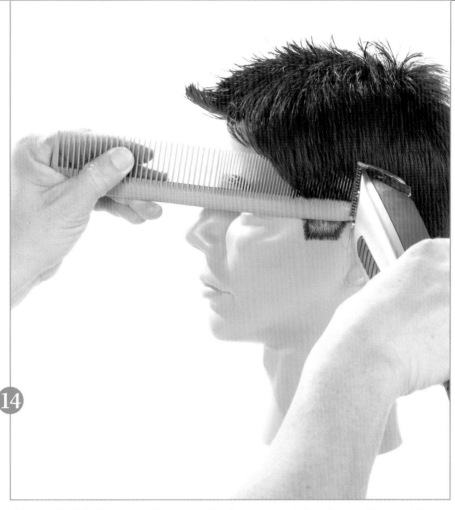

Move to the left side and continue using the clipper-over-comb technique. Begin sculpting at the sideburn area starting at the perimeter. Work from the front toward the back, sculpting high gradation.

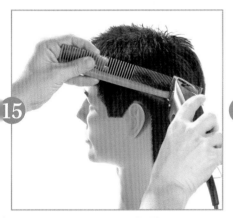

Angle the comb slightly to help blend the side and the back lengths.

Use the same clipper-over-comb techniques to sculpt on the opposite side. Work from the center back to the side.

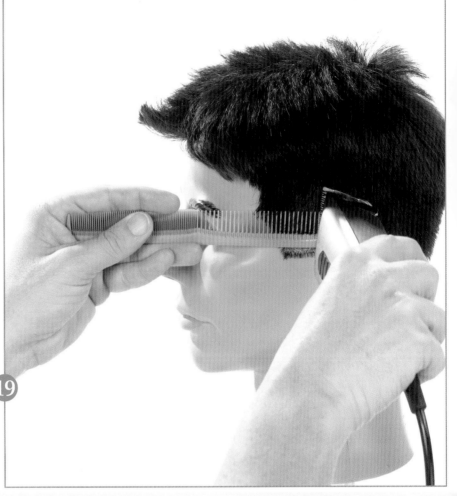

To refine the gradation, switch to the sculpting comb and use the wider teeth with the clipper-over-comb technique. Work from the center back toward the left side.

Move to the left side and continue refining the gradation with the clipper-over-comb technique. Angle the comb to blend the side and the back lengths.

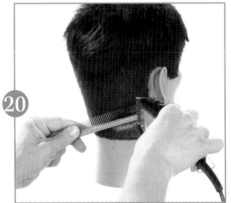

Repeat the same sculpting techniques on the opposite side. Work from the center back toward the right side. Then work from the side, blending to the back.

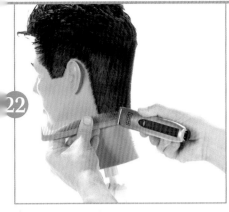

Next, refine the perimeter using the fine teeth of the sculpting comb and trimmers to achieve a closer effect.

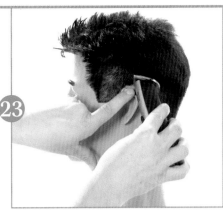

Outline the perimeter hairline using a freeform technique. Bend the ear slightly as needed and sculpt using the tip of the trimmers.

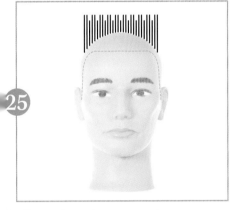

The art shows that tapering the ends removes weight and creates an alternation of length, to blend and create textural interest.

To complete the sculpture, project interior lengths straight up. Position your fingers horizontally and texturize the ends using the taper shears.

The finish shows a strong square form that is well-suited to many men's facial features.

DESIGN DECISIONS

Draw or fill in the boxes with the appropriate answers.

STRUCTURE:

SHAPE:

TEXTURE:

SECTIONING PATTERN:

INTERIOR: head position	parting	distribution	projection	finger/tool position	design line mobile/stationary

EXTERIOR: head position	parting	distribution	projection	finger/tool position	line of inclination
	N/A				

TOOLS:

variation
PLANAR/HIGH GRADUATION/UNIFORM

The angular shape of the planar form does not complement all face shapes and individual styles. As an option, the planar form can be rounded off to diminish its angularity. Many men have a receding hairline. Create the illusion of a fuller, straighter hairline by isolating it and sculpting with low projection.

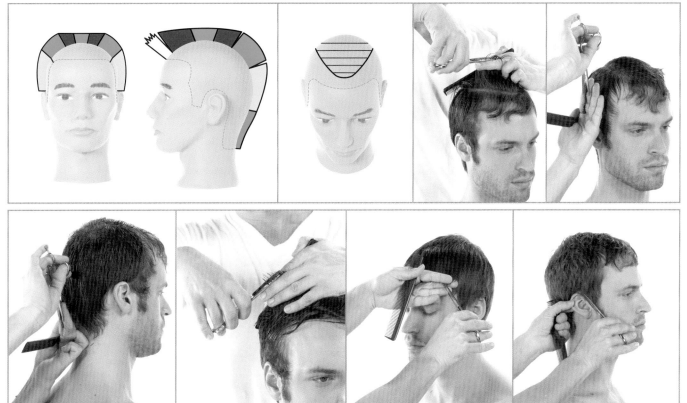

The interior is sectioned above the crest with the front hairline isolated to adapt to the recession. The planar sculpting technique is used in the interior to sculpt a horizontal plane. The exterior is sculpted with high graduation and short, uniform lengths in the nape. Vertical partings and 90° projection are used to round off the corners of the resulting weight area, when planar interior lengths and graduated exterior lengths meet. The front hairline is sculpted in low projection with the notching technique. The tips of the shears are used to define the perimeter.

SCULPTURE DESIGN RUBRIC

Chapter 4: Planar/High Gradation Combination Form–Clippers

This Rubric is a performance assessment tool designed to measure your ability to **create** Pivot Point sculpture designs.

Name _____ ID Number _____ Date _____

	In Progress Level 1	Getting Better Level 2	Entry-Level Proficiency Level 3
PREPARATION			
• Assemble sculpting essentials	☐	☐	☐
CREATE			
• Position head upright	☐	☐	☐
• Part horizontally in front of center panel; distribute straight up, position fingers horizontally and sculpt parallel to floor using mobile design line; work to back of center panel	☐	☐	☐
• Part horizontally in right front panel; use portion of center panel as length guide and sculpt using planar sculpting techniques; repeat same techniques on the left panel to complete interior	☐	☐	☐
• Cross-check interior along opposite line	☐	☐	☐
• Sculpt high gradation in exterior starting at center nape; use fine teeth of large comb and project at 90°; move clippers across comb to sculpt	☐	☐	☐
• Sculpt upward maintaining 90° projection holding the comb along intended line of inclination; work toward left side angling comb slightly to blend side and back	☐	☐	☐
• Sculpt using clipper-over-comb technique on the left side beginning at the perimeter of the sideburn area; work from the front toward the back	☐	☐	☐
• Repeat on opposite side working from center back and then from side	☐	☐	☐
• Refine gradation in back and sides using wider teeth of sculpting comb and same clipper-over-comb techniques	☐	☐	☐
• Refine nape perimeter using finer teeth of sculpting comb with trimmers	☐	☐	☐
• Outline perimeter hairline using trimmers and freeform technique; bend ear slightly and use tip of trimmers	☐	☐	☐
• Texturize ends in interior using taper shears	☐	☐	☐
• Finish sculpture design	☐	☐	☐

TOTAL POINTS = ☐ + ☐ + ☐

TOTAL POINTS _____ ÷ HIGHEST POSSIBLE SCORE 42 = _____ %

Record your time in comparison with the suggested salon speed. _____

To improve my performance on this procedure, I need to: _____

_____

FLAT TOP—CLIPPERS —
WORKSHOP

The flat top sculpture lends itself especially well to straighter hair textures and growth patterns, but can be worn by many men. Sometimes seen as a military cut, this design often requires little to no styling, but instead very frequent visits to the salon, which is a benefit for designers.

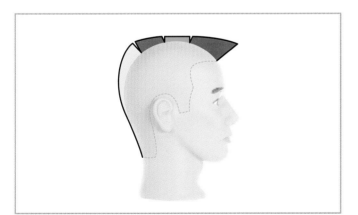

The structure graphic shows a very short planar form in the interior with very high gradation in the exterior.

Before sculpting, air form the hair to stand away from the head. Pay special attention to work against growth patterns as you dry the hair. This step may not be required if the client is already wearing this style.

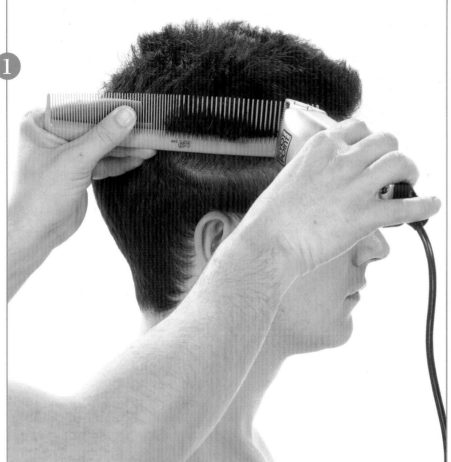

With the head upright, begin sculpting on one side. Use the wide teeth of a large comb and 90° projection. Position a large comb with the spine parallel to the crest and the large teeth of the comb pointing straight up. Move the clippers across the comb to sculpt high gradation.

NOTE: *The spine of the comb is positioned against the head.*

Work to the center back of the crest using the same technique.

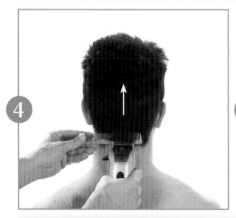

Then work from the opposite side to the center back. Check for symmetry before continuing.

Move to the center nape hairline. Use the wide teeth of a standard sculpting comb and 90° projection. Position the clippers parallel to the teeth of the comb and move the comb and clippers in unison up to the established line.

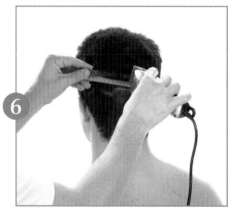

Work toward the right, sculpting another vertical panel and using the same technique.

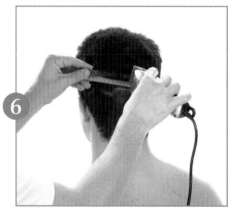

Then work toward the left using the same technique to establish the line of inclination. You may choose to move the clippers across the comb while blending to the previously sculpted line at the crest.

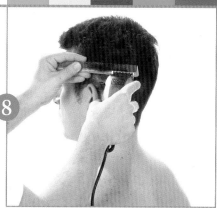

Work around the back of the ear, pivoting the comb until it is horizontal. Continue sculpting with the same technique.

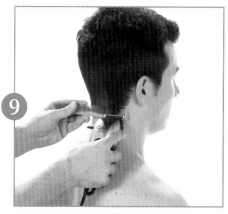

Then sculpt the opposite side of the nape using the wide teeth of the sculpting comb. Move both clippers and comb in unison. Work to the back of the ear on this side.

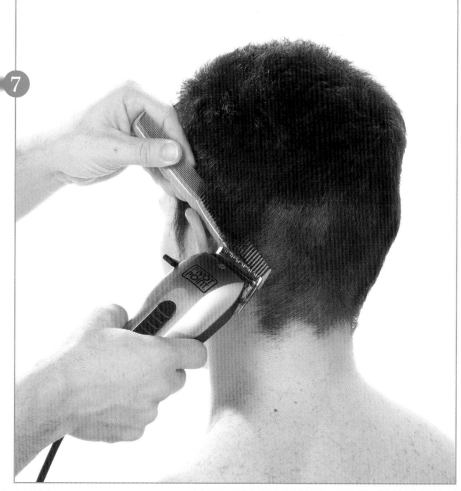

Continue working toward one side. Behind the ear, position the comb diagonally, or parallel to the hairline.

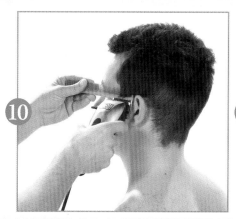

Return to the first side, moving to the front hairline. Position the wide teeth of the comb horizontally at the sideburn area, then move comb and clippers up in unison.

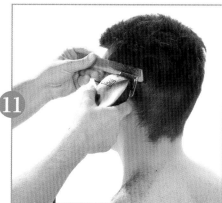

Work toward the back, blending to the previously sculpted lengths.

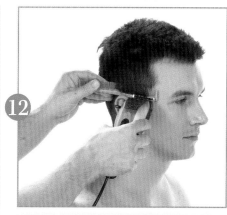

Then use the same technique to sculpt the opposite side. Check for balance and symmetry before continuing.

13 Move to the top and use the large comb to distribute the hair straight up. Position the wide teeth of the comb horizontally at the apex, with the teeth pointing to the crown. Move the clippers across the comb to sculpt.

14 Work toward the center back using the same technique to sculpt the horizontal plane. When you reach the crown, position the teeth of the comb to point forward to better control the lengths.

15 Then work from the apex to the front, pointing the teeth of the comb toward the apex and sculpting with the same technique.

16 Extend the horizontal plane toward either side as you work through the interior. Be sure to maintain a horizontal comb position.

17

To help you analyze the balance of the form before finalizing it, air form the remaining hair straight up.

18 19

Refine the shape in the interior. To cross-check the interior lengths, position the comb in the opposite direction. Make sure the head is upright and the comb is positioned along the horizontal plane.

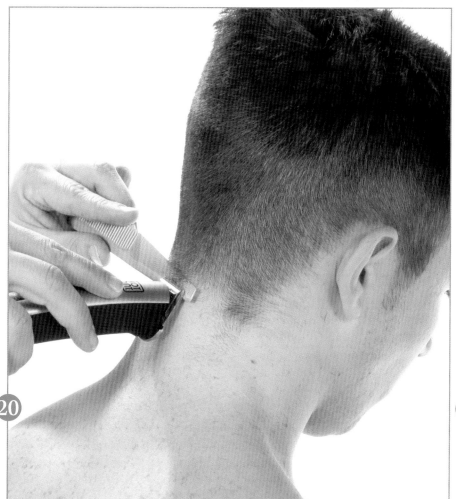

20

To refine the perimeter, use the fine teeth of a taper comb and trimmers, beginning at the center nape. Position the blade of the trimmers parallel to the teeth of the comb.

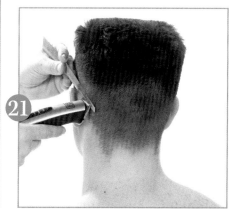

21

Work through the entire perimeter, adjusting the position of the comb and trimmers to work around the hairline. Sculpt from the center nape to one side.

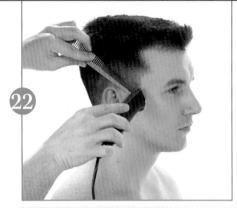

22

Then sculpt from the center nape to the other side.

23

Define the line around the ear, placing the trimmers against the skin. You may also choose to move the trimmers against hairline growth patterns to outline this area. The nape hairline may be defined or left as is, depending on the client.

24

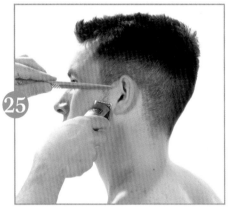

25

Use the trimmers to define the sideburn area as needed.

26

To complete the sculpture, position the large comb vertically and use the trimmers to check the form and blend any protruding lengths.

27

This strong, masculine form features high gradation contrasting with the flat top in the interior. Depending on the length of the interior and the texture of the hair, styling options may feature more or less angular finishes.

DESIGN DECISIONS
Draw or fill in the boxes with the appropriate answers.

SHAPE:

TEXTURE:

STRUCTURE:

SECTIONING PATTERN:

N/A

EXTERIOR:

head position	parting	distribution	projection	finger/tool position	line of inclination
	N/A				

INTERIOR:

head position	parting	distribution	projection	finger/tool position	design line mobile/stationary
	N/A				

TOOLS:

SCULPTURE DESIGN RUBRIC

Chapter 4: Flat Top-Clippers

This Rubric is a performance assessment tool designed to measure your ability to **create** Pivot Point sculpture designs.

Name _____ ID Number _____ Date _____

	In Progress Level 1	Getting Better Level 2	Entry-Level Proficiency Level 3
PREPARATION			
• Assemble sculpting essentials	☐	☐	☐
CREATE			
• Air form hair to stand away from the head	☐	☐	☐
• Position head upright	☐	☐	☐
• Sculpt high gradation in crest using large comb and clipper-over-comb sculpting technique; sculpt one side to center back then other side to center back	☐	☐	☐
• Sculpt high gradation in center nape using wide teeth of standard sculpting comb with clipper-over-comb sculpting technique; work toward left then right to establish line of inclination, blending with the previously sculpted line at the crest	☐	☐	☐
• Complete one side of nape then other; angle comb then pivot to work around back of ear	☐	☐	☐
• Return to front hairline of each side, sculpting with the clipper-over-comb technique and blending to the previously sculpted lengths	☐	☐	☐
• Sculpt flat top beginning at apex, distributing hair straight up while positioning the large comb horizontally; move clippers across comb horizontally working from apex to crown, then from apex to front	☐	☐	☐
• Extend the horizontal plane toward either side	☐	☐	☐
• Air form interior lengths straight up; analyze balance of form	☐	☐	☐
• Refine interior lengths using previous interior sculpting techniques	☐	☐	☐
• Refine perimeter using fine teeth of the taper comb and trimmers, beginning at the center nape and continuing through entire perimeter	☐	☐	☐
• Define the line around ear and nape hairline placing trimmers against skin	☐	☐	☐
• Position the large comb vertically to check form and remove any protruding lengths	☐	☐	☐
• Finish sculpture design	☐	☐	☐

TOTAL POINTS = ☐ + ☐ + ☐

TOTAL POINTS _____ ÷ HIGHEST POSSIBLE SCORE 45 = _____ %

Record your time in comparison with the suggested salon speed. _____

To improve my performance on this procedure, I need to: _____

BALD FADE—CLIPPERS —
WORKSHOP

A fade consists of extremely short lengths in the exterior gradually progressing to longer interior lengths. The bald fade is cut with the clippers positioned directly on the skin. The adjustable lever on the clippers is used to vary the distance of the cutting blade from the scalp. A guard is placed to vary the distance even more from the scalp. The bald fade gives the illusion of hair gradually fading into the skin.

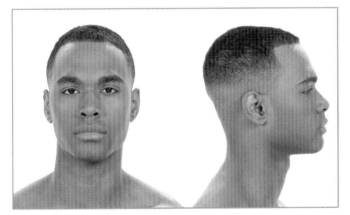

This sculpture features gradation along a horizontal line that gradually blends into the skin. Toward the top, gradation blends to short, uniform lengths.

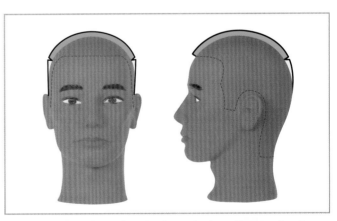

This exercise will be sculpted with very high gradation and uniform layers using the clippers with and without guards.

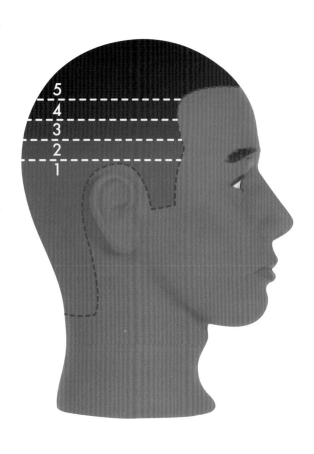

① Position the adjustable blade even with the cutting blade and position the head upright. Place the clippers flat on the scalp to create a horizontal line. Use the outside of the eyebrow as a guide. Extend the line to the center back.

This exercise will have five zones for a smooth transition from the shortest exterior lengths to the longer interior lengths. After the five zones are established, each will be further blended to remove weight, creating a gradual "fade" effect. Note that the width of each zone may vary.

② Repeat on the opposite side, extending the horizontal line to meet with the previously sculpted line at the center back.

③ Check for symmetry before proceeding. This horizontal line establishes the end of the first zone, which is "bald."

④ ⑤ Tilt the head slightly forward. With the blades in the same position, sculpt Zone 1 against the skin, starting at the center nape perimeter. Sculpt up to the established line, working from the center toward the right side.

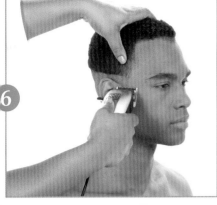

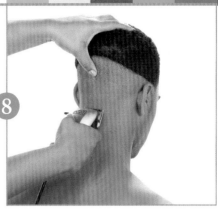

Continue using the same technique as you work to the front hairline on the right side. Then work from the center to the opposite side. If necessary, bend the ears forward to remove lengths behind them.

Use your thumb to pull the skin taut and go over the bald area to clean up lengths you may have missed. Sculpt against the skin in multiple directions, working against the growth direction.

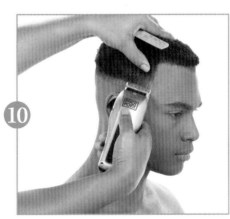

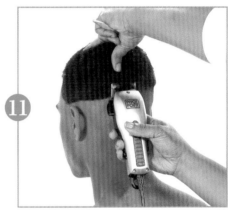

Extend the adjustable blade halfway to sculpt Zone 2, starting at the center back. Move the clippers outward at top of the zone. Comb the lengths downward as you proceed. Work to the front hairline on this side.

Work from the center back to the opposite side using same technique to complete Zone 2.

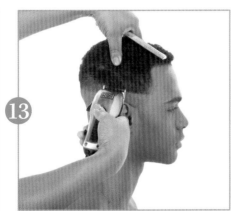

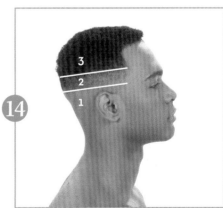

Now, fully extend the adjustable blade to sculpt Zone 3, starting at the center back. Begin the stroke within Zone 2 and move the clippers outward at the top of Zone 3. Continue to comb the lengths often as you proceed. Work from the center toward the right side. Then, work from the center to the left side using the same technique.

Note that Zones 1, 2, and 3 could be blended into the existing interior lengths at this point if desired.

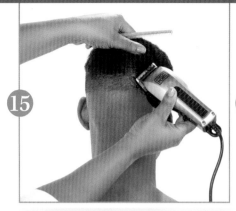

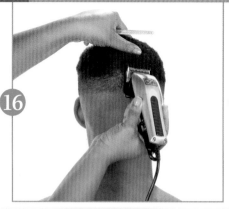

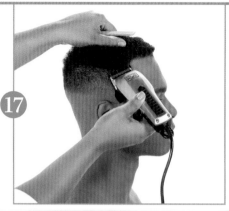

Next, add a small guard and fully extend the adjustable blade to sculpt Zone 4. Start at the center back and begin each stroke within Zone 3, moving the clippers outward at the top of Zone 4. Work from the center toward the right side, adjusting the direction to work against the growth patterns.

Work from the center to the left side using the same sculpting technique.

Next, position the cutting and adjustable blades even with one another and switch to a guard one size larger than the previous guard. Sculpt Zone 5 starting at the center front hairline, moving the clippers away from the face toward the crown. Comb the hair forward as you continue. Work from the center to the right side, then from the center to the left side using the same technique.

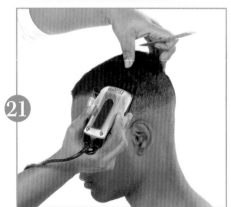

Move the clippers in multiple directions, working against the growth patterns.

Work toward the back using the same technique. Continue to work against the growth patterns in the crown area.

Next, position the adjustable blade halfway, without a guard attached, to blend Zones 1 and 2. Pull the skin taut and remove the weight line starting at the center back. Use an arcing motion moving away from the head. Comb lengths before moving to each section. Work from the center to the right side using the same technique. Repeat on the opposite side, again starting from the center.

Blend Zones 2 and 3 with the adjustable blade fully extended and no guard. Remove the weight line using the same technique. Work from the center to other side.

Extend the lever halfway and attach the smallest guard to blend Zones 3 and 4. Use the same sculpting technique. Sculpt against the growth patterns, working from the center to either side.

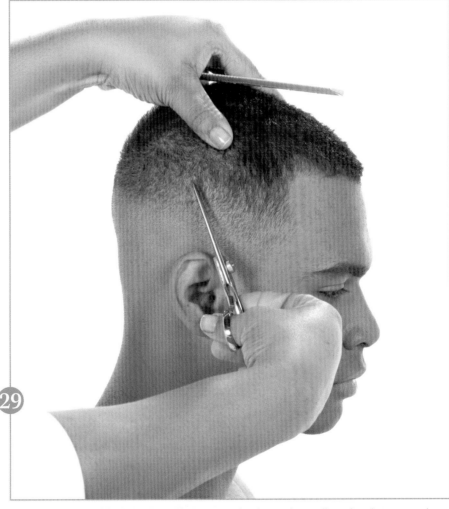

Fully extend the lever with the same guard attached and blend Zones 4 and 5 using the same sculpting technique. Sculpt against the growth patterns. Work from the center toward the other side.

As an option to further blend lengths, position the shears diagonally and sculpt against the skin in multiple directions.

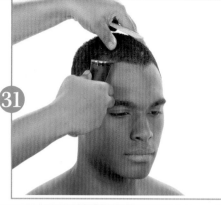

Next, outline the perimeter hairline using trimmers. Place the trimmers against the skin and sculpt working from the center front hairline to either side.

Position the trimmers and outline the sides as desired.

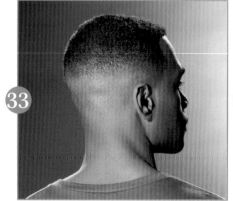

The finish displays a progression of lengths that seems to fade into the skin.

DESIGN DECISIONS

Draw or fill in the boxes with the appropriate answers.

STRUCTURE:

SHAPE:

TEXTURE:

SECTIONING PATTERN:

ZONE 1:

head position

sculpting direction

blade position
- [ ] fully extended
- [ ] half extended
- [ ] not extended

guard position
- [ ] guard
- [ ] no guard

ZONE 2:

head position

sculpting direction

blade position
- [ ] fully extended
- [ ] half extended
- [ ] not extended

guard position
- [ ] guard
- [ ] no guard

ZONE 3:

head position

sculpting direction

blade position
- [ ] fully extended
- [ ] half extended
- [ ] not extended

guard position
- [ ] guard
- [ ] no guard

ZONE 4:

head position

sculpting direction

blade position
- [ ] fully extended
- [ ] half extended
- [ ] not extended

guard position
- [ ] guard
- [ ] no guard

ZONE 5:

head position

sculpting direction

blade position
- [ ] fully extended
- [ ] half extended
- [ ] not extended

guard position
- [ ] guard
- [ ] no guard

TOOLS:

SCULPTURE DESIGN RUBRIC

Chapter 4: Bald Fade–Clippers

 This Rubric is a performance assessment tool designed to measure your ability to **create** Pivot Point sculpture designs.

Name _____ ID Number _____ Date _____

	In Progress Level 1	Getting Better Level 2	Entry-Level Proficiency Level 3
PREPARATION			
• Assemble sculpting essentials	☐	☐	☐
CREATE			
• Position head upright	☐	☐	☐
• Position adjustable blade of clippers even with cutting blade and establish first of five zones by placing clippers flat against scalp using outside of eyebrow as a guide and extending to center back; repeat on opposite side and check for symmetry	☐	☐	☐
• Position head tilted slightly forward; sculpt Zone 1 with clippers held against skin; starting at center nape perimeter, sculpt up to established line working from center to right side; return to center and work to opposite side	☐	☐	☐
• Sculpt same area moving in multiple directions and against direction of hair growth; hold skin taut	☐	☐	☐
• Position adjustable blade of clippers extended halfway to sculpt Zone 2	☐	☐	☐
• Sculpt Zone 2 starting at center back; move clippers outward at top of zone and comb lengths downward working to front hairline; work from center back to opposite side	☐	☐	☐
• Position adjustable blade of clippers fully extended to sculpt Zone 3	☐	☐	☐
• Sculpt Zone 3 starting at center back; begin stroke in Zone 2 and move clippers outward at top of Zone 3; comb lengths downward and continue working to front hairline; work from center back to opposite side	☐	☐	☐
• Position small guard on fully extended adjustable blade of clippers to sculpt Zone 4	☐	☐	☐
• Sculpt Zone 4 starting at center back; begin each stroke in Zone 3 and move clippers outward at top of Zone 4, adjusting direction to work against growth patterns; work from center back to opposite side	☐	☐	☐

SCULPTURE DESIGN RUBRIC

Chapter 4: Bald Fade–Clippers (continued)

	In Progress Level 1	Getting Better Level 2	Entry-Level Proficiency Level 3
• Position adjustable blade of clippers even with cutting blade and use guard one size larger than previous to sculpt Zone 5	☐	☐	☐
• Sculpt Zone 5 starting at center front hairline moving clippers away from face toward crown; comb hair forward and continue from center to right side and then center to left side	☐	☐	☐
• Sculpt moving clippers in multiple directions working against growth patterns; work through crown area	☐	☐	☐
• Position movable blade of clippers halfway and remove guard to blend Zones 1 and 2	☐	☐	☐
• Sculpt to blend by holding the skin taut and moving the clippers over Zones 1 and 2 in arcing motion combing each section before sculpting; work from center to right side and then center to left	☐	☐	☐
• Position moveable blade of clippers fully extended and sculpt to blend Zones 2 and 3	☐	☐	☐
• Position moveable blade of clippers halfway and attach smallest guard to blend Zones 3 and 4	☐	☐	☐
• Position moveable blade of clippers fully extended with same guard to blend Zones 4 and 5	☐	☐	☐

OPTIONAL:

• Sculpt with shears positioned diagonally against the skin moving in multiple directions	☐	☐	☐
• Sculpt with trimmers held against the skin to outline perimeter hairline working from center front hairline to either side; outline sides and front hairline as desired	☐	☐	☐
• Finish sculpture design	☐	☐	☐

TOTAL POINTS = ☐ + ☐ + ☐

TOTAL POINTS _____ ÷ HIGHEST POSSIBLE SCORE 66 = _____ %

Record your time in comparison with the suggested salon speed. _____

To improve my performance on this procedure, I need to: _____

_____

Voices of Success

The Salon Owner:

"IN OUR SALON, OUR DESIGNERS HAVE TO BE ABLE TO WORK AS WELL WITH THE MALE CLIENTS AS WITH THE FEMALE CLIENTS. HAVING THE SKILLS TO REALLY MAKE THE MALE CLIENTS FEEL LIKE THEY ARE GETTING A 'GUY'S CUT' AND NOT A VERSION OF A LADIES' IS KEY TO BUILDING—AND MAINTAINING—A SOLID MALE CLIENTELE."

The Educator:

"SOMETIMES IT SEEMS LIKE THE TECHNIQUES FOR SCULPTING MEN'S HAIR ARE EASIER FOR STUDENTS TO PICK UP ON, ESPECIALLY THE PLANAR SCULPTING TECHNIQUES WITH THE DIRECTIONAL DISTRIBUTION. ADDING THESE SKILLS TO THEIR WORKING KNOWLEDGE AND EXPERIENCE IN LADIES' SCULPTING MAKES THEM MORE WELL-ROUNDED DESIGNERS—READY TO TAKE ON THE SALON WORLD!"

The Client:

"I'M NOT EVEN THAT PARTICULAR ABOUT MY HAIR, BUT SOMETIMES I'LL LOOK AT OTHER GUYS AND WONDER: 'WHO DID THAT TO YOUR HAIR?' OR 'DUDE, DID YOU LET YOUR GIRLFRIEND CUT YOUR HAIR?' I'VE REALLY COME TO APPRECIATE THAT MY STYLIST HAS THE DESIGN SENSE AND TECHNICAL SKILL TO GIVE ME A HAIRCUT THAT LOOKS GREAT AND IS REALLY EASY TO TAKE CARE OF. I DON'T EVEN THINK ABOUT IT UNTIL IT'S TIME TO SHOW UP FOR MY NEXT APPOINTMENT! AND YES—THAT'S A PREBOOKED APPOINTMENT!"

IN OTHER WORDS:

The ability to adapt your sculpting skills and design specifically for male clients will make you a more versatile designer and will help you build your clientele.

Learning Challenge

This challenge contains a combination of multiple-choice and short-answer items. For multiple-choice items, circle the letter corresponding to the correct answer. For short-answer items, write the correct answer in the space provided.

1. The planar sculpting technique results in a form that appears to be:
   a. oval
   b. rounded
   c. triangular
   d. rectilinear or square

2. The angularity of a planar form can be more or less evident depending on the:
   a. head position
   b. styling direction
   c. distribution used
   d. sectioning pattern

3. To refine the form in a shear-over-comb technique designers use a:
   a. tail comb
   b. large comb
   c. small comb
   d. wide-tooth comb

4. Generally the taper-shear-over-comb technique is used for:
   a. blending
   b. removing bulk
   c. length reduction
   d. outlining the perimeter

5. In a fade the shortest lengths are usually positioned:
   a. in the lowest zone
   b. in the highest zone
   c. at the front hairline
   d. throughout the design

6. The planar sculpting technique is more commonly performed in the interior and shorter lengths are sculpted in the _____.

7. The shear-over–comb technique may be used to sculpt the majority of a hair sculpture or to _____ the perimeter.

8. In gradation, the hair is too short to be controlled with the fingers, therefore the _____ is used to control the hair.

9. Many designers may approach a fade by sculpting different length _____ first and then _____ them to create smooth transitions.

10. A tilted head position makes it near to impossible to judge the partings, _____ and _____ _____ during planar sculpting.

Lessons Learned

Planar sculpting and gradation are essential techniques that accommodate male clients' hair sculpture needs.

Designers adapt longer hair sculptures to take advantage of male clients' positive attributes, ensuring masculine-looking results despite the longer hair lengths.

Mid-length men's sculptures are very versatile and often incorporate planar form in the interior.

Short forms can make a strong fashion statement while offering low maintenance and carefree styling.

Courtesy of DF 284.

adapting as a designer
SCULPTURE

With all of your new hair sculpture skills, your next challenge is to expand your ability to select appropriate and flattering hair sculptures to best suit each client. Knowing what skills and techniques to use to achieve the specific outcome you envision is what helps set you apart from the average hair designer. Successful designers take the lifestyle and physical features of their clients into consideration to achieve flattering results.

Adapting sculpture has two components: composing and personalizing. Composing involves integrating all of your knowledge and skills into a single new hair sculpture. When you compose a hair sculpture, you show that you understand how your sculpting decisions and techniques yield the results you envision. Personalizing the sculpture you compose helps ensure that it is appropriate and flattering on each individual client. Taking into consideration hair density, growth patterns and other personal characteristics also helps you create a look that the client—with a little explanation—can duplicate at home to look great even between salon visits.

Courtesy of DF 286.

Your ability to adapt sculptures as a designer can also include finding inspiration in fashion or nature. By changing the shape, repositioning the weight and altering the surface texture, you can accentuate specific features or de-emphasize others. As you continue learning to adapt as a designer, you will become comfortable using different sources of inspiration and making design decisions that allow you to produce predictable results.

Within the pages of Pivot Point's *DF* (*Design Forum*®), examples of dynamic sculpture designs created by adapting as a designer may also serve as inspiration. As you look through *DF*, you will recognize that almost anything you visualize can be realized through adapting. Elevating your work from "satisfactory" to "wow" is why adapting as a designer reflects the ultimate in professional sculpture design.

Now you can start developing your ability to adapt sculpture as a designer. A personal portfolio where you will store "before and after" photographs of clients can be a great tool for tracking your success. Besides photos, keep notes describing your thought process for adapting hair sculptures for each client. Note the techniques used, what worked well, what didn't work well, and what you might have done differently. Your portfolio provides the chance for you to monitor your growth as a designer and your proficiency at adapting.

SCULPTURE TERMS:

Abstract - Theoretical; not of concrete substance.

Adaptable - To adjust or fit to the individual's anatomical structure, growth patterns, hair density and lifestyle.

Anatomy - The science of bodily structure.

Apex - The highest point or peak; top of the head; location where the comb leaves the scalp when placed flat on the head.

Asymmetry - Lack of symmetry.

Balance - Equilibrium of design elements; harmonious positioning of parts around a center axis.

Blend - To meet or join. Both lines and textures can be blended or not blended in hair sculpture.

CELESTIAL AXIS

A two-dimensional measurement system that identifies levels of space that surrounds the head.

Lines - horizontal, vertical, diagonal right, diagonal left

Angles - 0˚, 45˚, 90˚

Direction - upward, downward, forward, backward, left, right

Clipper-Over-Comb - A sculpting technique that achieves closeness to the head. A comb is used as a guide to hold the lengths while the hair protruding over the comb is sculpted with the clippers.

Comb Control - Sculpting technique in which the teeth of the comb, as opposed to the fingers, hold the hair in position while sculpting; places minimal tension on the hair.

Component - An element; a simple part of a larger system.

Composition - A putting together of elements to form a whole.

Concave - Curved like the interior of a sphere.

Concept - A general idea or understanding, especially one derived from specific instances or occurrences.

Converge - To come together toward a common point.

Conversion Layering - The primary sculpting technique used in increase layering. Hair is directed to a stationary design line opposite the area of the desired length increase.

Convex - Having a surface that curves outward, like the exterior of a sphere.

CREST AREA

The widest part around the head. It divides the interior from the exterior.

    Interior - The area of the head above the crest.

    Exterior - The area of the head below the crest.

Cross-check - A final stage in sculpting in which the accuracy of the sculpture is checked by using the line opposite the original sculpting pattern.

Curvilinear - Characterized by curved lines.

Density - The degree to which any area is occupied; i.e., the amount of hair per square centimeter.

Design - An arrangement of shapes, lines and ornamental effects that creates an artistic unit.

Design Decision - The determination made through proper consultation with the client in regard to the end result of the hair design.

DESIGN ELEMENT
Major components of an art form. In hair design, they are: form, texture and color.

Form - A three-dimensional representation of shape.

Texture - The quality of a surface influenced by sculpting techniques and curl patterns.

Color - The visual effect achieved when light reflects off a given object.

DESIGN LINE
The artistic pattern or length guide used while sculpting; it can be mobile or stationary.

Mobile Design Line - A length guide used in sculpting that moves throughout a given component area of the sculpture and serves as a design line to follow in creating the form.

Stationary Design Line - A constant, stable design line. Lengths are directed to this line in order to create a length increase in the opposite direction.

DESIGN PRINCIPLES
Arrangements or patterns for design elements to follow.

Alternation - Sequential repetition.

Contrast - A desirable relationship of opposites, which creates variety and stimulates interest in a design.

Progression - A succession of lengths that increases or decreases by proportional steps.

Repetition - Of identical nature throughout; a unit identical in all ways except position.

Diagonal - A line with a slanted or sloping direction.

Diagonal Back - A diagonal line that travels away from the face, resulting in a backward flow of hair.

Diagonal Forward - A diagonal line that travels toward the face.

Diagonal Left - A diagonal line that travels to the left.

Diagonal Right - A diagonal line that travels to the right.

Direction - The path taken by a line or plane.

DISTRIBUTION
The direction the hair is combed in relation to its base parting. There are four types of distribution: directional, natural, perpendicular and shifted.

Directional - The hair is combed straight up or straight out from the curve of the head.

Natural - The direction the hair assumes in relation to its natural growth patterns.

Perpendicular - The direction hair assumes when it is combed at a 90° angle to its base parting.

Shifted - The direction hair assumes when it is combed out of natural distribution in any direction but perpendicular to its base parting. Shifting is primarily used for extreme length increases and blending in activated forms.

Fade - A sculpting technique that is a very short version of gradation. In many instances, areas of the head are sculpted to the skin with the use of clippers.

Form Line - The outline or outer boundary of a form.

Freehand Sculpting - A sculpting technique in which the eye and hand are the only means of control.

Fringe - Hair that partially or completely covers the forehead in a design. The fringe is one of the most variable portions of a style.

Gradated - A progression of shorter lengths toward the top of the head, creating an activated surface.

Graduated Texture - A progression of lengths in which the ends of the hair appear to stack upon one another. It creates a combination of unactivated and activated sculpted texture.

GRADUATION
The sculpting technique that produces a stacked effect in hair.

Decreasing Graduation - Graduation within two nonparallel lines; it diminishes as it moves back from the face.

Increasing Graduation - Graduation within two nonparallel lines; it increases as it moves back away from the face.

Parallel Graduation - Graduation within two parallel lines for an equally graduated effect throughout a given area.

Horizontal - Near, on or parallel to the horizon.

Layered Texture - Texture in which the ends of the hair are most visible. There are two types of layered texture: uniformly layered and increase layered.

Line - A series of points.

Line of Inclination - The angle at which graduation progresses in length. The three basic types are low, medium and high.

Mass - The quantity of matter in any given body.

Multiple Design Lines - Two or more stationary design lines used with a conversion layering technique to achieve increase-layered texture.

Natural Fall - The natural position the hair assumes due to gravitational pull.

Nonparallel Sculpting - Angling your fingers in any direction other than parallel to your base parting while sculpting.

Normal Projection - Hair held uniformly at 90° in relation to the position of the head. Normal projection views are used to analyze the structure of a sculpture. It is also the projection angle at which uniform layering is performed.

One-Finger Projection - A projection angle equal to the width of one finger.

Parallel - A line, or point on a line, that maintains an equal distance from another line or point.

Parallel Sculpting - A technique in which a section is sculpted parallel to its base parting.

Perimeter - Circumference, border or outer boundary; the hair around the hairline.

Pivotal Parting - A parting pattern that radiates from a central point and conforms to the curve of the head; allows easy sculpting around the crown; creates triangular sections.

Planar Sculpting - A technique in which the lengths are sculpted along a plane.

Plane - A surface containing every line connecting any two points lying within it; any flat or level surface.

Project - To extend forward or out.

PROJECTION
The angle the hair is held in relation to the curve of the head while sculpting.

Zero - Flat to the surface of the head.

Natural Fall - The position the hair assumes due to gravitational pull. This may be 0° in some areas of the head.

High - Above 60°, below 90°

Medium - Above 30°, below 60° (45° is standard)

Low - Above 0°, below 30°

Proportion - The relationship between things or parts of things in respect to comparative magnitude, quantity or degree.

Qualitative Analysis - To list all the parts of a whole.

Quantitative Analysis - Determining the amount of each part and the proportion of the parts to the whole.

Razor Etching - A razor sculpting technique in which length is removed with a short razor stroke; performed on the ends of the hair.

Rectilinear - Characterized by straight lines; usually more adaptable to men because straight lines are considered more masculine than curved lines; square forms are considered rectilinear.

Ridge Line - The line that divides two textures in graduated forms.

SEVEN SCULPTING PROCEDURES
Sequential steps used to perform a hair sculpture.

Sectioning - Dividing the head into workable areas for control.

Head Position - The position of the client's head while sculpting.

Parting - Lines that subdivide the sections to separate, distribute and control hair while sculpting.

Distribution - The direction the hair is combed in relation to its base parting.

Projection - The angle at which the hair is held while sculpting.

Finger/Shear Position - The finger position and the sculpted line in relation to the parting pattern.

Design Line - The artistic pattern or length guide used while sculpting. It can be stationary or mobile.

Shape - The contour of an object. In hair sculpture, shape implies two dimensions.

Shear-Over-Comb - A sculpting technique that achieves closeness to the head. A comb is used as a guide to hold the lengths in position for sculpting. The angle of the comb determines the amount of length removed.

Silhouette - The outer contour of an object or design.

Slide Cutting - Sculpting technique in which the shank of the shears slides along the strand to remove length vertically; often used when rapid length increases are desired.

Space - A continuum in three dimensions; distance extending without limit in all directions.

Structure - The arrangement of lengths across the curve of the head.

STRUCTURE GRAPHIC

A diagram that represents the proportional relationship of the lengths within a sculpture as they occur across the curve of the head. This graphic serves as a blueprint for the final sculpture. The structure graphics that identify the length arrangements are color-coded as follows:

 Solid Form - A length progression that increases toward the top of the head with all lengths falling to the same level in natural fall; produces an unactivated sculpted texture; it is color-coded blue.

 Graduated Form - A form in which the lengths gradually become longer toward the interior; in natural fall, the ends stack above one another; produces an unactivated and activated sculpture texture; it is color-coded yellow.

 Gradated Form (Gradation) - A very short graduated form that gradually progresses in length toward the top of the head; produces an activated sculpted texture; it is color-coded yellow.

 Increase-Layered Form - A form in which lengths become progressively longer toward the exterior; produces an activated sculpted texture; it is color-coded red.

 Uniformly Layered Form - A form in which all lengths are equal; produces an activated sculpted texture; it is color-coded green.

 Combination Form - A form in which two or more basic forms are combined by using different techniques or by sculpting along a plane.

 Planar Form - A combination form that is the result of sculpting along horizontal and/or vertical planes; multiple forms occur automatically due to the curves of the head. Short planar forms are also called square forms.

Surface - The outer or the topmost boundary of an object; the boundary of any three dimensional figure.

Symmetrical - A balanced or harmonious arrangement.

Symmetry - Having equal sides or parts.

Tapering Shears - A tool used for irregular removal of lengths within a form. One blade is straight and the other is serrated. These shears include taper 8 (teeth are spaced $1/8$" apart), taper 16 (teeth are spaced $1/16$" apart) and taper 32 (teeth are spaced $1/32$" apart).

Tension - The art of stretching or the condition of being stretched.

TEXTURE

The quality of a surface influenced by sculpting techniques and curl patterns; may be unactivated, activated or a combination.

Sculpted Texture - Texture achieved through sculpting.

Unactivated - A smooth surface in which the ends are not visible.

Activated - A rough hair surface in which the ends are visible.

Combination - Unactivated and activated surface.

TEXTURIZING

Sculpting at the perimeter or within the form to achieve textural qualities, design mobility or expansion.

Contour Tapering - Texturizing technique that reduces hair density to achieve a degree of closeness within a form.

Expansion Tapering - Texturizing technique that produces volume through sculpting shorter lengths, which then support the longer ones within a form.

Form Line Tapering - Texturizing technique that reduces the concentration of bulk or weight at the ends, encouraging mobility.

Notching - Technique used to create irregular lengths, usually for a chunkier texture at the hair ends.

Pointing - A texturizing technique in which the tips of straight shears are moved from the fingers toward the ends.

Razor Rotation - A texturizing technique in which a comb and razor are rotated with light pressure in a circular motion to reduce bulk and blend the form.

Slicing - A texturizing technique in which the open shears glide along the surface of the hair to achieve mobility.

Three-Dimensional - Having length, width and depth fullness or hollowness.

Triangular - Of, pertaining to or shaped like a triangle; three-sided.

Two-Dimensional - Having length and width (flat).

Uniformly Layered Texture - A totally activated surface created by uniform length throughout.

Vertical - Upright; perpendicular to the horizon.

Volume - Mass or fullness.

Weight - Mass in form and space; also the length concentration in a hair design.

Weight Area - The area within a sculpture where there is a concentration of longer lengths.

Zone - Intervals of 2" (5 cm) that echo out in space from the curve of the head and are used to analyze hair length.

INDEX